THE BATSFORD BOOK OF
KNITTING AND CROCHET

THE BATSFORD BOOK OF

KNITTING AND CROCHET

Edited by Thelma M. Nye

B.T. BATSFORD LTD
London

This book was originally developed and
produced by Kammgarnspinnerei
Schachenmayr, Mann & Cie,
in Salach, Württemberg, Germany
© Otto Maier Verlag, Ravensburg, 1968

First English Language Edition 1973

Filmset by Servis Filmsetting Ltd, Manchester
Printed and bound by Cox & Wyman Ltd,
London, Fakenham and Reading
for the publishers B. T. Batsford Ltd
4 Fitzhardinge Street, London W1

ISBN 0 7134 2658 6

Contents

Practical Hints

Crochet

Introduction and Basic Stitches

(See p. 299 for List of Abbreviations)

1 The Starting Loop

Hold the thread between thumb and fore-finger of left hand. With the working thread form a loop from right to left so that working thread lies on top. Put working thread behind loop above your forefinger, and hold it between little and ring finger. From the front insert hook through the loop, thr.o., and dr. l.thr. The loop remains on the hook to start the Ch.-st chain.

2 Chain Stitch

With the crochet hook continuously draw working thread through loop (thr.o., dr.thr.). Almost all crochet work starts with this Ch.-st chain (chain-stitch foundation).

3 The Chain or Slip Stitch

Insert hook from the front through the 2nd Ch. from hook, catch thread with hook—this is known as 'thread over'—draw thread through the 2 loops on hook. Insert hook into next Ch. and repeat as before to end of row.

4   Single Crochet

Insert into the 2nd-last st of foundation, thr.o., dr.thr., thr.o. and draw this thread through the 2 loops on hook. Insert into the next st, thr.o., dr.thr., thr.o. and again draw this thread through the 2 loops on hook. Rep.

2nd and all following rows: turn work, Ch.1, insert hook into 2nd SC of previous row, thr.o., dr.thr., thr.o. and dr.thr. the 2 loops. Insert hook from the front into the next st, etc., etc.

5   Double Crochet

1st row: thr.o., insert hook into the 4th Ch. from hook, thr.o. and dr.thr., thr.o. and dr.thr. 2 loops, thr.o. again and dr.thr. 2 remaining loops. Thr.o., insert hook into next Ch., thr.o., dr.thr. and so on. The illustration shows the forward and backward rows. One turns work as follows:

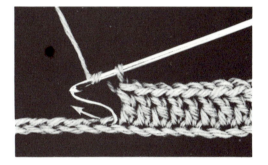

2nd row: to replace the 1st DC, Ch.3 then thr.o. Insert into the 2nd DC (the 1st of each row is always missed) it is optional to insert under the 2 horizontal links or through the back horizontal link. Thr.o., dr.thr., thr.o., dr.thr. 2 loops, thr.o. and dr.thr. 2 remaining loops, etc., etc.

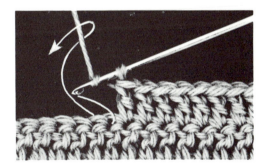

6   Half-double Crochet

1st row: thr.o., insert into the 3rd Ch. from hook, thr.o., dr.thr., thr.o. and pull through 3 loops on hook. Thr.o., insert hook into next Ch., rep. The illustration shows the half-DC only in forward row. One turns work as

follows: to replace the 1st half-DC, Ch.2, thr.o., insert into 2nd half-DC, thr.o., dr.thr., thr.o. and pull through 3 loops on hook, etc., etc.

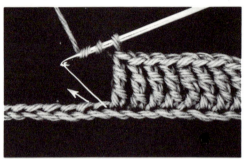

7 Treble Crochet

1st row: thr.o. twice, insert into 5th Ch. from hook. Thr.o., dr.thr., thr.o. and pull through 2 loops, thr.o. and pull through 2 loops, thr.o. and pull through last 2 loops. Thr.o. twice, insert hook into next Ch., etc. Turn work.
2nd row: Ch.4, work into the 2nd TC from hook, again a TC, and so on.

8 Quadruple and Multiple Crochet

Here the thread is put over the hook 3 or more times, and drawn through 2 loops at a time. When turning the work, the number of turning Ch.sts depends on how high the crochet is to be worked at the beginning of the next row.

9 Cross Crochet

This consists of 4 DCs which lie crosswise above each other, and are separated by 2 Ch.sts. The lower right DC is worked 1st, then the lower left, the upper right then the upper left, in sequence.
Working method: on beginning the row, as substitute for the lower left crochet, Ch.3; for the space in between, miss 2 Ch.sts,

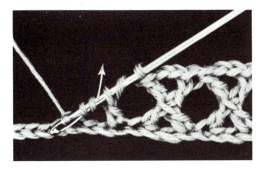

thr.o., insert into the 6th Ch.st of foundation and work the lower left DC.

Ch.5 (3 for upper right DC, and 2 for the intervening space) thr.o., in the crossing point join the 2 lower links and work the upper left DC. All the other cross crochets are worked in the following manner: thr.o., twice (once for upper right and once for the lower right DC), insert into the next loop of

previous row, thr.o., pull through, thr.o. and pull once through 2 loops, thr.o., insert into the 3rd following st, thr.o., pull through, thr.o. and dr.thr. 2 loops, thr.o. again, dr.thr. 2 loops. Rep. twice more. Ch.2, thr.o., in the crossing point join the 2 lower links, thr.o., pull through, thr.o. and pull through 2 loops at a time. The individual cross DCs can also be separated from each other by Ch.sts.

10 Double Chain Foundation

Begin by making 2 Ch.sts. In the 1st of these work 1 SC, insert with hook into the left vertical link of SC, and work 1 SC, continuously insert into the left vertical link and work 1 SC.

11 Double Stitch *(Wickel-stitch)*

Is worked like No. 6. The illustration shows a treble thread-over; insert hook, dr.thr., thr.o. and pull through all the loops.

This illustration shows the long double stitch, with 5 thread-overs. The method of working is the same as above.

12   Cluster Crochet I

This only worked in forward row. With this type of st, one leaves between each cluster stitch 1 to 2 Chs of foundation free. Begin with 1 thread-over, insert hook into 4th Ch., dr.thr. and pull up into a loop, thr.o., insert into the same st, thr.o., dr.thr. and pull up, thr.o., get a 3rd loop out of the same st, thr.o., get 4th loop and now draw together all the loops present on hook. Ch.1, and rep. the cluster.

2nd and all subsequent rows: Ch.2 to turn, each cluster st begins with a thread-over. Insert hook, draw thread through and up into a loop (to height as required), rep. the same 3 times. Thr.o. and draw all loops tog. Finish by making 1 Ch.st. In all the following rows, work 1 cluster between 2 of the previous rows; always insert under 2 links.

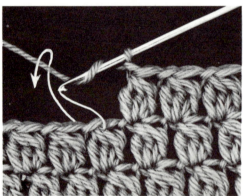

13   Cluster Crochet II

The 1st cluster group: thr.o., insert into 3rd Ch. from hook, draw wool through, thr.o. and pull through 2 loops, thr.o., insert into the same st, draw wool through, thr.o. and dr.thr. 2 loops. Thr.o. and pull through remaining loops on hook. It is optional to finish each group with 1 Ch.st. Thr.o., insert hook into 2nd following Ch. of foundation, draw wool through, pull through 2 loops, thr.o., insert into the same Ch., draw wool through and pull through 2 loops, thr.o., insert into the same st, draw wool through, pull through 2 loops. Thr.o. and pull through remaining loops on hook. The illustrations show the cluster st in backward and forward row. Work always between the 1st and 2nd cluster of previous row.

14 Plain Knit Stitch

This can only be worked in forward rows.
1st row: consists of DC.
2nd row: insert into 2 horizontal crochet links, draw wool through, thr.o. and pull through the 2 loops on hook.

15 Double Knit Stitch

Insert hook as in ordinary crochet and draw thread through; thr.o. and pull through 1 loop on hook, again thr.o., and pull through the 2 loops. This is repeated to the end of the row. It is worked in forward rows. At the beg. of each row, work 1 sl.st. In the 2nd and all following rows, insert hook into the upper st from the back and crochet as described above.

16 Knot Stitch

Worked only in forward rows.
1st row: SCs.
2nd row: insert to the right of the st of previous row, to the back, thr.o., dr.thr.,

insert into the left of the same st, draw wool through, thr.o. and pull through all loops on hook. Insert into the same place as before, to the right of the following st, dr.thr., insert to the left of the st, dr.thr., thr.o. and pull through all loops on hook.

17 Gretchen Stitch

Insert into 2nd Ch. from hook, thr.o. (the thread must lie in front of hook) dr.thr., thr.o. and pull through 2 loops. The illustration shows the pattern worked in forward row; the hook is always inserted under 2 links.

18 Rose Stitch

One begins with 1 thr.o.; insert hook into basic or previous row through the 2 loops of st, dr.thr., and pull through the 1st thread-over, thr.o. and pull through the loops on hook. Only forward rows are worked. So begin each row with a sl.st.

19 Plait Stitch

The foundation is the SC. Only the insertion of the hook gives a different appearance to the st. It is only worked in forward rows. The 1st row is SC. In the following rows, leave the 2 links, and insert into the cross-thread at the back of the st, and work SC. Through that, the 2 links are pushed forward.

20 Bosnian Crochet

The basic technique here is the sl.st. Only by the method of inserting can one achieve an interesting form of work. The illustration shows the smooth Bosnian stitch. This is worked only in forward rows. Insert hook into the back loop of st, draw wool through, and pull direct through loop on hook. The 1st row can optionally be worked as SC.

21 Roumanian Crochet Stitch

Only forward rows are being worked. The hook picks up the back horizontal loop from the front to the back, then the next loop from back to front; draw thread through these 2 crossed loops, thread wool over, and through 2 loops on hook, so that the base is a SC. Now insert hook from front to back into the link which has been used already with previous st in reverse direction. Through the next link from back to front and finish st as described before. The front link is never touched.

22 Zig-zag Stitch

Ch.-st foundation. Work 1 DC into the 4th Ch. from hook, thr.o., insert into the same Ch., thr.o., dr.thr., thr.o., pull through 2 loops, thr.o., insert into the next-but-one Ch. of foundation, thr.o., dr.thr., pull through 2 loops, thr.o. and pull through all remaining loops on hook. Rep. to the end of row. Thr.o., insert into the same place as before, thr.o., dr.thr., thr.o., pull through 2 loops, thr.o., insert into the next-but-one Ch., thr.o., dr.thr., thr.o., pull through 2 loops, thr.o. and pull through all remaining loops on hook.
2nd and all subsequent rows: after turning of work, make 3 Ch.sts, work 1 DC (from now on, one always inserts into space between 2 groups). Continue to draw 2 DCs tog. To achieve a good result, one must crochet loosely, especially draw sts up well.

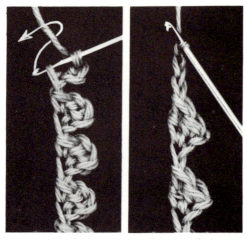

23 Picots and Edgings

Ch.5; into 1st Ch.st Cr.1, Ch.5, back into the 1st Ch. of the 5, Cr.1, Ch.5, etc., etc. Ch.3 * insert into the 2nd-last Ch., Cr.1, into the 1st Ch., DC1, Ch.3, from * rep.

For edging: 1 sl.st into previous row * Ch.4, insert back into the 1st Ch. and Cr.1, insert into the 2nd or 3rd st of previous row, work 1 sl.st, from * rep.

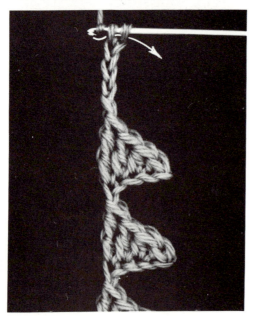

Ch.5, * insert into 2nd-last Ch.st, Cr.1, into the next Ch. make a half-DC, into the following Ch. a DC, and into the last Ch. a TC, from * rep.

Patterns

Simple Crochet Patterns

24 Different Patterns with Single Crochet

As the illustration shows, there are two ways of working the SC st. Every 2nd and following row, insert into 2 loops of previous row, *or,* insert into 1 loop.
The illustration shows the SC in forward and backward row, always inserted into 2 loops.

25 Crochet Pattern

In forward and backward row, here one inserts into the back loop.

26 Rib Pattern

The 1st row is SC. It is worked only in forward rows, so you break thread at end of each row, and start again at the beg. The 2nd and all following rows are worked in SC; insert hook into 2 loops of previous row.

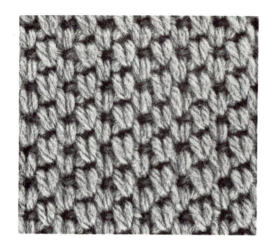

27 Crochet Pattern

Ch.-st foundation.
1st row: into the 2nd-last Ch.st work 1 SC *
Ch.1, miss 1 Ch. of foundation row, into the
next Ch. work 1 SC, from * rep.
2nd row: turn, Ch.2, 1 SC into the first free
Ch. of foundation; thus, one reaches below
the 1st row * Ch.1, SC1, into the next free Ch.
of foundation, from * rep.
3rd row: the SCs of this row are worked
into the SCs of last-but-one row, the loops
are pulled up. After every SC Ch.1.
3rd row: rep. continuously.

28 Crochet Pattern

Into every 2nd Ch. of foundation row, work 2
SCs. Always insert under 2 links. Only forward
rows are being worked. In every following
row, insert between the 2 SCs.

29 Crochet Pattern

Work into each of the last 2 Chs, 1 SC.
Ch.2, miss 2 Chs of foundation row, and
work into each of the 2 following Chs 1 SC.
Again Ch.2, miss 2 of foundation, work into
the next 2, 1 SC each, etc. In the following
rows work 2 SCs around the 2 Ch.sts of
previous row; above the SC work 2 ch.sts.
Forward and backward rows are worked. Turn
with 1 Ch.st.

30 Crochet Pattern

Into each Ch. of foundation row, work 1 DC and 1 SC alternately. If the row ends with a DC, turn with 1 Ch.st, and work onto the DC of previous row, a SC. On to every SC of previous row, work a DC, and on to every DC, work a single. If the row ends with a SC, turn with 3 Ch.sts. Work the 3rd and every subsequent row as the 2nd row.

31 Crochet Pattern

Ch.-st foundation.
Insert into the 3rd-last Ch. * thr.o., dr.thr., thr.o., pull through 2nd loop, thr.o. and pull through the 2 loops. Ch.1, miss 1 Ch. of foundation row, insert, from * rep.
Only work in forward rows.

32 Small Tree Pattern

The 1st st after foundation row work as previous picture shows. Now insert hook into the 1st of Ch. foundation, and work 1 SC. Then follows the st as described above, and then 1 SC. Work only in forward row.

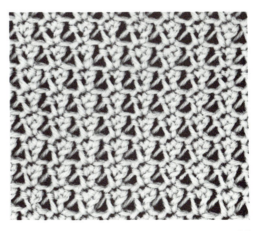

33 Crochet Pattern

In backward and forward rows the pattern is worked as follows:

Ch.-st foundation.
1st row: insert into the 3rd-last Ch. * draw thread through, thr.o., work 2 Chs, thr.o. and pull through both loops. Into the 1st Ch.st of the 2 just made, make 1 SC, insert into the next-but-one. From * rep. The row ends: insert into the last st, draw wool through, Ch.2, thr.o., pull through both loops and make 2 Chs to turn.
2nd row: into every st work 1 SC.
1st and 2nd rows: rep. continuously.

34 Crochet Pattern

On to the Ch.-st foundation, work into every 2nd Ch. alternately, 2 DCs, then 2 SCs. In the 2nd and all following rows, work between the 2 SCs 2 DCs, and between the 2 DCs, 2 SCs. Work in forward and backward rows. If the row ends with a SC, turn with 3 Ch.sts, otherwise 1 is enough.

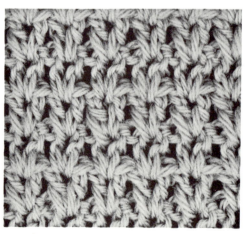

35 Crochet Pattern

Foundation Ch.
1st row: work into the 3rd Ch., 1 DC; miss 1 Ch., into the next work 2 DCs, into the next-but-one, again 2 DCs, etc., etc. So, into every 2nd Ch., work 2 DCs. Turn with 3 Ch.sts, and work between the 1st DC group 1 DC. Between each following group work 2 DCs. Insert hook between the 2 DCs. The pattern can be worked in forward and backward row (as illustrated), or just in forward row.

36 Crochet Pattern

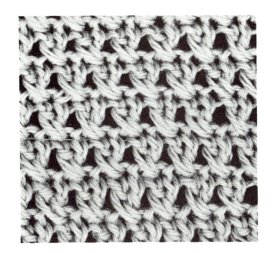

Only worked in forward row.

1st row: into the 4th Ch. from hook of the foundation-row, work 1 DC. Hereafter, work 1 DC into the 6th Ch., then insert back into the 5th and work 1 DC. Continue always with 1 DC into the 8th, 7th, 10th, 9th, 12th, 11th Ch. etc., etc. So miss 1 Ch., and then go back into it.

2nd and all subsequent rows: as illustration shows, one works the 1st DC on to the 2nd group of previous row, and the 2nd DC on to the 1st group. Thus, the 2nd DC is worked into the same st as the 1st DC of previous row. In this way the DCs are crossed.

If one wishes to work forward and backward, one works into the back of each DC group, 1 SC, 1 Ch.st.

37 Crochet Pattern

Ch. foundation.

1st row: insert into the last-but-one Ch., draw thread through, rep. this with the next Ch. Pull the 3 loops on hook to the same height and crochet together. Ch.1 * insert into the following Ch.st., draw thread through, rep. with the next Ch. and pull the 3 loops to the same height and crochet together. Ch.1, from * rep.

2nd row: * Ch.1, insert 1st from right, then from the left of the standing crochet link, draw thread through each, so that again you have 3 loops on hook. Crochet tog. From * rep.

2nd row: rep. continuously.

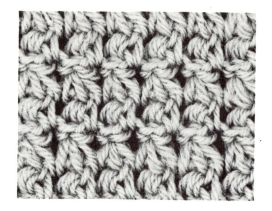

38 Crochet Pattern

Ch.-st foundation.
1st row: insert into the 2nd-last Ch., draw loop through, insert into the next Ch. and again draw wool through into a loop, thr.o. and crochet these 3 loops tog., Ch.1. * Insert again into the same Ch., draw loop through, insert into the following Ch. and draw through, thr.o., crochet all 3 loops on hook tog. Ch.1. From * rep.
2nd row: as 1st, and all subsequent rows. One crochets always around the Ch.st of previous rows.

39 Crochet Pattern

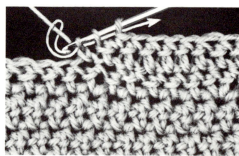

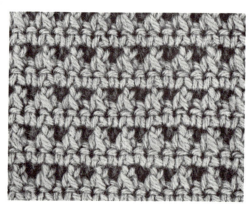

Ch.-st foundation.
Only forward row is worked.
1st row: 1 DC * now one inserts hook into the lower left link of DC, draw wool through, thread over and pull through 1 loop, insert into the next Ch. of foundation, draw wool through, thr.o. and pull through 1 loop; then thr.o., pull wool through 3 loops on hook (see lower illustration). From * rep. Always insert into the left lower link of previous st.
Every following row begins with the DC. As the upper illustration shows, one inserts into the two links of st in previous row.

40 Crochet Pattern

Ch.-st foundation.
1st row: draw out of the 4th and 5th Ch. of foundation each 1 loop, thr.o., dr.thr. 2, thr.o., dr.thr. 2, * Ch.1, draw out of each of the following 2 Chs, 1 loop, thr.o., dr.thr. 2 loops, thr.o., dr.thr. 2 loops. From   rep.
2nd row: to turn, Ch.1. To the right and left of each vertical link, SC1.
3rd row: to turn, Ch.3. Out of each of 2nd and 3rd SCs of previous row, draw 1 loop, crochet tog. as in 1st row.
2nd and 3rd rows: rep.

41 Crochet Pattern

Ch. foundation.
1st row: SCs with 2 Ch.sts to turn.
2nd row: * insert into the first SC, thr.o., dr.thr., thr.o., insert into the next SC, thr.o., dr.thr., thr.o., and pull through all 4 loops on hook. Ch.1, from * rep. Turn with 1 Ch.st.
3rd row: into every st (including Ch.-st) SC1.
2nd and 3rd rows: rep. continuously.

42 Crochet Pattern

Ch.st foundation.
1st row: insert into the 3rd-last Ch., and into the following 2 Chs. Out of each draw 1 loop, thr.o. and pull through all 4 loops on hook. * Ch.1, insert into the same st as before, draw wool through, rep. with the 2 following sts, thr.o. and pull through all 4 loops. From * rep. Turn with 2 Ch.sts.
2nd row: insert into the gap before Cl.st of previous row, into the st itself and into the gap beyond. Draw wool through each, thr.o. and pull through all 4 loops. * Ch.1, insert into the gap into which inserted last, into the Cl.st and into the gap beyond. Draw wool through each into a loop, thr.o. and pull through all 4 loops. From * rep.
2nd row: rep. continuously.

43 Crochet Pattern

Ch.-st foundation.
1st row: work 1 DC each into the 4th and into the 5th-last Ch. * Ch.1, DC3 (with the Ch.st always miss one Ch. of foundation). From * rep.
2nd row: into each DC and Ch.st work a sl.st.
3rd row: Ch.3, to turn. DC2 * Ch.1, DC3 (with the Ch.st miss every 4th sl.st) from * rep.
2nd and 3rd rows: rep. continuously.

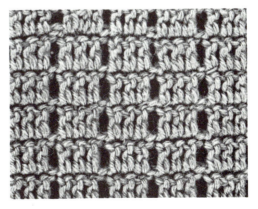

44   Crochet Pattern

On to the Ch.-foundation crochet into the 3rd-last and the following 3 Chs., 1 DC each. Make 1 Ch.st and miss 1 of foundation, then work into the following 4 Chs. 1 DC each. Rep. continuously as before, Ch.1, DC4. Ch.5, turn. Insert into the Ch. between the 1st and 2nd group of DC, and work 1 SC, Ch.4, and insert between the 3rd and 4th group, SC1, etc., etc. In the 3rd row work 4 DCs around the 4 Ch.sts of previous row. Separate the groups with 1 Ch.st. Work the 4th row, as the 2nd, the 5th row as the 3rd, and so on.

45   Crochet Pattern

Ch.-st foundation.
1st row: into each of the 4th-, 5th-, 6th- and 7th-last Ch. work 1 DC. ★ Into the following Ch. work 3 DCs; into each of the next 5 Chs work 1 DC. Now miss 2 Chs of foundation and into the next 5 Chs work 1 DC each.

From ★ rep. The row finishes with 5 DCs after the 3 DCs.
2nd row: and all following rows: into every DC of previous row, work 1 DC; into the centre crochet of the 3 always work 3 DCs. Instead of missing 2 Ch.st, as in first row, miss 1 DC on each side of previous row, so forming a hole. Note that before and after each centre 3, work 5 DCs.

46 Crochet Pattern

Ch. foundation.
1st row: insert into the 3rd-last Ch.st, draw wool through, thr.o., insert into the same st, dr.thr., thr.o., into the same st insert again, dr.thr., thr.o. and pull through all loops. * Ch.1, miss 1 Ch. in foundation, insert into the next Ch., dr.thr., thr.o., insert, dr.thr., thr.o., and again into the same st insert, dr.thr., thr.o. and pull through all loops. From * rep. Ch.2, turn.
2nd row: as the 1st row, but work Cl.sts into the gap below Ch.st of previous row.
2nd row: rep. continuously.

47 Crochet Pattern

Ch.-st foundation.
Out of the 3rd-last Ch. and out of each of the 2 following Chs draw 1 loop, draw these well up, put wool over hook and dr.thr. all 4 loops. Ch.1, draw 1 loop out of each of the following 3 Chs, again put wool on hook and dr.thr. all loops, Ch.1. In this way work to the end of the row. Work only in forward rows, so that at the end of each row, break thread and start at the beginning again, either with Ch.3 or dr.thr. 1 loop. Then get the 3 loops which belong tog., in the following manner: the 1st loop from the right of lower group, the 2nd out of the middle (insert into the st which keeps loop tog.) the 3rd from left of group. Insert for the 3rd loop in front of the last thread of lower group. Thr.o., and dr.thr.

all loops. Finish with a Ch.st. Between every group of loops one has a single vertical thread, which separates the groups from each other. One inserts for the 1st and 3rd loop, to the left and right of this thread. Always insert under full Ch.st.

Shell Pattern

48 Crochet Pattern

Ch.-st foundation.
1st row: into the 4th-last Ch. of foundation, DC1 * into the next Ch. work 2 DCs, 1 Ch.st

and 2 DCs, thr.o., insert into the next Ch., thr.o., dr.thr., thr.o. and dr.thr. 2 loops. Thr.o., miss 3 Ch.sts of foundation, insert into the 4th Ch., thr.o., dr.thr., thr.o., dr.thr. 2 loops, thr.o., dr.thr. 2 loops, thr.o. and dr.thr. the last 2 loops. From * rep. The row ends with 2 DCs, drawn tog. after the group.

2nd and all following rows: Ch.3, 1 DC into the st before the Ch.-st gap, which lies between the 4 DCs * Around the Ch.sts work again the described group: 2 DCs, 1 Ch.st, 2 DCs, thr.o., insert into the next st, thr.o., dr.thr., thr.o. and pull through 2 loops, thr.o., miss 3 st, insert into the 1st st before the gap, thr.o., dr.thr. (see illustration). Repeat 3 times; thr.o. and pull through 2 loops. From the * rep.

49 Crochet Pattern

Ch. foundation

1st row: work into the 4th-last Ch. of foundation, 4 DCs * Miss 2 Chs of foundation, into the next work 1 SC, miss 2 Chs, and into the next work 5 DCs. From * rep. The row ends with 1 SC.

2nd row: to turn, Ch.3. Into the last SC of previous row, DC2. From now on, one inserts only into the back cross-link of the SC. Through this the st is pushed forward * 1 SC into the middle of the 5 DCs of previous row (insert into the 2 cross links) 5 DCs into the SC of previous row, here again insert only into the back cross-link. From * rep.

2nd and 3rd rows: rep.

50 Crochet Pattern

Ch. foundation.

1st row: 1 SC into the 2nd Ch. of foundation. Miss 4 Chs * into the 5th Ch. work 12 DCs, miss 4 Chs, into the next 1 SC, miss 4 Chs, from * rep. The row ends with 1 SC and 3 Ch.sts to turn.

2nd row: into the SC of previous row, 1 DC * Ch.4, into the middle of the 12 DCs work 1 SC, again Ch.4; into the next SC make 2 DCs; from * rep. The row ends with 2 DCs.

3rd row: Ch.1 * between the 2 DCs work 1 SC, on to the SC above the 12 DCs, work again 12 DCs. From * rep. The row ends with 1 SC.
2nd and 3rd rows: rep.

51   Crochet Pattern

After Ch.-st foundation, work into the 4th last Ch., 2 DCs, then miss 2 Chs, into the 3rd Ch. make 1 sl.st, 2 Chs and 2 DCs; miss 2 Chs. Into the next Ch., again work 1 sl.st, 2 Chs and 2 DCs, miss 2. Into the next, work 1 sl.st, 2 Chs and 2 DCs. Finish the row with 1 sl.st. Turn with 4 Chs, and into the 2 Chs of previous row, work 1 sl.st. 2 Ch.sts and 2 DCs. Work the same into 2nd and all following rows. This pattern (Shell) can also be worked in 2 colours. E.g. if white and green are used in alternate rows, and green in forward row, a good effect will be achieved, as these lie slightly back.

52   Crochet Pattern

On to the Ch.-st foundation work 1 SC, miss 2 Chs and into the following work 5 DCs, miss 2 Chs, work 5 DCs into the next, etc., etc. to the end of row. To achieve a straight edge, finish row with a SC.
2nd row: Ch.3, turn: 2 DCs into the SC of previous row, on to the 3rd DC of DC group of previous row work 1 SC. On to the SC of previous row work 5 DCs, etc., etc. This row ends with 3 DCs. Ch.1, turn: 5 DCs on to the SC, etc., etc.

53 Crochet Pattern
(Closed tufts)

Work 2 rows of SC (insert into the rear loop). With the 3rd row the pattern is formed. First work 2 or 3 SCs, insert from the back into the 1st SC of previous row, and work 4 or 5 DCs, only half-finished. i.e. thr.o., insert, thr.o. and dr.thr., thr.o. and dr.thr. 2 loops; rep. this again 3 or 4 times, then, dr.thr. all loops at the same time. Follow up by working 3 SCs, then the tuft pattern as before etc., etc. Ch.1, turn, then work 1 row of SC. The tufts in the next row are moved. One works into the middle SC of previous pattern row. The tufts form on reverse side. The illustration shows the reverse side, hence arrow points to the left.

Star Pattern

Ch.-st foundation.
1st row: draw out of the 2nd to 6th Ch. of foundation, 1 loop each. Pull loops well up. Draw all 6 loops on hook tog. Finish with Ch.st. * For the following star, the 1st loop lies already on the hook, the next loop draw out of the finishing Ch., for the 3rd loop, insert into the back link of stitch out of which the 6th loop for previous star pattern came, and dr.thr. The 4th loop out of the st of which the 6th loop came, and the 2 next loops out of the following Ch.sts of foundation. With 1 Ch.st draw all the loops tog. From * rep.
2nd and all following backward rows:

54 Crochet Pattern

SC.
3rd and all following forward rows: Ch.3, out of the 2nd and 1st of these Ch.st, and out of the 3 following SCs draw 1 loop each, and draw tog. Ch.1 * for the following star st, get second loop through previous Ch.st, the 3rd loop out of the back link of the 6th loop of previous star st. The 4th loop draw out of the st of which the 6th loop of previous star st was drawn. Through the 2 following SCs, take 1 loop each, draw all loops tog. and finish with a Ch.st. From * rep.
2nd and 3rd rows: rep. continuously.

55   Crochet Pattern

1st row: Into every 3rd Ch. of foundation row, work 3 DCs.
2nd row: Ch.3, turn. On to each of the DCs, of group of 3 in previous row, work half a DC, i.e. thr.o., insert, thr.o., dr.thr. 2 loops, thr.o., insert into the next st, thr.o., dr.thr., thr.o. and pull through 2 loops, thr.o., insert above the 3rd DC, thr.o., dr.thr., thr.o., pull through 2 loops, thr.o., and pull through all 4 loops (as illustration), 1 Ch. before beg. the next DC group. At the end of row, turn with 3 Chs.
3rd row: as 1st row. One always works the 3 DCs in the upper loop which keeps the 3 loops tog.
2nd and 3rd rows: rep. continuously.

56   Crochet Pattern

Ch.-st foundation.
1st row: into every Ch. work 1 DC (one should be able to divide the number of DCs by 2). After turning, Ch.3 to replace the 1st DC.
2nd row: Ch.3, insert into the 1st of the 3 Ch.sts, draw thread through into a loop. Out of the 2nd and 3rd DCs of previous row draw 1 loop each, so that one has 4 loops on hook. Thr.o. and dr.thr. all loops. Ch.1 to close ring. * Insert into back link of previous st, thr.o. and dr.thr. into a loop. Out of each of the next 2 DCs draw 1 loop, so that there are 4 loops on hook. Draw all 4 tog. Finish with 1 Ch.st. From * rep.
3rd row: work into the middle of the little star, and into the Ch.sts of previous row, 2 DCs each.
2nd and 3rd rows: rep. continuously.

57 Large Star Pattern

Every star is formed with two rows.

1st row: SC into the last-but-one Ch. of foundation. Miss 3 Chs, into 4th Ch. work 9 DCs (thus forming half a star—see illustration), miss 3 Ch.sts, and into the next work 1 SC, again miss 3 Chs and work 9 DCs into the next, etc., etc.

2nd row: after one ends the 1st row with a SC, and turns with 3 Ch.sts, work on each of the next 4 DCs half a DC, i.e. thr.o., insert, thr.o. and dr.thr., thr.o. and pull through 2 loops. Draw loops well up. Thr.o., and now draw all 5 loops on hook tog. Close with 1 Ch.st. Ch.3, work 1 SC, into the 5th DC of arch, Ch.3, on the following 4 DCs, the SC and the next 4 DCs (tog. 9 sts) work half a DC each. One has now 9 half-DCs on hook. Continue with thr.o., and dr.thr. all loops, close with 1 Ch.st. Ch.3, etc., etc. The row always ends with half an arch.

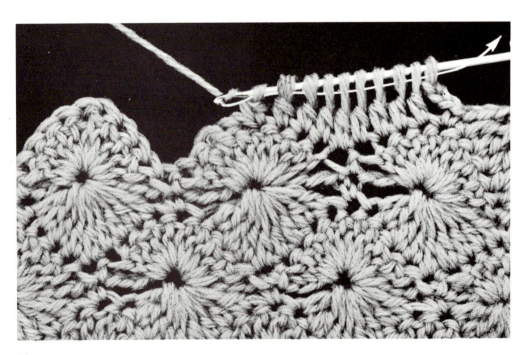

3rd row: Ch.3, insert into the closing Ch.st of the 4 dr.-tog. DCs, and work 4 DCs; on the SC of previous row, 1 SC. Work 9 DCs in the closing Ch. of the 9 dr.-tog. DCs. 1 SC on to the SC of previous row, etc., etc. At the end of row, 4 DCs on to the half-arch of previous row. Turn with 3 Ch.sts. Make 9 half-DCs, etc., etc.

2nd and 3rd rows: rep. continuously.

Pattern in Relief

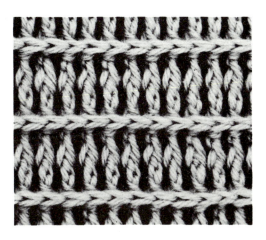

58   Crochet Pattern

Ch.-st foundation.
1st row: DC.
2nd row: DC, but work around the DCs of previous row.
2nd row: rep. continuously.

59   Crochet Pattern

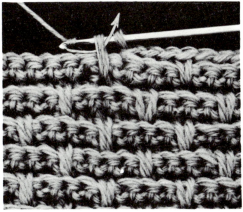

Forward and backward rows. First work two rows of SCs, insert into the upper back link of previous row, in the 3rd row crochet every 4th st as relief st, i.e. for every 4th crochet, insert into the row *below*, draw thread through, and pull loop loosely so long until it reaches the last row. Finish the SC.
In the 2nd following row, move the relief sts.

60   Crochet Pattern

Ch.-st foundation.
1st row: SC.
2nd row: 1 SC, 1 DC, alternately.
3rd row: SC.
4th row: 1 SC, 1 relief DC. The SCs are worked on the SCs of previous row, the relief DCs are worked around the DCs of the 2nd row, and afterwards around the relief DCs.
3rd and 4th rows: rep. continuously.

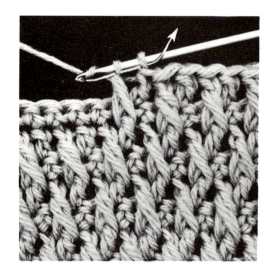

61 Crochet Pattern

Ch.-st foundation.
1st row: DC.
2nd row: SC.
3rd row: DC1, the next DC work around the upright st of the DCs of the 1st row. For that, insert hook from right to left behind the st, thr.o., dr.l.thr. behind the st and up to the middle of SC, and finish the DC. Work 1 DC, for the next DC, insert again into the 1st row, etc., etc.
4th row: SC.
3rd and 4th row: rep. continuously.
The relief sts are moved in each DC row.

62 Relief Plate Pattern

Ch.-st foundation.
1st row: DC.
2nd row: work 3 DCs (for details *see* Pattern 61) into the front and 3 into the back of row. The latter are worked exactly as the 1st, but insert from the back around the upright st of previous row. With the 3rd and all following rows, work the relief DCs lying back, to the front, and vice-versa.

63 Crochet Pattern

The illustration shows the pattern being worked in 2 colours. The 1st row, after the Ch. foundation, is made with DCs. Only work in forward rows. Every row begins with a sl.st. The 2nd row is made with 3 Ch.sts and 1 sl.st alternately. With the 3 Ch.sts, miss 2 DCs of previous row. The 3rd row shows 2 DCs and 1 relief DC alternately (*see* details in Pattern 61). As the illustration shows, the DCs are worked on the DCs of previous row, the relief DC covers the sl.st. Work the following row as the 2nd row.

64 Crochet Pattern

Ch.-st foundation.

1st row: in every 2nd Ch. of foundation, 1 DC, Ch.1.

2nd row: Ch.3 * 1 relief DC (from the front insert around the upright st of previous row) Ch.1, one relief DC, Ch.1, DC1, with that insert from the back around the upright st of previous row, Ch.1, DC1 from the back again, Ch.1. From * rep.

3rd row: Ch.3 * on the relief DCs of previous row, work one DC from the back, Ch.1 and vice-versa.

4th row: Ch.3 * from the back work 1 DC, Ch.1, from the back 1 DC, Ch.1, one relief DC, Ch.1. From * rep.

5th row: as 3rd row.

2nd–5th rows: rep. continuously.

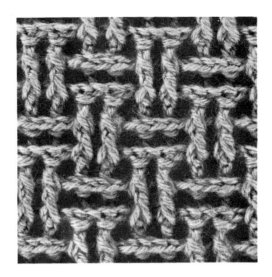

65 Crochet Pattern

Ch.-st foundation.

1st row: DC.

2nd row: SC.

3rd row: * 3 DCs on the 1st SC of previous row, now thr.o. twice, and insert hook from right to left around the upright st of the SC, below the 1st DC of the group of 3, and work 1 TC. From * rep.

4th row: SC on DC only.

5th row: here the TCs lie in reverse direction. First work 3 Ch.sts * then the TC into the 4th st, so, above the TC of previous row, then the 3 DCs. Leave the TC to the foreground.

2nd–5th rows: rep. continuously. The backward row is always worked with SC.

66 Crochet Pattern

Ch.-st foundation.

1st row: into the 4th-last Ch. of foundation, work 1 DC. (3 Chs replace 1 DC) * in the next-but-one Ch., work 1 tuft pattern, (consisting of 3 half-finished DCs which are simultaneously dr.tog.; 1 Ch.st closes the tuft pattern), in the next-but-one Ch. work 2 DCs. From * rep.

2nd and all following rows, as 1st row: the DC group is worked between the 2 DCs, and the tuft pattern around the tuft pattern. Insert around the lower upright sts from right to left.

67 Crochet Pattern

Ch.-st foundation.

1st row: thr.o., insert in the last-but-one Ch., thr.o. and draw direct through a loop, and a thr.-o. Thr.o. again, and dr.thr. the last 2 loops * thr.o., insert in the next Ch., thr.o. and dr.thr. direct through loop and thr.o. Thr.o. again and dr.thr. 2 loops. From * rep. To turn, Ch.3.

2nd row: * miss the 1st st, work into the next 1 DC, then insert back into the 1st st and work one DC. The 2nd DC winds loosely round the 1st. From * rep. To turn, Ch.1.

3rd row: * thr.o., insert into the next st, thr.o., dr.thr. and direct through 1 loop and the thr.o. Thr.o. again and dr.thr. last 2 loops on hook. From * rep. To turn, Ch.3.

4th row: as 2nd row, but with the pattern moved on.

5th row: as 3rd row.

2nd–5th rows: rep. continuously.

Openwork Patterns

(With these patterns, the abbreviations given on p. 299 are used.)

68 Crochet Pattern

Ch. foundation

In the 8th-last Ch. work 1 SL * Ch.4, miss 3 foundation sts, SL1, from * rep.

2nd and all following rows: begin with Ch.4, the SL is worked in the arch of Ch.sts.

69 Crochet Pattern

Ch. foundation.

1st row: SC.

2nd row: 1 SC and 2 Ch. alternately. With the 2 Ch. always miss the 2 Ch. of previous row.

3rd row: SC, on the SC of previous row, always work 1 SC, around the Ch.sts, work 2 SC.

2nd and 3rd rows: rep. continuously.

70 Crochet Pattern

Ch.-st foundation.
1st row: 1 DC into the 8th-last Ch. Ch.2 *
1 DC, 2 Ch., leave 2 Ch. of foundation.
From * rep.
2nd row: 3 SC and 1 Ch. alternately. Work
the SCs always around the 2 Chs. of previous
row.
3rd row: 5 Ch., then continue as in 1st row,
as described from *. The DC work always
around the Ch., of previous row, missing the
3 SCs.
2nd and 3rd rows: rep. continuously.

71 Crochet Pattern

On to the Ch. foundation, work 1 DC and 1
Ch. alternately, between each missing 1 Ch.
of foundation. Turn with 4 Ch. and work, in
the following rows, the DCs on the DCs of
previous row. Insert through the 2 links of st.

72 Crochet Pattern

Ch. foundation.
1st row: work 1 DC into the 6th-last Ch *
miss 2 Ch. of foundation, 1 DC, 2 Ch., 1 DC
in the next Ch. of foundation. From * rep.
2nd and all following rows: 5 Ch.1 DC in
the arch of Ch. Into every arch of Ch. work
DC group as described in 1st row.

73 Crochet Pattern

Ch. foundation.
1st row: into the 5th-last Ch. of foundation,
1 DC * miss 1 Ch. of foundation, 1 DC, miss
1 Ch. 1 DC, Ch.1, and work into the same st a
2nd DC. From * rep. The row ends with a
DC.
2nd row: 3 Ch. * Into the crochet-group of
previous row work 1 DC. On to the next
single DC work a crochet-group (1 DC, 3 Ch.
1 DC). From * rep. The row ends with 1 DC.
2nd row: rep. continuously.

74 Crochet Pattern

Ch. foundation.
Work forward and backward rows.
1st row: into the 6th Ch. of foundation work
1 DC * miss 2 Ch. In the following Ch. work
1 DC, 2 Ch. and 1 DC. From * rep.
2nd row: Ch.3, DC3 into the 2 Ch. of
previous row * 4 DC into the next 2 Ch. of
previous row. From * rep.
3rd row: 5 Ch. 1 DC above the next DC of
previous row * 1 DC, 2 Ch., 1 DC (work the
2 DCs between the crochet-group of previous
row). From * rep.
4th row: 3 Ch. 1 DC * 4 DC into the 2 Ch.
of previous row. From * rep.
5th row: as 1st row, but the 2 DCs between
the DC group of previous row.
2nd–5th rows: rep. continuously.

75 Crochet Pattern

Ch. foundation.
Into the 8th-last Ch. work 1 SC * Ch.3,
miss 3 Ch. of previous row, 1 SC. From * rep.
2nd row: Ch.4, around the 1st 3 Ch. DC1 *
1 Ch. around the next 3 Ch. DC4, Ch.1, DC1
around the next 3 Ch. From * rep.
3rd row: * Ch.3. Work 1 SC in front of the
DC of previous row, Ch.3. Now 1 SC behind
the DC. From * rep.
4th row: as 2nd row, but begin with 3 DCs.
Rep. 3rd and 4th rows continuously. In
each row the pattern is being transposed, as
shown in illustration.

76 Crochet Pattern

Ch. foundation.
1st row: into the 4th-last Ch. work 1 DC *
Ch.1, in the 3rd-following Ch. of foundation
work 2 DCs. From * rep. The row ends with
1 DC.
2nd and all following rows: Ch.4 to turn,
work 2 DCs into the arch of Ch. * Ch.1, DC2
into the next Ch.-arch. From * rep.

77 Crochet Pattern

Ch. foundation.

1st row: thr.o., insert into the 3rd-last Ch. *
Thr.o., dr.thr., thr.o., insert into the next Ch.,
thr.o., dr.thr., thr.o., dr.thr. 4 loops, thr.o. and
dr.thr. the last 2 loops. Ch.1, thr.o., insert into
the next Ch. From * rep. Ch.3 to turn.
2nd and all following rows: thr.o., insert
into the st which pulled loops of previous
row tog., draw wool through, thr.o., insert
into the Ch. between 1st 2 groups of pattern
of previous row, thr.o., dr.thr., thr.o., dr.thr.

4 loops, thr.o. and dr.thr. the last 2 loops * Ch.1,
thr.o., insert into st which pulled loops of
previous row tog., thr.o., dr.thr., thr.o., insert
into next Ch.st of previous row, thr.o.,
dr.thr., thr.o., dr.thr. 4 loops, thr.o. and dr.thr.
the last 2 loops. From * rep. Finish with 1 Ch.st.
Thr.o., insert into the st which pulled last
group tog. in previous row, thr.o., dr.thr.,
insert into the Ch. which was made for the
turn, draw wool through, thr.o., dr.thr. 4
loops, thr.o. and dr.thr. the last 2 loops. Turn
with 3 Ch.sts.

78 Crochet Pattern

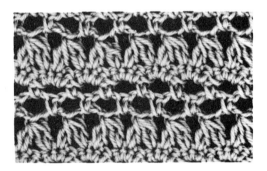

Ch.-st foundation.

1st row: into the 4th-last Ch. work 1 DC
(only half-finished), miss 2 Ch. of foundation,
in the next Ch. work 2 half-finished DCs,
draw the 4 loops on hook tog. * Miss 3 Ch.
Into the next Ch. work 2 DCs, but only half-
finished, miss 2 Ch. and into the next again
2 half-finished DCs, draw the 5 loops on hook
tog. From * rep.
2nd row: Ch.3, into the arch of Chs of
previous row, work 1 SC * Ch.3, into the
following arch of Chs, SC1. From * rep.

3rd row: as 2nd row.
4th row: Ch.2, and into every arch of Chs
work 4 SCs. Into the 1st and last arch work
only 2 SCs.
5th row: Ch.3 into the 1st SC work 1 half-
finished DC, miss 2 SCs, and into the next st
work 2 half-finished DCs, and crochet the
4 loops on hook tog. * Ch.3, into the next SC
work 2 half-finished DCs, miss 2 SCs of
previous row, into the 3rd SC, work a half-
finished DC, and now draw the 5 loops on
hook tog. From * rep.
2nd–6th rows: rep. continuously.

79　Crochet Pattern

Ch.-st foundation.
1st row: into every Ch.st, 1 SC.
2nd row: Ch.3 * thr.o., insert into the 2nd SC of previous row, draw thread through, draw up, thr.o., insert into the same st and draw wool through, pull up, thr.o., again insert into the same st to draw wool through, pull up, thr.o., and pull through all loops. Ch.3, miss 1 st of previous row, SC1, Ch.2, miss 1 st of previous row. From * rep.
3rd row: * above the tuft of SC, Ch.5 sts. From * rep.
4th row: * above the SC, one tuft, as described in 2nd row. Ch.3, SC1 into the middle of the 5 Ch.sts of previous row, Ch.2. From * rep.
3rd–4th rows: rep. continuously.

80　Crochet Pattern

Ch.-st foundation.
1st row: into the 2nd-last Ch., work 1 SC * Ch.4, miss 4 Ch. of foundation, into the next Ch. work 1 SC. From * rep. For the turn, Ch.2.
2nd row: 1 DC into the 1st SC * into the arch of Ch.sts of previous row, work 1 SC, 2 DCs and 1 SC. Ch.5. From * rep. End row with 1 SC, 2 DCs and 1 SC. Into the last arch, DC1 into the turning-stitch of previous row. Ch.1 to turn.
3rd row: 1 SC into the 1st DC, Ch.5. * Round the arch of Ch.sts, 1 SC, Ch.5. From * rep. End with 1 SC into the last DC. To turn, Ch.2.
2nd and 3rd rows: rep. continuously.

81　Crochet Pattern

Ch.-st foundation.
1st row: into 4th Ch. SC1 * Ch.3, miss 2 Chs of foundation, into the next, work 1 SC. From * rep.
2nd row: Ch.3 to turn * DC 3 into the SC, into the arch of Ch.sts work 1 SC. From * rep.
3rd row: Ch.3 to turn. 1 SC into the middle of the three DCs, Ch.3. From * rep.
2nd and 3rd rows: rep. continuously.

82　Crochet Pattern

Ch.-st foundation.
1st row: into the 4th-last Ch. of foundation work 1 DC, 2 Ch and 2 DCs * Ch.2, miss 3 Ch. of foundation and into the following Ch. DC2, Ch.2 and DC2. From * rep.
2nd row: between each group of DC, work 2 DCs, Ch.2, 2 DCs. These 4 DCs form a tooth; between each tooth crochet around the Ch.sts of previous row 1 SC. Continuously rep. these 2 rows.

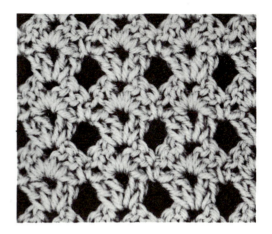

83　Crochet Pattern

Ch.-st foundation.
1st row: Work into the 4th-last Ch. of foundation, 1 DC * Ch.2, and DC2 into the same Ch.st. Miss 2 Ch. of foundation, DC1 miss 2 Ch. of foundation and DC2. From * rep.
2nd and all following: as 1st row. The one DC is worked onto the DC, and the DC group *between* the group of previous row.

84　Crochet Pattern

Ch.-st foundation.
1st row: into the 5th Ch. of foundation, DC1 * Ch.2, miss 5 Ch. of foundation, DC1, Ch.2, DC1 into the same st. From * rep.
2nd row: Ch.2. * Into the Chs between the 2 DCs, work 8 DCs, miss the next arch of Ch.st, and from * rep.
3rd row: with sl.st go back to the 5th DC, Ch.4, DC1 into the same st, (the 5th DC). * Ch.2, into 5th DC of next group, 1 DC, Ch.2, DC1. From * rep.
2nd and 3rd rows: rep. continuously.

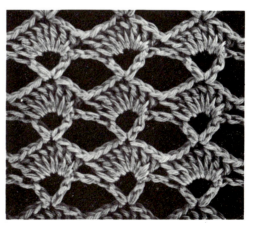

85　Crochet Pattern

Ch.-st foundation.
1st row: into the 3rd-last Ch., 1 SC * Ch.3, miss 5 of foundation, work into next Ch. 5 DCs, miss 5 Ch. Ch.3, into the following Ch. work 1 SC. From * rep. Ch.2 to turn.
2nd row: into every SC, again SC1, but only make 1 Ch.st in between.
3rd row: in the 1st SC, DC3 * Ch.3, into the 3rd (middle) DC of previous row, SC1. Ch.3, into the SC of previous row DC5. From * rep. At the end of row, work into the last SC only 3 DCs. Ch.2 to turn.
4th row: as 2nd.
5th row: * into the 3rd DC work 1 SC, Ch.3. Into the SC work 5 DCs, Ch.3. From * rep. Into the last DC, 1 SC, Ch.2, turn.
2nd to 5th rows: rep. continuously.

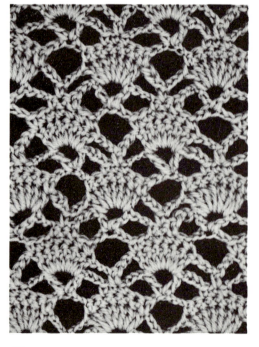

86　Crochet Pattern

Ch.-st foundation.
1st row: into the 2nd-last Ch. work 1 SC * Ch.3, miss 2 Ch. of foundation, into the next Ch. work 1 DC, Ch.3, DC1, Ch.3, miss 2 Ch.sts, work 3 SCs. From * rep.
2nd row: Ch.4 * between the two DCs of previous row, work 7 DCs, Ch.3. Into the middle one of the 3 SCs, SC1, Ch.3. From * rep.
3rd row: Ch.6 * 7 SCs into the 7 DCs of previous row, Ch.5. From * rep.
4th row: Ch.4, 1 DC into 1st st of previous row. * Ch.3, SC3, into the middle 3 SCs of previous row. Into the 3rd Ch.st of previous row, DC1. From * rep.
5th row: Ch.3, DC2 between the 2 DCs of previous row. * Ch.3, into the middle SC of group of 3 SCs in previous row, work 1 SC, Ch.3. 7 DCs between the 2 DCs of previous row. From * rep.
6th row: Ch.1, SC3 * Ch.5, SC7. From * rep.
1st–6th rows: rep. continuously.

87 Crochet Pattern

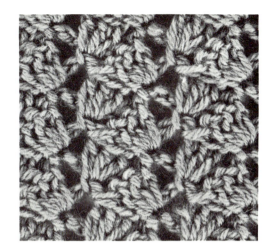

Ch.-st foundation.

1st row: into the 2nd-last Ch. of foundation, work 1 sl.st * miss 2 Chs of foundation, into the next DC3; Ch.3, miss 3, into the following, 1 sl.st. From * rep. Row ends with 1 sl.st.

2nd row: Ch.3 to turn. Into 1st sl.st of previous row, DC2, Ch.3 * into the Ch.-arch, close to the DC group of previous row, 1 sl.st. DC3 on to the sl.st of previous row, Ch.3. From * rep. The row ends with 3 Ch.sts.

3rd row: Ch.1 to turn. On to the last DC of previous row, 1 sl.st * on to the sl.st of previous row, 3 DCs; Ch.3. Into the arch of chain of previous row, close to the DC group, 1 sl.st. From * rep. The row ends with 1 sl.st.

2nd and 3rd rows: rep. continuously.

88 Crochet Pattern

Ch.-st foundation.

1st row: into the 5th-last Ch. of foundation, 1 DC * 1 SC into the next Ch., the loops on the hook draw up about $\frac{1}{2}$ inch high, into the 4th following Ch. 1 DC, Ch.1, DC1. From * rep. The row ends with 1 SC.

2nd and all following rows: Ch.4, DC1 into the last DC of previous row. * 1 SC between the 2 DCs. Draw loops on hook to about $\frac{1}{2}$ inch; into the next SC, DC1, Ch.1, DC1. From * rep. Row ends with 1 SC.

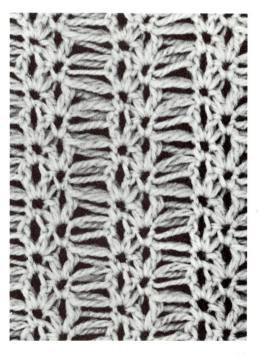

89. Crochet Pattern

Ch.-st foundation.

1st row: 4 DCs * Ch.2, miss 1 Ch. of foundation, 1 SC, Ch.2, miss 1 Ch. of foundation, 1 DC, Ch.3, into the same st a 2nd DC, Ch.2, miss 1 Ch. of foundation, 1 SC, Ch.3, again miss 1 Ch. of foundation, DC4. From * rep.

2nd row: into the 4 DCs of previous row, again work 4 DCs (when turning, instead of 1 DC, Ch.3) * Ch.5, work 7 DCs into the arch of Ch.sts between the 2 DCs of previous row, Ch.5, DC4. From * rep.

3rd row: 4 DCs * Ch.2, 1 SC into the lower arch, Ch.5, 1 SC into the middle of the lower DC group, Ch.5. 1 SC into the next lower arch, Ch.3, DC4. From * rep.

4th row: DC4 * Ch.5, 1 SC into the 2nd arch, Ch.5, SC1 into the next arch, Ch.5, DC4. From * rep.

5th row: 4 DCs * Ch.2, 1 SC into the 1st arch, Ch.2, into the 3rd Ch. of 2nd arch, 1 DC. Ch.3, and again 1 DC, then Ch.2, 1 SC into the 3rd arch, Ch.2, 4 DCs. From * rep.

2nd—5th rows: rep. continuously.

90 Crochet Pattern

The number of sts should be divisible by 9, and 1 st for the 1st SC.

Ch.-st foundation.

1st row: miss 1 st of foundation, into the next 3 Ch.sts work 3 SCs * Ch.3, miss 2 of foundation, work 7 SCs. From * rep. Row ends with 4 SCs.

2nd row: Ch.1, SC2 * Ch.3, SC1, Ch.3, SC5 (the 5 SCs always go into the middle of the 7 SCs: the single SC into the middle of the 3 Ch.sts always insert under 2 links). From * rep.

3rd row: Ch.1, SC1 * Ch.3, SC1 into the arch of Ch., SC1 into the SC of previous row. 1 SC in the arch of Ch., Ch.3, 1 SC into each of the middle 3 of group of 5 SCs of previous row. From * rep.

4th row: Ch.5 * 5 SCs into the 3 SCs of previous row, Ch.3, 1 SC into middle SC of group of 3 in previous row, Ch.3. From * rep.

5th row: * Ch.3, SC7, Ch.3, SC7. From * rep.

6th row: Ch.3 * 1 SC into each of the middle 5 of group of 7 SCs in previous row, Ch.3, 1 SC into arch of Ch.sts, Ch.3. From * rep.

7th row: Ch.1, SC1 * Ch.3, 1 SC into the arch of Ch.sts, 1 SC in the SC of previous row, 1 SC into the arch of Ch.sts, 3 Ch., 1 SC into each of the middle 3 SCs of group of 5 in previous row. From * rep.

8th row: Ch.1, SC2 * Ch.3, SC1, Ch.3, 5 SCs. From * rep.

1st—8th rows: rep. continuously.

91 Crochet Pattern

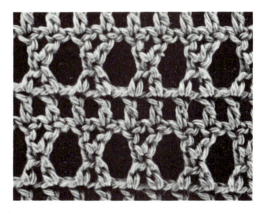

The number of sts should be divisible by 10, plus 2.

Ch.-st foundation.

1st row: into the 2nd, 3rd and 4th st of foundation, 1 SC each * Ch.4, miss 2 sts of foundation, into the next DC1, Ch.4, miss 2 sts of foundation and into the following 5 sts, work 1 SC each. From * rep. The row ends with Ch.4, DC1, Ch.4, SC3, Ch.1 to turn.

2nd row: 1 SC into each of the last 2 SCs of previous row * Ch.4, miss next SC and the 3 Ch.sts of arch of Ch., into 4th Ch. of the same arch, into the DC and following Ch.st, 1 SC each. Ch.4, miss next 3 Ch.sts and the 1st SC of SC group, into 2nd, 3rd and 4th SC, work 1 SC each. From * rep. Row ends with Ch.4, 1 SC into each of the 2 last SCs, Ch.3 to turn.

3rd row: 1 DC into the last SC of previous row * Ch.4, miss the next SC and the following 3 Ch.sts of Ch.-arch, into the 4th Ch.st work 1 SC, and 1 SC each into the 3 SCs of previous row. 1 SC in the following Ch.st. Ch.4, 1 DC into the middle of the three SCs of previous row. From * rep. Ch.1 to turn.

4th row: 1 SC into the DC and another into the 1st Ch.st of àrch * Ch.4, SC into each of middle 3 sts of SC group, Ch.4, miss 3 sts of arch of Ch.; SC1 into the 4th Ch.st. From * rep. Row ends as it begins, Ch.1 to turn.

5th row: 1 SC into each of the SCs of previous row, and into the next Ch.st * Ch.4, 1 DC into the middle of the 3 SCs of previous row, Ch.4, miss 3 sts of arch of Chs, and into the 4th Ch., SC1. 1 SC into each of the 3 SCs of previous row, and 1 SC into the next Ch.st. From * rep. Row ends as it begins.

2nd–5th rows: rep. continuously.

92 Crochet Pattern

Ch.-st foundation.

1st row: DC1 and Ch.1 alternately. Miss 1 Ch.st of foundation between each DC.

2nd row: cross crochet (*see* Pattern 9).

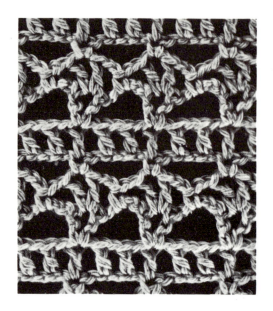

93 Crochet Pattern

Ch.-st foundation.
1st row: 1 DC, 1 Ch., 1 DC, 1 Ch., etc., etc.
With every Ch.st miss 1 Ch. of foundation.
2nd row: 1 DC (for the 1st DC Ch.3), Ch.1,
DC1 * Ch.5, miss 2 DCs of previous row, into
next DC work 1 DC, Ch.2, DC1. From *
rep.
3rd row: here one works between the 2 DCs
of previous row, 1 DC, 2 Chs, 1 DC; around
the 5 Ch.sts of previous row work 1 SC,
Ch.2. Between the 2 following DCs, DC1 and
Ch.2 and DC1.
4th row: * 1 SC between the 2 DCs of
previous row. Ch.5. From * rep.
1st–4th rows: rep. continuously.

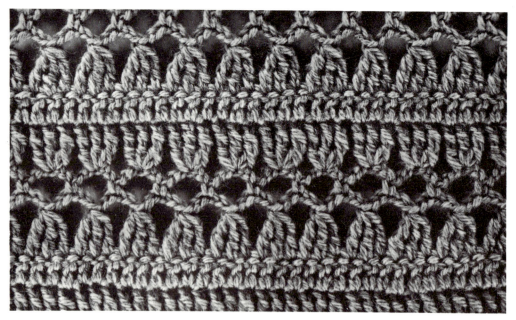

94 Crochet Pattern

Ch.-st foundation.

1st row: into every Ch.st of foundation 1
DC.
2nd row: Ch.5 * into the following 3 DCs,
TC1 each, but leave the last loop on hook,
and after every 3rd TC, draw loops completely
through. Ch.5. From * rep.
3rd row: * Ch.5, into 3rd Ch. of previous row
1 SC. From * rep. At the end of row Ch.5,
work the last SC at the edge into the st after
the 3 TCs of previous row.
4th row: Ch.5 * in every 3rd Ch.st of previous
row, TC3. From * rep.
5th row: into every TC work 1 DC.
2nd–5th rows: rep. continuously.

95 Cross-over Crochet

Ch.-st foundation.
1st row: DC, at the end of row turn with 5 Ch.sts.
2nd row: into the 5th, 6th and 7th DCs of previous row, work 1 TC each, then go back into 2nd, 3rd and 4th DCs and work into these also 1 TC each. * Miss 3 DCs of previous row and into the next 3, TC1 each, then go back and work into the 3DCs which were missed 1 TC each. From * rep. Turn with 3 Ch.sts.
3rd row: into each TC work 1 DC, at the end of row turn with 5 Ch.sts. The illustration shows the crossed stitches at the point where one inserts after the 3 TCs.

96 Crochet Pattern

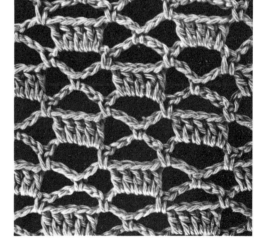

Ch.-st foundation.
1st row: into every Ch.st 1 SC.
2nd row: * Ch.5, miss 4 SCs of previous row, then SC1. From * rep. Row ends with 1 SC.
3rd row: Ch.3 * into the arch of Ch.sts of previous row work 5 DCs, Ch.3, into the middle of the next arch of Ch.sts work 1 SC, Ch.3. From * rep. At the end of row, 1 DC.
4th row: * Ch.5, before the group of DCs, work 1 SC, Ch.5, after the group of DCs again work 1 SC. From * rep.
5th row: * Ch.3, into the middle of arch of Ch.sts of previous row, SC1. Ch.3, into next arch work 5 DCs. From * rep.
6th row: * Ch.5, before the 1st group of DCs work 1 SC; Ch.5, after group of DCs, 1 SC. From * rep.
3rd–6th rows: rep. continuously.

97 Crochet Pattern

Ch.-st foundation.
1st row: 11 DCs, Ch.9, miss 9 Chs of foundation, 11 DCs, Ch.9, etc., etc.
2nd and 3rd rows: as 1st.
4th row: DC11, Ch.5, with 1 SC draw tog. the 3 previous bars of Ch.sts, Ch.5, DC11, etc., etc.
5th row: DC11, Ch.9, DC11, Ch.9, DC11, etc., etc.
From here on, one shifts the pattern.

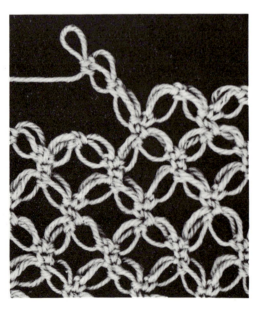

98 Knot Stitch

Ch.-st foundation.
1st row: into 2nd-last st of foundation, 1 SC, and ⋆ draw st up to approximately $\frac{3}{4}$ cm long loop. Thr.o. and dr.thr.; into the back link of the Ch.st work 1 SC, draw st up to loop, thr.o., dr.thr., and into the back link of the Ch.st work 1 SC, so that now there are 2 loops, 1 above the other (*see* illustration). Miss 3 Ch.sts and into the 4th st of foundation work 1 SC. From ⋆ rep.
1st row: rep. continuously.
The SC in these rows are worked into the upper knots of previous rows.

Various Shapes

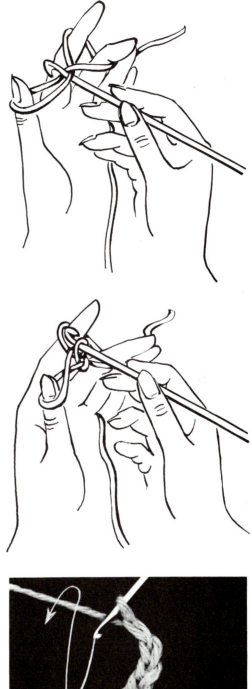

99 Round Beginning without Chain-stitch Ring

Put the thread around the left hand as with crochet. With end of thread, from bottom to top, lay around the thumb of the left hand, a loop. Hold end of thread with ring and middle finger. Insert hook from below through loop on thumb, thread working-thread over, dr.thr.; with this the loop is twisted once. Now insert from above, thr.o. and dr.thr., thr.o. and dr.thr. the 2 loops on hook. Into the loops, work now SC or DC as pattern requires. Lastly, draw the loop at end of thread tog.

100 Chain-stitch Ring

For the beg. of a cap, round cushion, etc., one needs a ring of Ch.sts. One makes 3–5 Ch.sts, closes them with a sl.st to form a ring. Fill ring with SCs or DCs as pattern requires.

101 The Round Crochet Plate

Ch.3, into the 1st Ch.st (beg.) work 16 DCs, close circle with 1 sl.st. Start the following round again with 3 Ch.sts.

2nd round: in every st of previous row inc. Work 2 DCs into 1 st of previous round.

3rd round: in every 2nd st of previous round inc. by 1.

4th round: in every 3rd st of previous round inc. by 1.

5th round: in every 4th st of previous round inc. by 1 and so on.

One must not work loosely. Should it still happen that the plate is not lying flat, omit the increasing in 1 round.

102 Square, Crocheted from the Centre

1st round: Ch.4 (all DCs of 1st round are worked into the 1st Ch.st, the remaining 3 Ch-sts are instead of 1 DC). Into the 1st Ch.st, DC1, Ch.1, DC4, Ch.1, DC4, Ch.1, DC4, Ch.1, DC2, 1 sl.st (with the latter, insert into the upper of the 3 Ch.sts of the beg. of the round, thr.o., dr.thr. and pull through loop on hook).

2nd round: Ch.3, 1 DC into the next DC of previous row. Now into the Ch.st (corner-st) work 3 DCs, 1 Ch.st and 3 DCs * work 4 DCs above the next 4 DCs. 3 DCs, 1 Ch. and 3 DCs above the corner st. From * rep. twice.

At the end, 2 DCs, 1 sl.st. In the 3rd and following rounds, work above each DC of previous row 1 DC into the Ch.st (corner-st) 3 DCs, 1 Ch.st, 3 DCs.
Work continuously in this way. Watch the place at which the round closes. At the beg. of every new round, the 1st DC is replaced by 3 Ch.sts. The following DC comes above the next DC. Each side of the square should have the same number of sts. If the work is too loosely crocheted, it will not lie flat any more after the 5th or 6th round. In this case, work only 2 DCs, 1 Ch., 2 DCs into the corner.

103 Square in Single Crochet

Work from the corner.
Begin with 2 Ch.sts, and into the 1st Ch.st work 3 SCs. Turn with 1 Ch.st, instead of 1 SC. Then into the middle SC of previous row work 3 SCs, again 1 SC, and with 1 Ch.st turn. In the following rows, work always 1 SC above the SC of previous row, and in the middle SC, work 3 SCs to form the corner.

104 To Increase in the Crocheting of Symmetrical Patterns

If it is necessary to inc. quickly, one increases on both sides, by turning with 1 Ch.st, then into the 1st SC of previous row, work 2 SCs. In the last SC of previous row, as well as the Ch.st, 1 SC each.

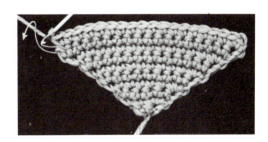

105 To Decrease in the Crocheting of Symmetrical Patterns

To make a sharp slope, begin with 1 Ch.st, then work 1 SC into the 3rd SC of previous row. At the end of each row, miss 1 st of previous row.

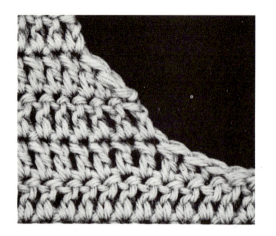

106 Crochet Armhole

Depending on how deep the armhole is to be, begin according to pattern with 3 to 5 sl.sts (illustration shows 4 sl.sts). Follow with 1 SC, half a DC, 1 DC then continue with your crochet pattern. If you crochet back to the armhole, do so only to the st before the last DC. The following row begins again with 1 sl.st, followed by half a DC, 1 DC. Again continue with your pattern. Should the armhole have to deepen even more, then miss 1 at the beg. of row.

107 Crochet Buttonhole

Miss (depending on size) with 3–5 Ch.sts, the same amount of sts of previous row. In the next row, crochet into each of the Ch.sts. If the buttonhole should have to be vertical, work first the right, then the left half, upwards, until the required size is reached. Close buttonhole in following row.

Irish Crochet

108 Motif 1

Into a Ch.st ring (Pattern 100) work 8 Cl.sts (Pattern 13). Separate them with 3 Ch.sts. 1st cluster, DC: Ch.4, work the next st up to 2 loops, the 3rd up to 3 loops, thr.o. and dr.thr. all 3 loops on hook. Ch.3. With the next Cl.st, work the 1st DC up to 2 loops, with the 2nd DC leave a further loop on hook, the same with the 3rd DC, so that it leaves you with 4 loops to draw tog. After the 8th Cl.st, work 3 Ch.sts, and 1 sl.st on to the 1st Cl.st.

109 Motif 2

1st round: into a Ch.-st ring (*see* Pattern 100) work 4 times 6 TCs, separate each group with 5 Ch.sts, 4 Ch.sts replace the 1st TC. Close round with 1 sl.st.

2nd round: into the 2nd, 3rd, 4th and 5th TCs of previous row, work 1 cluster pattern (Pattern 13), Ch.6, 1 SC into arch of Ch.sts of previous row. Ch.6, 1 cluster pattern, etc., etc. With 1 sl.st into the 1st Cl.st, close the round.

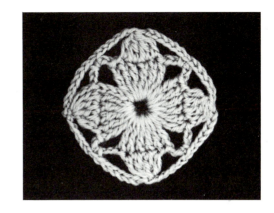

110 Motif 3

Ch.5, and close to form a ring. Again make 5 Ch.sts, work back on them, and work into each Ch. 1 SC, fasten this petal (or spoke) with a sl.st to a ring. In this way work 8 petals to a ring. Then break the thread. Into every petal point work 1 sl.st, and in between, Ch.5. In the last row, work in every arch of Ch.sts, 2 SCs, then 1 picot (Ch.3, back into 1 Ch.st, SC1). 2 SCs, 1 picot, 2 SCs, 1 picot, 2 SCs.

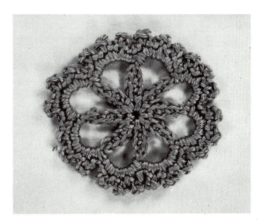

111 Motif 4

1st round: into a Ch.-st ring, work 6 DCs, separated by 3 Ch.sts. 3 Ch.sts replace the 1st DC. The round ends with 1 sl.st.

2nd round: in every Ch.-st arch of previous row work 4 DCs; separate each with 1 Ch.st. Again the 1st DC is replaced by 3 Ch.sts. End round with 1 sl.st.

3rd round: Ch.10, between the 2nd and 3rd following DC of previous row work 1 DC. Ch. 7, miss 2 DCs, then work 1 DC, etc., etc. The round ends again with 1 sl.st.

4th round: into the next 4 Ch.sts work 4 sl.sts. ★ Ch.1, work 1 cross-crochat (Pattern 9). After the cross-crochet work 1 Ch.st and 1 SC in the middle of the Ch.-st arch. From ★ rep.

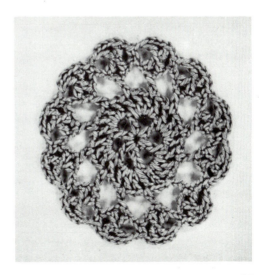

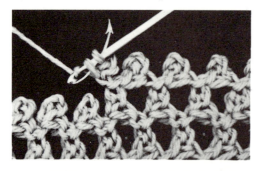

112   Picot Pattern

Ch.-st foundation as required.
Into the 4th-last Ch. work 1 SC, miss 3 Chs of foundation and make 1 sl-st. Ch.4, insert into the 1st of the 4 Chs, and work 1 SC. Miss 3 Chs of foundation, into the next Ch. work 1 sl.st, Ch.4, back in the 1st of the 4 Chs work 1 SC, etc., etc. Turn at end of row with 4 Ch.sts, and in the middle Ch.st of previous picot work 1 sl.st. Ch.4, back in 1st Ch.st work 1 SC. Into the middle Ch.st of the next picot, 1 sl.st, etc., etc.

(The 2nd illustration shows the same pattern and where to insert for sl.st.)

113   Crochet Pattern

Ch.-st foundation.
In the 5th st of foundation 1 SC. Miss 2 Ch.sts, 1 DC * miss 5 of foundation, and into the next work 1 DC, 1 picot, 1 DC (1 picot = 4 Ch.sts, and into the 1st Ch. work 1 SC). From * rep.
2nd row: Ch.7: into 3rd st of Ch.-st arch, 1 DC, 1 picot, 1 DC * Ch. 5, into the 3rd Ch. of arch, 1 DC, 1 picot, 1 DC. From * rep.

End row with 3 Ch.sts and 1 DC which will be behind the last picot of previous row.
3rd row: Ch.7, into the 4th-last work 1 SC. Work 1 DC on to the last DC of previous row. * Ch.5, into the middle of the 2nd Ch. arch of previous row, work 1 DC, 1 picot, 1 DC. From * rep.

2nd and 3rd rows: rep. continuously.

114 Crochet Pattern

Ch.-st foundation.
1st row: into the 4th-last Ch.st work 1 SC. Miss 6 Ch.sts of foundation and make 1 DC * Ch.3, miss 3 of foundation, DC1, work 1 picot (Ch.4, back into 1st Ch. make 1 SC). Miss 3 Chs of foundation, DC1. From * rep. Finish with 1 picot and 1 DC.
2nd row: The position of the picot has moved. Ch.6, DC1 on to the 2nd DC of previous row. * 1 picot, 1 DC on to the next DC, Ch.3, 1 DC on to the next DC. From * rep.
3rd row: Ch.6, into the 4th-last Ch., 1 SC * 1 DC on to the next DC, Ch.3, 1 DC on to the next, 1 picot. From * rep.
2nd and 3rd rows: rep. continuously.

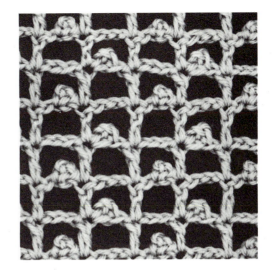

115 Crochet Pattern

Ch.-st foundation.

1st row: into the 2nd-last Ch. of foundation SC1 * Ch.4, into 2nd-last Ch., SC1, into the 3rd-last Ch., DC1. Ch.4, into the 2nd-last Ch. SC1, into the 3rd-last Ch., DC1. Ch.1. Miss 3 Chs of foundation, and into the following Ch., SC1. From * rep. Turn.
2nd row: * Ch.4, into the 2nd-last Ch., SC1. Into the 3rd-last Ch. DC1. Ch.4. Into the 2nd-last Ch. SC1 and into the 3rd-last Ch. DC1. 1 Ch.st and 1 SC into the middle of the 1st pattern group of previous row. From * rep.
2nd row: rep. continuously.

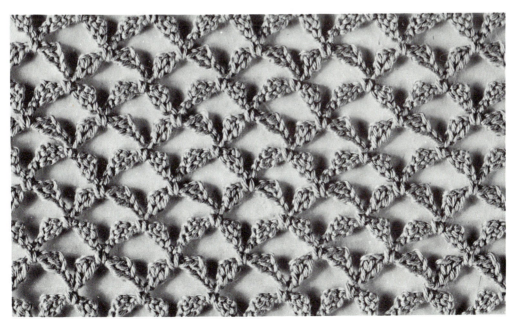

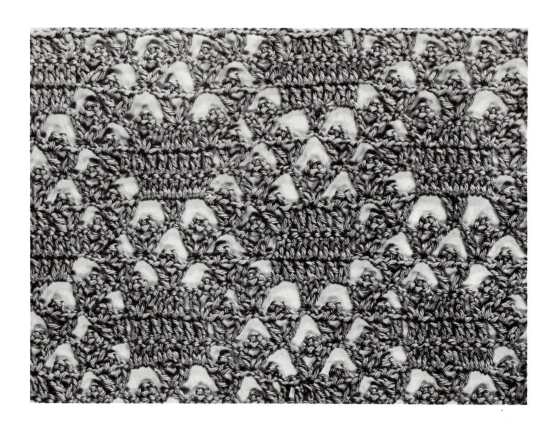

116   Crochet Pattern

Ch.-st foundation.

1st row: into the 4th-last Ch. 1 DC. Into the next 5 Chs 1 DC each. * Ch.3, 1 DC into that 5th following Ch.st, 1 picot (=4 Ch.sts, into the 1st Ch.st, SC1). 1 DC into the same Ch.st as the last DC. Ch.3, 1 DC into the 5th following Ch.st, 1 picot, 1 DC into the same Ch.st as the last DC, Ch.3, 1 DC into the 5th following Ch.st, 1 picot, 1 DC into the same Ch.st as the last DC. Ch.3, miss 4 Ch.sts of foundation, DC7. From * rep. Row ends with 7 DCs.

2nd row: Ch.3, on to each of the next 6 DCs, 1 DC * Ch.1, 1 DC into the middle of the 3 Ch.sts of previous row, 1 picot, 1 DC into the same Ch.st as the last DC, Ch.3, 1 DC into the middle of the next 3 DCs, 1 picot, 1 DC into the same Ch.st as the last DC. Ch.3, 1 DC into the middle of the next 3 Ch.sts, 1 picot. 1 DC into the same Ch.st, Ch.3, 1 DC into the middle of the next 3 Ch.sts, 1 picot, 1 DC into the same Ch.st, Ch.1, DC7. From * rep.

3rd row: Ch.5 * 3 DCs above the middle 3 DCs of previous row. Ch.1, DC1 into the 7th DC of previous row, 1 picot, 1 DC into the same DC as the last DC. Ch.3, 1 DC into the middle of the next 3 Ch.sts of previous row, 1 picot, 1 DC into the same Ch.st as the last DC, Ch.3, 1 DC into the middle of the next 3 Ch.sts of previous row, Ch.1, 1 DC into the same Ch.st as the last DC. Ch.3, 1 DC into the middle of the next 3 Ch.sts of previous row, 1 picot, 1 DC into the same Ch.st, Ch.3, 1 DC into the 1st DC of previous row, 1 picot, 1 DC into the same DC, 1 Ch.st.

From * rep. Row ends with 2 Ch.sts, 1 DC.

4th row: Ch.5 * 1 DC into the middle of the 3 DCs of previous row, 1 picot, 1 DC into the same DC, Ch.3, 1 DC into the middle of the next 3 Ch.sts of previous row, 1 picot, 1 DC into the same Ch.st as the last DC, Ch.3, DC7 (the 1st 2 into the Ch.st arch, the 3rd DC into the DC, the 4th on to the picot, the 5th on to the DC, the 6th and 7th into the arch). Ch.3, 1 DC into the middle of the next 3 Ch.sts of previous row, 1 picot, 1 DC into the same Ch.st, Ch.3. From * rep. Row ends with 2 Ch.sts and 1 DC.

5th row: Ch.7, into the 4th-last Ch. 1 SC (picot), 1 DC into the last DC of previous row. * Ch.3, 1 DC into the middle of the next 3 Ch.sts, 1 picot, 1 DC into the same Ch.st, Ch.3, 1 DC in the middle of the 3 Ch.sts, 1 picot, 1 DC into the same Ch.st as the last DC. Ch.1, DC7 into the 7 DCs of previous row, Ch.1, 1 DC into the middle of the next 3 Ch.sts, 1 picot, 1 DC into the same Ch.st as the last DC, Ch.3, 1 DC into the middle of the next 3 Ch.sts, 1 picot, 1 DC into the same Ch.st as the last DC. From * rep. Row ends with 1 DC, 1 picot, 1 DC.

6th row: Ch.5 * 1 DC into the middle of the next 3 Ch.sts, Ch.1, 1 DC into the same Ch.st as the last DC, Ch.3, 1 DC into the middle of the next 3 Ch.sts, 1 picot, 1 DC into the same Ch.st. as the last DC, Ch.3, 1 DC into the 1st of the 7 DCs, 1 picot, 1 DC into the same st, Ch.1, 3 DCs into the 3rd, 4th and 5th DCs of previous row, Ch.1, 1 DC into the last of the 7 DCs, 1 picot, 1 DC into the same st, Ch.3, 1 DC into the middle of the next 3 Ch.sts, 1 picot, 1 DC into the same Ch.st, Ch.3. From * rep. Row ends with 2 Ch.sts and 1 DC.

1st–6th rows: rep. continuously.

Chart

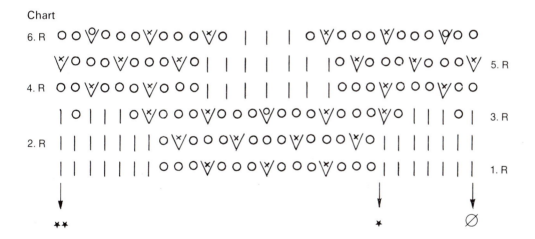

Key to the signs used:

| | DC
o Ch.st
$\vee$ DC, picot, DC
$\vee$ DC, Ch.st, DC

It is easiest to work in accordance with the diagram above. One crochets in forward rows *once* from ⌀ to *; *continuously* from * to **. In backward rows *continuously* from ** to *, and *once* from * to ⌀.

57

117 Lace Pattern for Collars

Ch.-st foundation.

1st row: * 1 DC, 1 Ch.st, in between, miss 1 Ch. of foundation. From * rep.

2nd row: Ch.1 to turn * SC1, Ch.4, miss 3 DCs of previous row, then work 2 DCs, Ch.5, work 2 DCs into 1 Ch. Ch.4, miss 3 DCs of previous row. From * rep. Finish with 4 Ch.sts and 1 SC.

3rd row: to turn, Ch.1 * SC1, Ch.5, into Ch. of arch of DC group work 2 DCs, Ch.5, and DC2, Ch.5. From * rep.

4th row: to turn, Ch.1 * SC1, Ch.6, into the arch of chain DC2, Ch.5, DC2, Ch.6. From * rep.

5th row: to turn Ch.1 * SC1, Ch.7, into arch of Ch., DC2, Ch.5, DC2, Ch.7. From * rep.

On the foundation row of Ch.sts, work now 1 row of DC, between each Ch.1. If this lace is being used as a collar, dec. slightly in this last row.

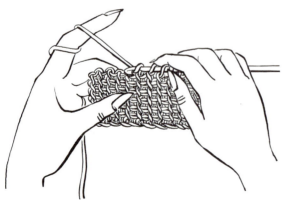

Tunisian Crochet

While in the usual crochet, each st is completed next to each other, in the Tunisian technique a forward and backward method is essential over the whole width of the work, in order to complete the sts of a row. The forward row forms loops on the hook, the backward row completes the sts.

118 Forming Tunisian Loops on Foundation

Ch.-st foundation.
Insert a long, strong hook of even thickness through 2nd-last Ch.st, thr.o., dr.thr. into a loop. In this way draw out of each Ch.st 1 loop, thus forming the forward row. The illustration shows the position of the Ch.-st foundation and the insert of the hook. The completion of the st is described in the following paragraph.

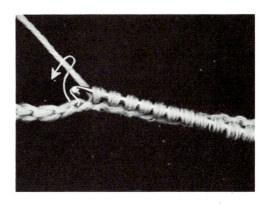

119 The Simple Right Tunisian Stitch

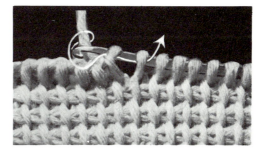

Forward and backward rows are worked with an evenly thick crochet hook. Forward row (=forming of loops) on an appropriate Ch.-st foundation, miss last Ch.st and draw out of each following Ch., 1 loop. Insert hook from front to back, thr.o. and draw thread through into a loop (take care that all loops are drawn up evenly). Backward row: after thread-over

once, draw thread first through 1 loop, thr.o. again and from now on, draw thread to the 1st 2 loops on hook. So, after every thread-over, dr.thr. 2 loops. Pull loops up slightly.

With every following forward row, draw loops through vertical link (see left illustration). With every backward row, draw working thread always through 2 loops (see right illustration), except 1st loop, which is worked singly.

120 Right Tunisian Stitch with Chain Stitches. I

On to a Ch.-st foundation work the forward row: insert, thr.o., dr.thr., thr.o., dr.thr. 1 loop on hook (the newly formed loop remains on hook). Insert into the next Ch.st, thr.o., dr.thr., thr.o. and dr.thr. 1 loop on hook (again leave the newly formed loop on hook), etc., etc. When the row of loops is formed, work the backward row as with the 'Simple *right* Tunisian Stitch'.

With the 2nd and all following rows, insert hook exactly as with the 'Right Tunisian Stitch'. Dr.l.thr., thr.o. and dr.thr. newly-formed loop. Always leave last loop on hook.

121 Right Tunisian Stitch with Chain Stitches. II

The illustration shows the same technique, only here between each loop, 1 Ch.st is worked. This technique requires loose working. Backward row: thread over to form a Ch.st. After working off the 1st loop, make the Ch.st, at the same time work off next loop. Again make a Ch.st and with it, work off next loop, etc., etc.

122 Left Tunisian Stitch

1st row: Right Tunisian.
2nd row: here, in the forward row, the left st is formed. As in the left knitted st, the thread lies in front of hook, insert from right to left through the vertical link of previous row, and draw thread through as follows: in front of vertical link, put thread under hook to the back, thr.o. by putting hook under the thread to the back and dr.thr. into a loop. Finish loop as with Right Tunisian Stitch.

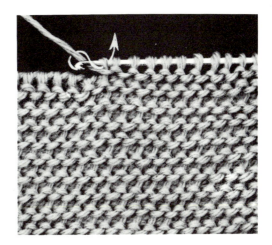

123 Tunisian Cross Stitch I

1st row: Right Tunisian Stitch.
2nd row (forward row): out of the 2nd st of previous row draw 1 loop, then insert into the missed st (1st st), draw out a loop, after this draw a loop out of each, 4th, 3rd, 6th, 5th, 8th, 7th, 10th, 9th st, etc., etc. Thus a loop is always drawn out of the next-but-one, then out of the next st. In this way the vertical links are crossed. Work loops off as with Right Tunisian Stitch. Also in the 3rd and following rows, the loops are drawn out of the 2nd, 1st, 4th, 3rd st of previous row, etc., etc.

124 Tunisian Cross Stitch II

This pattern is worked as the previous one, except that the cross-sts are transposed. This is achieved by inserting at the beg. of every 2nd row through the single link of 1st st.

125 Two Right, Two Left Tunisian Stitch

1st row: Right Tunisian.
2nd row: 2 Right Tunisian, 2 Left Tunisian, alternately. In all following rows the right sts are worked on to the left sts, and vice-versa.

126 One Right, One Left Tunisian Stitch

1st row: Right Tunisian.
2nd row: 1 Right Tunisian, 1 Left Tunisian, alternately. In all the following rows, work the Right Tunisian on to the Left, and vice-versa.

127 Thread-Over Pattern

The type of stitch used here is the Right Tunisian. Ch.-st foundation, then draw out of every 2nd Ch.st 1 loop, after every loop thr.o. once. Work loops off as usual, the thread-over makes a loop.
2nd and all following rows: out of every vertical link of st in previous row, draw 1 loop, between each loop thr.o. once, then work off loops.

128 Filling Stitch

1st row: Right Tunisian Stitch.
2nd and all following rows: always insert into the link between the 2 vertical sts. The loops are worked off as usual. Note the insertion at the beg. of row. Insert in the 2nd row, in front of the 1st vertical link, and in the 3rd row, *behind* the 1st vertical link of previous row. At the end of 2nd row, draw last loop in front of last vertical link, and in the 3rd row, from *behind* the vertical link, forward.

129 Knit Stitch

1st row: Right Tunisian Stitch.
2nd and all following rows: in forming the loops, the hook is not inserted as usual from right to left through vertical link, but between the backward- and forward-lying link towards the back, and from there, draw loop forward. Work off loops as in the Right Tunisian Stitch.

130 Weave Stitch

1st row: Right Tunisian.
2nd row: insert from left to right into the 1st vertical link, thr.o., dr.thr., pull up loosely, insert into the 2nd vertical link from right to left, thr.o., dr.thr. and pull up loosely, etc., etc. Work off loops as usual.
3rd row: as 2nd, but vice-versa.

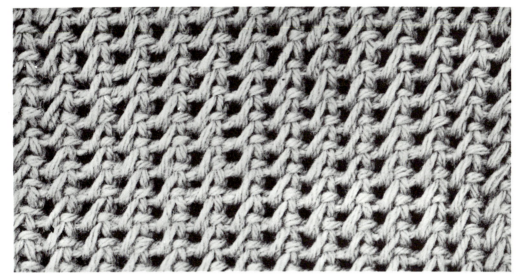

131   Net Stitch

1st row: Right Tunisian.
2nd row: lay thread in front of work (*not* on hook), insert hook through 2nd and 3rd vertical links of previous row (the 1st link is the edge st). Work the *left* Tunisian way. Draw-up loosely, then insert between the 3rd and 4th links, draw thread through and pull up into loop. The next 2 links work tog. as above, then out of the following space between, draw 1 loop, etc., etc. The row ends in the following way: out of the last space between, draw 1 loop, insert into the edge st and draw a loop through, thr.o. and work off 2 by 2.

132   Trellis, or Lattice Stitch

1st row: Right Tunisian.
2nd row and all following rows: in forward row, always insert under the 2 upper horizontal links, which lie between the vertical. Begin behind the 1st edge st, and behind the 1st vertical link. At the end of row, draw 1 loop each, out of the last link and edge st, then thr.o., and work off 2 by 2.

133   Nomotta Stitch

1st row: Right Tunisian.
2nd row: insert hook through two vertical links of previous row, and draw 1 loop through, which with a thread-over, is worked-off. Between the 2 links which were worked tog. and the following 3 links, Cr.2 sts (like a SC, but with the difference that the 2nd time, the thread is only drawn through 1 loop). Insert under both horizontal links. The next 3 links again work tog. with 1 loop, and work-off with 1 thread-over, now follow 2 SCs. Again work tog. the next 2 links, etc., etc. Rep. the 2nd row continuously, and work tog. the same links as in previous row.

134   Chaining-off Tunisian

Every Tunisian work must at the end be chained-off. For this, the hook is inserted in the usual way for the forming of loops, so through the 1st vertical link of st, draw thread through and at the same time draw through loop on hook. In this way work-off all loops.

135   Decreasing of Stitch at Beginning of Row

In forward row (forming of loops) miss the edge st and the 1st vertical link, and draw loop out of the 2nd link of previous row.

136 Decreasing of Stitch at End of Row

Out of the last two vertical links of previous row, draw only 1 loop.

137 Increasing a Stitch at Beginning of Row

Insert hook so that the upper horizontal link between the edge st and the 1st vertical link, and draw loop out.

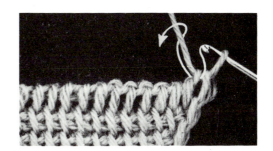

138 Increasing a Stitch at End of Row

At the end of forward row, draw edge st sideways and insert under the upper horizontal link, which is visible between the last vertical link and the edge st, draw thread through, out of the edge st also draw loop.

139 Buttonhole in Tunisian Stitch

As required for size, miss with 3–5 thread-overs, the same amount of sts. In the backward row work-off the thread-overs like ordinary loops, the illustration shows how the loops are drawn out of the thread-overs.

140 Sloping for Shoulder

The right shoulder-sloping: depending on how much the shoulder should be sloped, work off at the beg. of each row 4–8 sts. In the backward row, draw thread through 3 loops, at the same time, and in the next forward row, work into the 2nd vertical link of previous row the 1st SC.

The left shoulder: here leave required amount of sts at the end of forward row, and draw working-thread in backward row through the 2 last loops tog.

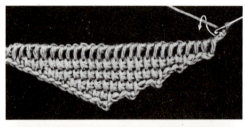

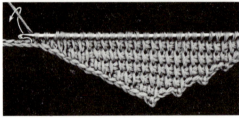

141 To Increase on Both Sides

After working-off loops, one increases at the beg. of row with as many Ch.sts as future sts are required. Out of these Ch.sts draw now the necessary loops. Should the inc. be necessary at the end of row, then the required Ch.sts must be worked at the beg. of the work, and leave them hanging. At the end of every forward row, draw out of the Ch.sts as many loops as required.

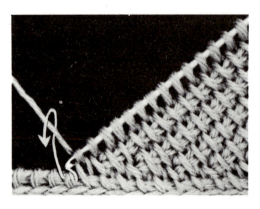

142 Forming a Wedge by Lengthening or Shortening a Row

If it is necessary to crochet a wedge on to a row, one divides the number of sts on this row into as many equal parts as the total number of rows on the wide side of the wedge. The 1st part of the row is worked with the backward-and-forward techniques. With the following row, crochet on to the 1st and 2nd part, in the subsequent row, the 1st, 2nd and 3rd part, etc., etc., until again the whole row is being worked.

143 To Form a Wedge in Forward Row

Here the wedge is formed in reverse direction. Divide the row into equal parts. Here in the 1st row, leave the last part free, in the 2nd row, the last and previous part, and so on, until only the 1st small part has been crocheted. From here on, work again the whole width. The illustration shows how to draw the loops out of various steps.

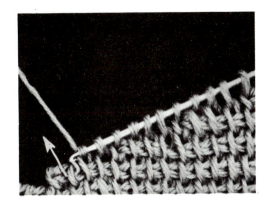

Borders

144 Border I

To crochet around borders of pullovers, waistcoats, etc., work 1 Ch.st and 1 sl.st alternately. Take care to keep even spaces between sts.

145 Border II

For covers, blankets, etc., which demand an even finish, work 1 SC and 1 Ch.st alternately. The SC is worked into the last-but-one row. After drawing thread through, draw up to border and finish with SC st.

146 Border III

1 SC, 2 Ch.sts * again insert into the last-but-one row, draw thread through into a loop, and pull well up, miss 3 sts, and again draw out loop, thr.o., and dr.thr. all 3 loops on hook. Ch.2, SC1, into the 5th st of last row. Miss 2 sts, Ch.2. From * rep.

147 Border IV

For this you need 2 colours. With the 1st colour, work into the border 1 SC, 3 Ch.sts, miss 2 sts of border, SC1. The hook is taken out of loop and the loop thread is put to the front. With the 2nd colour, work into the 1st missed st, 1 SC (working thread lies to the front). Ch.3, then SC1, into the following st of border. Draw out hook and lay loop and thread to front. Now pick up loop of 1st colour and Ch.3, then SC1 into the 2nd following st, draw hook out. Take loop of 2nd colour, Ch.3, etc., etc. This border can be worked more loosely. For this, work 4—6 Ch.sts as desired and miss corresponding number of sts in border.

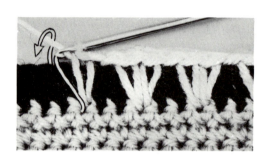

148 Border V

With a darker colour (with light ground-colour) work a forward row and backward row in SC. With the ground-colour, partly cover these 2 rows. Into every 3rd st, work 2 SCs. These, as illustration shows, are worked into the last row of ground-colour. Between each 2 SCs, work 1 Ch.st.

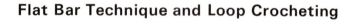

Flat Bar Technique and Loop Crocheting

149 Flat Bar Technique

For this use a wooden slat of even width. Ch.-st foundation.
1st row: SC, the last loop is drawn up to the width of the wooden slat.
2nd row: the slat is put behind the last loop, then working thread is brought under slat, up the back and drawn through the loop at edge of slat. Insert into the next SC (*see* illustration), draw thread from behind slat into loop up to edge, thr.o., dr.thr. 1 loop,

thr.o., dr.thr. 2 loops (that is 1 SC). The SCs lie on top edge of slat. Take care not to draw these down, when hook is inserted into next st. By drawing loop tight this can be avoided. Draw slat out.

3rd row: into the SCs of reverse row, work again SCs, but when inserting hook, grip both links, also the last thread of every loop-group.

2nd and 3rd rows: rep. continuously.

150   Loop Crocheting

1st row of loops: after a Ch.-st foundation insert into every Ch.st. Put thread twice around hook and slat (e.g. a pencil), draw hook through (*see* illustration), thr.o. hook and dr.thr. the 2 last loops on hook. The illustration shows the reverse side after several rows of loops have been worked. Here one always inserts into the SC of previous row. After every row of loops follows 1 row of SCs.

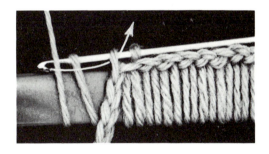

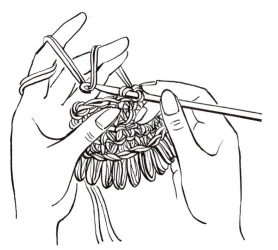

151   Crocheting Loops Over the Fingers

Ch.-st foundation.

1st row: insert into the 2nd-last Ch.st. As with crocheting, wind thread round the index finger; the middle and the ring fingers (depending on size of loops) are put in front of thread. Insert, thr.o., and dr.thr. Ch.st, again thr.o. and dr.thr. both loops on hook. Remove fingers from loop, insert into the next Ch.st, lay fingers again in front of thread, thr.o., dr.thr. Ch.st, thr.o., dr.thr. the 2 loops on hook, etc. The loops lie on reverse side.

2nd row: SC.

1st and 2nd rows: rep. continuously.

Fork or Hairpin Crocheting

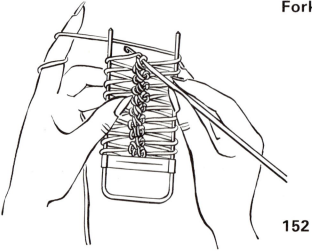

152   Correct Way of Holding the Fork

153 Border I

Working method: begin work with 1 Ch.st. Now draw hook out of loop, and put the right prong of fork upwards through the loop. Hold prong in the left hand between thumb and middle finger. The knot of loop should lie in the middle of fork. Put thread from the front to the back, around the left prong of fork. Twist fork. Insert hook up through loop on left prong, draw thread through, insert into the right loop, draw thread through, and work a SC. Now put hook above right prong to the back of fork, then turn fork from right to left, with which the thread goes automatically around the left prong. Insert into the left loop, draw thread through loop, work the 2 loops on hook into 1 SC. Put crochet hook to the back, turn fork, draw thread out of left loop, work 1 SC, etc., etc. When the fork is filled with loops, draw it out of the loops, and carefully push only the last 4 or 5 loops on to fork.

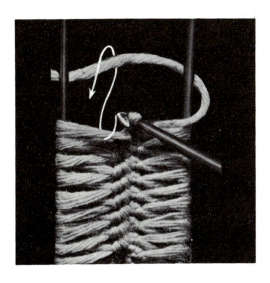

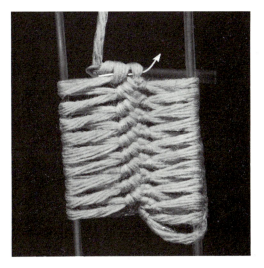

154 Firm Edge

As the illustration shows, the hook is inserted through the back into each loop and 1 SC is worked.

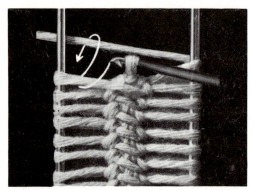

155 Border II With Wide Rib

This border is worked as Border I, only when inserting grip the full loop on to hook, and work the SC.

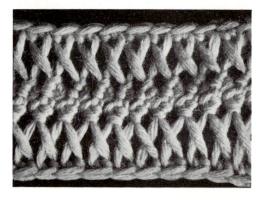

156 Border III

This border shows a still wider rib. Work as Border I, with the difference that into every loop, 2 SCs are worked.

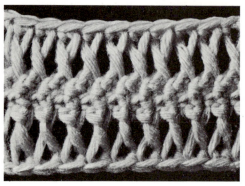

157 Border IV

Here into every loop work 3 SCs. Crochet tog.: 1 SC, 1 Ch.st, alternately.

158 Border V

In this border, work into every loop 2 DCs, crochet tog.: 1 SC, 2 Ch.sts, alternately.

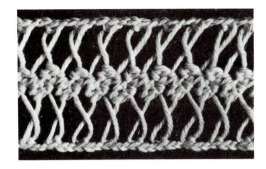

159 Border VI

This border offers a pretty change. The rib shows 1 SC and 2 DCs in each loop. Crochet tog. 2 loops at a time, Ch.3, etc., etc.

160 Firm Edge

Here, insert into 3 loops and work 1 SC. To the next group of loops work 2 or 3 Ch.sts, so that the loops will be in the right position, always insert from back to front.

161 Firm Edge with Twisted Loops

Insert into every loop from back to front. Every 2nd loop twist 2 or 3 times in form of circle, then work the SC.

Connecting of Edges

162 Connecting Without New Working Thread I

The illustration shows the connecting of loops without new working thread. As arrow indicates, the hook inserts into loops alternately from one edge to another, each loop being drawn through the other.

163 Connecting Without New Working Thread II

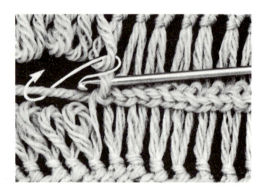

As arrow shows, here, 2 loops are gripped (from 1 edge to another, alternately), and these are drawn through the 2 loops on hook.

164 Connecting With New Thread I

With new thread, draw alternately from each edge a loop and work-off with a sl.st. As arrow indicates, get thread and dr.thr. loop on hook.

165 Connecting With New Thread II

A pretty connection is made with the help of Ch.sts. Insert the hook, as arrow indicates, through 2 loops at a time. Pull working-thread through, and draw at the same time through 2 loops on hook, then make 2 Ch.sts. Rep. preceding work on 2nd edge.

Knitting

Introduction, and Basic Stitches

(See p. 299 for List of Abbreviations.)

Handling the Yarn while knitting

To start every piece of knitting work, the thread has to be put correctly around the fingers of the left hand. The palm of the left hand faces downward. The working thread is brought between the little finger and the ring finger, then put above three fingers and once again around the forefinger.

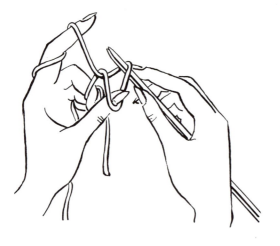

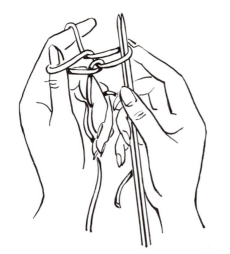

1   Single Cross Cast-on

This form of casting-on is nice and durable and is for all work which requires a firm edge, e.g. stockings and socks.

To cast-on about 10 sts one requires 1 needle-length of wool thread. It is drawn between the little and ring fingers to the outside, put around 3 fingers and wound once again round the forefinger. The end of the thread is put from right to left around the thumb, brought above the yarn between the fingers and gripped. With the needle in the right hand, insert from below into the loop of the thumb, pass the yarn which comes from the forefinger, over (the working yarn lies here always in front of the needle) and draw through loop. Take thumb out of loop and draw loop tight.

With the 2nd and all following sts, form loop with thumb, by putting thumb above yarn coming and ring and middle fingers, insert into loop from below, pass over, dr.thr., take thumb out of loop and tighten loop.

So that the casting-on is not done too tightly, it is advisable to use 2 needles of the same size (*see* illustration).

Should the cast-on still require more strength and durability, then double yarn may be used.

2   To Cast-on out of a Stitch

The end of the yarn is held in the right hand
and the yarn is wound around the left hand
as with knitting. Put a loop round the thumb
from right to left; here the end of the yarn is
held with the ring and middle fingers. With
the needle in the right hand insert from below
into the loop of the thumb, pass the thread
which comes from the forefinger, over, draw
through loop, pull loop tight. Take needle
with st into the left hand; take the 2nd needle
in the right hand; from below insert into st on
left needle, pass yarn over right needle and
draw through st. Do not slip the stitch! With
the left needle insert into st on right needle,
put yarn around the right needle, dr.thr.; do
not slip. The sts on the left needle inc.; on
the right needle there remains always 1 st.

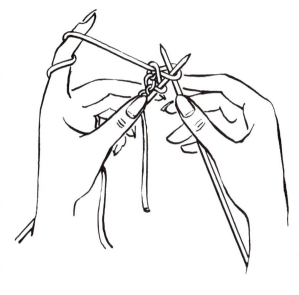

This form of casting-on, also called Knitting-
on, is mainly used when a loose edge is
required, and when the cast-on sts have to
be picked up, e.g. with a hem. If the cast-on
serves as a self-edge, this form of casting-on
is not recommended.

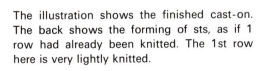

The illustration shows the finished cast-on.
The back shows the forming of sts, as if 1
row had already been knitted. The 1st row
here is very lightly knitted.

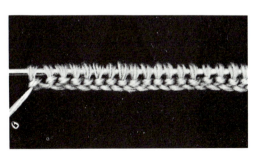

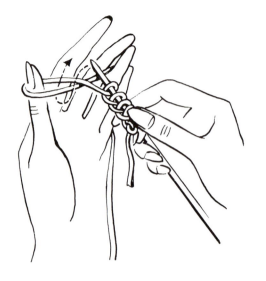

3 Increasing of Stitches at the End of Row

Should a work already started need to be extended, the following cross cast-on can be used. Hold the yarn as for knitting (or as illustration shows, only around your thumb), form a loop around the thumb from right to left, insert needle upwards through this loop, and sl off on to the needle, draw tight.

Crochet sl.st-chain as foundation sts for knitwork: insert needle through upper links of sl.st sts from the front to the back, and k.

One differentiates between a closed and an open knitting. The closed knitting is worked with 3 or more needles or a round needle. For the open knitting 2 long, straight needles are used in forward and backward rows.

4 Cast-on for Closed Knitting

The cast-on sts are so divided that on the 1st needle there are 2 sts more than on the 2nd and 3rd needles. The 4th needle has 2 sts less.
The 1st 2 sts of the 1st needle are now knitted with the 4th needle, and so the work is closed (rounded). With the 5th needle k the sts of the 1st needle.

5   Casting-off for Rib-stitch Patterns: K1, P1

This method of casting-on increases the elasticity of the edge. The impression is created that the sts run from the right to the left of the knitting without interruption.

With the following sketches and explanations it will be possible for you to learn this method of casting-on so that it will soon come as easy to you as the single cross cast-on.

To cast-on 1 st requires about 1—1·5 cm of wool. Now measure an appropriate length of thread and let this hang free. Always choose an even number of sts, and lay a loop around the needle.

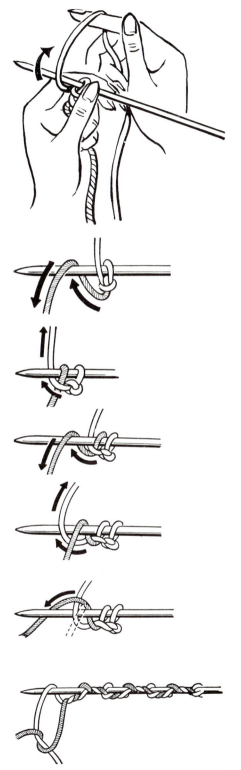

Hold loop with thumb and forefinger of left hand, bring thread from the ball-needle to the front and over needle back again.

Hold loop with thumb and forefinger of right hand, and bring loose hanging thread from the back over the needle to the front.

Hold loop with thumb and forefinger of left hand, and lay thread from ball in front over hanging thread, then under needle to the back.

Hold loops with thumb and forefinger of the right hand, and bring the loose hanging thread from the back, over the needle to the front.

Hold loop with thumb and forefinger of left hand and bring the ball-thread under the needle to the front and over the needle back again.

Hold loops with thumb and forefinger of right hand and first lay loose hanging thread over the ball-thread, then bring it under needle from back to the front. There are now 2 sts, plus the starting loop, on the needle. Rep. the 6 operations continuously.

When enough sts have been cast-on, join loose hanging thread and ball-thread over the needle.

The next 2 rows are worked as follows:
1st row: k1 * p1 (the thread lies in front of st) k1. From * rep.

2nd row: * k1, p1 (thread lies in front of st). From * rep.
From here continue in rib-pattern; k1, p1.

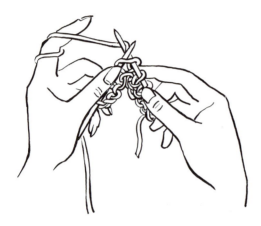

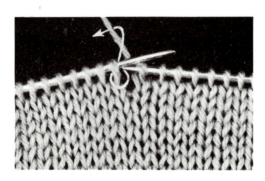

6   Knitting Stitch

Into the st on left needle insert from front to back; throw the yarn, coming from the forefinger, around needle (working thread lies in front of needle), dr.thr.st and sl.st from the left needle.

7   Twisted Knit-stitch

Insert into the back of the st, thr.o., draw yarn through, sl.st from left needle.

8 Purl Stitch

Put the yarn on to the left needle in front of st, insert behind the yarn from right to left into st, thr.o., dr.thr., sl.st off left needle.

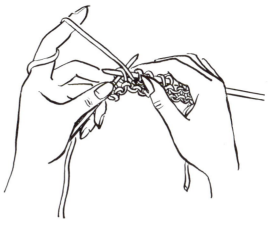

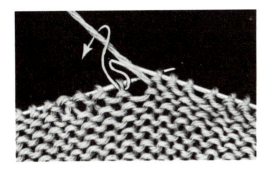

9 'Curl' stitch

Backward and forward rows are knitted continuously.

10 K1, P1, Alternately

If the instructions read 'k1, p1, k1, p1' then continue in this way to the end of row.

11 P1, K1, Twisted Stitch

The twisted st looks pleasant and even when used alternately with the p.st. On the backward row, for twisted k.st, twist 1 p.st.

12 K2, P2, Alternately

This form is popular for tops and ribbings. The number of sts must be divisible by 4.
1st row: k2, p2, alternately.
2nd and all following rows: k sts as they appear.

13 Cast-off

1. Cast-off by drawing st over; k the 1st 2 sts as usual, then draw the 1st knitted st over the 2nd st, leaving 1 st on right-hand needle.
K 3rd st, draw 2nd over 3rd etc., so on till sts are cast-off. Through the last st on needle draw the yarn and sew into the back of the work.

2. Cast-off by knitting tog. This way k2 sts twisted tog., put back the new st on to needle, k tog. with the following st, again in twisted form and so on.

3. Cast-off by crocheting. For this, 1 crochet hook is required. If a loose edge is wanted, use a large hook; for the medium edge use the same size hook as the knitting needle, and for a very tight edge use a thin hook. Lift the 1st 2 sts on to the hook, and with a Ch.st cast-off (with the crochet-hook draw yarn through 2 sts). From now on always slip the next st on to the hook, and with the st already on hook, cast-off with a Ch.st.

14 Cast-off the Ribbed Pattern. —K1, P1—with Darning Needle

This form of casting-off increases the elasticity of the edge. It is invisible and gives the impression of an uninterrupted flow of sts (k1, p1).
With the help of the following illustrations and explanations it will be possible to learn this form of casting-off so that it will soon be as easy as other methods.

When finishing the last row of knitting leave a long enough thread to cast-off with, put its end through a darning needle (the right side of the work is to the front). Insert with the darning needle from right to left into the 1st knitted st, draw the yarn through and lift st off the knitting needle.

Miss the following p.st, insert into the next k. st, draw yarn through (leave st on knitting needle).

Insert into the missed p.st from right to left, draw yarn through, and lift both sts off knitting needle.

Into the following p.st insert from left to right, draw thread through (leave st on knitting needle).

Insert into the previous lifted k.st from right to left, and draw yarn through.

Into the next k.st insert from right to left and draw yarn through. Rep. the last 4 working methods until all sts are cast-off. Draw end of yarn through a few sts.

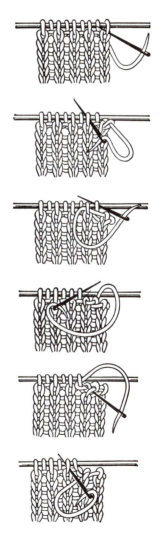

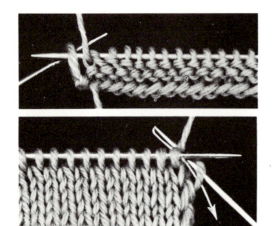

15 Side Self Edge

When the fabric is formed by knitting backwards and forwards, every row is finished with an edge st as follows:
The last st of every row is not knitted, put the yarn as for the p.st forwards and lift the last st off.

After turning, k the sl.st in twisted form.

16 Knotted Edge

For all edges which have to be worked as seams this form of strong, firm edge is recommended. In the forward row the last st is knitted, and in the backward row, put the yarn behind the needle, insert as if to p, lift st, draw yarn tight. The edge is the same as formed with 'curled' st.

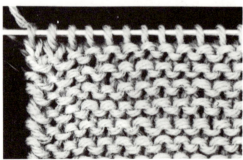

17 Picking-up Edge Stitches

When a collar is knitted on to a cardigan, pullover, etc., one picks up on to the hook the loops of the edge sts lying to the front.

18 Increasing by One Stitch at Beginning of Row

Pick up vertical thread between the edge- and the 2nd st, and k as twisted st (cross st). Should the increase be necessary at the end of the row, then k to the last st, pick up the last vertical thread and k twisted st (cross st).

19 Increasing Stitches within the Knitting Row

If the number of sts in a row is to be invisibly increased, it can be worked in 2 ways:

1st method: K2 sts; out of 1 st, k1, but do not lift from needle. Out of the same st make a 2nd crossed (or twisted) st.

2nd method: Out of the vertical thread between 2 sts, make a new st, by picking up the thread with the left needle and k in twisted form.

Should it be required that more sts have to be increased within 1 row, rep. the process at regular intervals.

If the increasing with a row has to be repeated several times during the work, above the same point, mark the place with a coloured thread.

Should only 1 st be increased at every increasing point, pick up in the 1st increasing row the cross link in front of marked st, and in the next increasing row the cross link *behind* the marked st. Work it with a crossed k.st.

Should 2 sts have to be increased on marked points, then pick up cross links before and behind marked places and work crossed k.sts.

20 Decreasing

The usual way to dec. is to k2 sts tog. This can be done either with knitted p edge, or twisted st. The number of sts can also be dec. by 1 or 2 by slipping a st over. Should the number have to be reduced by 1, lift the 1st st off the left to the right needle (insert as for knitting), then k the 2nd st and draw the lifted st over.

If the number of sts has to be reduced by 2, slip the 1st st, k the 2nd and 3rd tog., then draw the slipped st over the knitted st. Should the middle st continue, then put it on to a relief needle. Now k the 1st and 3rd sts tog. and draw the middle st over.

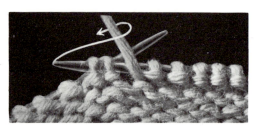

In slipping a st to dec. in k row, it should always be slipped knitwise. Should the decreasing be left (purl), slip crossed-wise.

If within a row several sts have to be decreased, it is done at regular intervals, in the manner already described.

Should several sts in 1 row have to be decreased, and this has to be repeated at the same place during the work, e.g. with a bell-shaped skirt, which is worked from bottom to top, the decreasing points are marked with coloured thread. If at every point only 1 st is to be decreased in the 1st row (round) the marked st is knitted tog., with the st in front of it; in the 2nd round the marked st with the following st.

Rep. these 2 decreasing rounds continuously. If on every decreasing point 2 sts have to be decreased, the 2 sts in front of the marked point are knitted twisted or knitted tog. by drawing over. The 2 sts after the marked point are knitted tog.

If, at the beginning or end of the row, 1–2 sts are to be decreased, e.g. raglan sloping or cut-outs (sleeves, neck, etc.), the edge sts at the beg. can be knitted with 1 or 2 following sts in twisted form. At the end of the row, 1 or 2 sts are knitted tog. with the edge st. * If at the beg. or end of a row several sts are to be reduced, this is done in the form of chain-decreasing.

One other way of decreasing at the beg. or end of a row is to let the sts first run up and then k tog. either after or before, as described.

Correcting Mistakes

21 Picking-up Knit-stitches

With the right needle pick up the cross thread and the st from back to front and put both on to the left needle (the thread lies to the right of st). With the right needle pick up st from the side to the front, and lift over thread.
If the st lies several rows below, pick up the lowest cross thread and continue working in the same way.

22 To Crochet-up Knit-stitch

With the help of a crochet-hook (if possible the same size as the needle), the dropped sts can easily be picked up. As the picture shows, the dropped st lies on the crochet-hook. Pick up the next cross thread and draw through the dropped st (as in chain st). Rep. the process to the top, then lift the st on to the left needle so that the right link of st lies in front of needle.

23 Picking-up Dropped Purl stitches

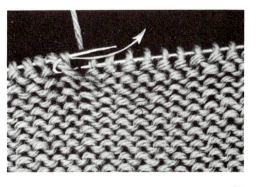

With p.sts, the dropped st lies on the left needle to the right of the cross thread. With the right needle insert from the side to the front into the picked-up st, and draw the cross thread through the st. An easier way to correct this mistake is to turn the work and pick up the dropped st knit-way.

Round Edges, Curves, Slopes, Buttonholes

24   The Armhole

As material, size of needle and size of armhole are important, the exact number of sts to be decreased cannot be given. It is best to work with a pattern. Before beginning the armhole, the work is put on to the pattern, so that one can now count the number of sts needing to be decreased in the next row. The illustration shows the armhole of a back. The wool used was of medium strength and the needles were 3 mm. The armhole was worked as follows:

At the start of the needle dec. 5 sts by drawing st over, finish row. After turning start the left armhole by decreasing 5, again drawing 1 st over the other; k to the end of row, turn, beg. row by decreasing 3 sts; dec. the same number of sts after turning for the 2nd armhole.

Again dec. 2–3 sts, then continue to dec. 1 st only on each side until the correct width of back is reached. If the armhole does not need to be so deep, or if thicker wool is used, the decreasing is achieved thus: 4, 3, 2, and then 1 st until the correct size. But the easiest way is to work to a good pattern; the work is put repeatedly on to the paper and the decreasing sts are continuously controlled.

25   V-Neck

It requires a little more calculation as to the number of sts to be decreased, for the shaping of the V-neck. It depends on the material, the needles and the type of neck. First, the number of sts are counted. Divide the work in half, into a right and a left shoulder part. Again, most necklines are worked to a pattern, and the work is put repeatedly on to this from the outset. It is easily seen if the shaping of the V is even, or if it has a slight curve. With an evenly sloping neckline 1 st is decreased in the neckline of the left shoulder part, by slipping the 4th-last, knitting the 3rd-last and passing the slipped st over (*see* illustration). On the right shoulder dec. at the beginning by knitting the 3rd and 4th sts tog. If the neckline shows a curved (rounded)

pattern, 1 st is decreased on forward and backward rows. It is often sufficient to dec. only in every 2nd or 3rd forward row. As already stated, the pattern is decisive; the work is placed repeatedly on it, to be assured of the correct measurements.

26   Vertical Buttonholes

First k the garment to the beginning of the hole. The knitting then has to be carried on in 2 parts. The illustration shows the connection of both parts. After turning, the 1st st on the buttonhole edge is slipped.

27   Horizontal Buttonholes

Before one begins on the buttonhole, consider how wide to make it. For a cardigan, etc., 3 sts are usually needed. Bind-off the sts in 1 row, and on the return row, cast-on above the bound-off.

28   Knitting the Slope of a Shoulder

As previously mentioned, the sloping of the shoulder depends on the pattern. To get a sloping shoulderline, leave stepwise 4—10 sts unknitted on the needle. After turning, always slip the 1st st, in the forward row knit-wise, and in the return row, purl-wise. Continue

in this way until the length of the shoulderline is reached. At the end, bind-off the sts.

One other way to slope the shoulder is to bind-off 4—10 sts, stepwise, as pattern requires.

29 Shortened Rows

With worked-in darts, shoulder slopings, heightening the backs of trousers, horizontally worked skirts, and with all shapes worked out in detail, the shortened rows are used. How unpleasing it is to see a dart in a cardigan, etc., marked by holes. This can be avoided by putting yarn over once before turning. In the next row the thread-over is knitted tog. with the following st. The same applies when working with a handknitting machine.

Knitting Patterns

Patent Patterns

30 Plain Patent

Knitting method no. 1: even number of sts.
1st row: edge st * yarn over, next st sl purlwise, k1. From * rep., edge st.
2nd row: edge st * yarn over, sl st purlwise, k and thread-over of previous row with the slipped st tog. From * rep. Edge st. Rep. the 2nd row continuously.

Knitting method no. 2: even number of sts.
1st row: k.
2nd row: edge st * k1, k1 but insert under the p.st, which undoes the st. From * rep. Rep. the 2nd row continuously, and move the knitted st so that on the deep-knitted st comes the normal k.st, and so on.

90

31 Half-Patent Stitch

Even number of sts.
1st row : * k1, thr.o., sl1 purlwise. From * rep.
2nd row : * k slipped st with thread-over tog., p1. From * rep.
1st and 2nd rows : rep. continuously.

32 Knitting Pattern

Even number of sts.
1st row : edge st * p1, next, p1 but insert 1 row deeper (which undoes the st). From * rep. Edge st.
2nd row : p.
3rd row : edge st * p1 and when inserting grip the lower horizontal link as well, next st p. From * rep. Edge st.
4th row : p.
5th row : edge st * p1, next st p but insert under the lower horizontal link. From * rep. Edge st.
2nd–5th rows : rep. continuously.

33 New Patent Pattern

The pattern appears on the reverse side. Even number of sts.
1st row : edge st * thr.o., next st sl purlwise, k1. From * rep. Edge st.
2nd row : edge st * k2, sl the thread-over of previous row purlwise (yarn lies behind the thread-over). From * rep. Edge st.
3rd row : edge st * k the following st with the thread-over tog. Thr.o. once, sl1 purlwise. From * rep. Edge st.
4th row : Edge st, k1 * sl the thread-over of previous row purlwise (yarn lies behind the thread-over). K2. From * rep. Row ends: sl thread-over of previous row purlwise (yarn to the back), k1, edge st.
5th row : edge st * thr.o., sl1 purlwise, k next st with the thread-over tog. From * rep. Edge st.
2nd–5th rows : rep. continuously.

34 Knitting Pattern

Pattern appears on reverse side. Even number of sts.
1st row: edge st * thr.o., sl the following st purlwise. From * rep.
2nd row: edge st * k1, k the next st with the thread-over twisted tog. From * rep. Edge st.

3rd row: edge st * k1, thr.o., sl1 purlwise. From * rep. Edge st.
4th row: edge st * k the next st with the thread-over twisted tog. K1. From * rep. Edge st.
1st–4th rows: rep. continuously.

35 Cross Pattern

Number of sts to be divisible by 3, plus 2. Edge sts.
1st row: edge st * sl1 purlwise (thread lies behind st), thr.o., k2 tog. From * rep. Edge st.
2nd row: edge st, k1 * sl the thread over purlwise (yarn lies behind the work), thr.o., k2 tog. From * rep. Row ends: sl thread over purlwise (yarn to the back), thr.o., k1, edge st.
3rd row: edge st, k1 * sl1, thr.o. purlwise, thr.o., the 2nd thread-over k tog. with the following st. From * rep. Edge st.
3rd row: rep. continuously.

36 Double Patent Pattern

Even number of sts.
1st row: k1, thr.o., alternately.
2nd row: k the thread-over of previous row, knitted st sl purlwise (yarn lies in front of sts).
3rd row: k the slipped st of previous row, the knitted st sl purlwise (yarn lies in front of sts). Rep. this 3rd row continuously. The work will show a knitted pattern on both sides.

Tight Patterns

37 Small Pearl Pattern

Even number of sts.
1st row: * k1, p1. From * rep.
2nd row: * p1, k1. From * rep.
1st and 2nd rows: rep. continuously.

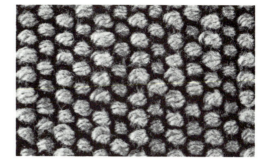

38 Large Pearl Pattern

Even number of sts.
1st row: edge st * k1, p1. From * rep. Edge st.
2nd row: sts are worked as they appear.
3rd row: edge st * p1, k1. From * rep. Edge st.
4th row: sts are worked as they appear.
1st–4th rows: rep. continuously.

39 Knitting Pattern

Even number of sts.
1st row: edge st * k1, p1. From * rep. Edge st.
2nd and 3rd rows: sts are worked as they appear.
4th row: p the knitted st and k the p.st of previous row.
5th and 6th rows: sts are worked as they appear.
1st–6th rows: rep. continuously.

40 Knitting Pattern

Number of sts to be divisible by 6, plus 5 sts (2 edge sts and 3 sts).
1st row: edge st * k3, p3. From * rep. Row ends with k3 and edge st.
2nd row: work sts as they appear.
3rd row: edge st * p3, k3. From * rep. Row ends with p3 and edge st.
4th row: work sts as they appear.
1st–4th rows: rep. continuously.

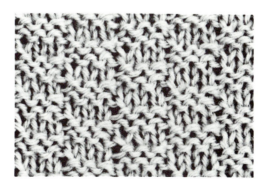

41   Knitting Pattern

Number of sts to be divisible by 4, plus 2 edge sts.
1st and every further forward row: k.
2nd, 4th and 6th rows: edge st * k2, p2. From * rep. Edge st.
8th, 10th and 12th rows: edge st * p2, k2. From * rep. Edge st.
1st–12th rows: rep. continuously.

42   Knitting Pattern

Sts to be divisible by 6, plus 1 st.
1st and every further forward row: k.
2nd row: edge st * k5, p1. From * rep. Row ends with k5, edge st.
4th, 6th and 8th rows: as 2nd row.
10th row: edge st, k2 * p1, k5. From * rep. Row ends with p1, k2, edge st.
12th, 14th and 16th rows: as 10th row.
1st–16th rows: rep. continuously.

43   Knitting Pattern

The number of sts are to be divisible by 8, plus 2 edge sts.
1st and all forward rows: k.
2nd row: edge st * k7, p1. From * rep.
4th row: edge st, p1 * k5, p3. From * rep. Row ends with k5, p2, edge st.
6th row: edge st, p2 * k3, p5. From * rep. Row ends with k3, p3, edge st.
8th row: edge st, p3 * k1, p7. From * rep. Row ends with k1, p4, edge st.

10th row: edge st * p1, k7. From * rep. Row ends with p1, k4, edge st.
12th row: edge st, k2 * p3, k5. From * rep. Row ends with p3, k3, edge st.
14th row: edge st, k1 * p5, k3. From * rep. Row ends with p5, k2, edge st.
16th row: edge st * p7, k1. From * rep. Edge st.

1st–16th rows: rep. continuously.

44   Knitting Pattern

Number of sts to be divisible by 6, plus 2 edge sts.

1st row: edge st * p1, k5. From * rep. Edge st.

2nd row: edge st * p4, k2. From * rep. Edge st.

3rd row: edge st * p3, k3. From * rep. Edge st.

4th row: edge st * p2, k4. From * rep. Edge st.

5th row: edge st * p5, k1. From * rep. Edge st.

6th row: k.

7th row: as 5th

8th row: as 4th.

9th row: as 3rd.

10th row: as 2nd.

11th row: as 1st.

12th row: p.

1st–12th rows: rep. continuously.

45   Knitting Pattern

Number of sts to be divisible by 8, plus 1 st.

1st row: edge st * k7, p1. From * rep. Row ends with k7, edge st.

2nd row: edge st, k1 * p5, k1, p1, k1. From * rep. Row ends with p5, k1, edge st.

3rd row: edge st, k1, p1 * k3, p1. From * rep. Row ends with k1, edge st.

4th row: edge st, p2 * k1, p1, k1, p5. From * rep. Row ends with k1, p1, k1, p2, edge st.

5th row: edge st, k3 * p1, k7. From * rep. Row ends with p1, k3, edge st.

6th row: as 4th.

7th row: as 3rd.

8th row: as 2nd.

1st–8th rows: rep. continuously.

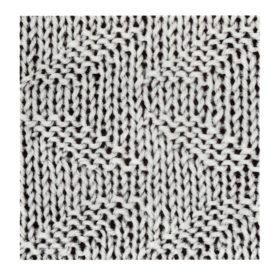

46 Knitting Pattern

Number of sts to be divisible by 8, plus 2 edge sts.

1st and 2nd rows: plain knitting (forward row k, backward row p).
3rd row: edge st * k4, p4. From * rep. Edge st.
4th row: edge st, p1 * k4, p4. From * rep. Edge st. Row ends with k4, p3, edge st.
5th row: edge st, k2 * p4, k4. From * rep. Row ends with p4, k2, edge st.
6th row: edge st, p3 * k4, p4. From * rep. Row ends with k4, p1, edge st.
7th row: edge st * p4, k4. From * rep. Edge st.
8th row: p.
9th and 10th rows: plain knitting.
11th row: as 7th.
12th row: as 6th.
13th row: as 5th.
14th row: as 4th.
15th row: as 3rd.
16th row: p.
1st–16th rows: rep. continuously.

47 Knitting Pattern

Number of sts to be divisible by 8, plus 2 edge sts.

1st row: edge st * k5, p3. From * rep. Edge st.
2nd–5th rows: work sts as they appear.
6th row: edge st * p5, k3. From * rep. Edge st.
7th–10th rows: work sts as they appear.
11th row: edge st, k3 * p3, k5. From * rep. Row ends with p3, k2, edge st.
12th–15th rows: work sts as they appear.
16th row: edge st, k2 * p5, k3. From * rep. Row ends with p5, k1, edge st.

17th–20th rows: work sts as they appear.
21st row: edge st, k1 * p3, k5. From * rep. Row ends with p3, k4, edge st.
22nd–25th rows: work sts as they appear.
26th row: edge st, p1 * k3, p5. From * rep. Row ends with k3, p4, edge st.
27th–30th rows: work sts as they appear.
31st row: edge st, p2 * k5, p3. From * rep. Row ends with k5, p1, edge st.
32nd–35th rows: work sts as they appear.
36th row: edge st, p3 * k3, p5. From * rep. Row ends with k3, p2, edge st.
37th–40th rows: work sts as they appear.
1st–40th rows: rep. continuously.

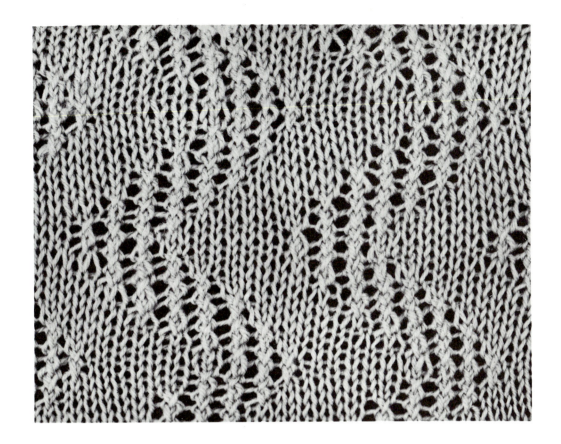

48   Knitting Pattern

Number of sts to be divisible by 14, plus 2 edge sts.

1st row: edge st * k8, 3 times k2 sts crossed (1st, k the 2nd st, pull-up and draw over the 1st st, then k the 1st st). From * rep. Edge st.

2nd row: edge st * 3 times p2 sts crossed (as in 1st row, only p), p8. From * rep. Edge st.

3rd row: edge st, k2 sts crossed * k8, 3 times k2 sts crossed. From * rep. Row ends with k8, k twice 2 sts crossed, edge st.

4th row: into the crossed sts of previous row, work crossed sts purlwise; p the p.sts of previous row.

5th row: edge st, k twice 2 sts crosswise * k8, 3 times k2 sts crossed. From * rep. Row ends with k8, k2 sts crossed, edge st.

6th row: as 4th.

7th row: edge st * 3 times k2 sts crosswise, k8. From * rep. Edge st.

8th row: as 4th.

9th row: edge st, k2 * k 3 times 2 sts crossed, k8. From * rep. Row ends with k 3 times 2 sts crossed, k6, edge st.

10th row: as 4th.

11th row: edge st, k * k 3 times 2 sts crossed, k8. From * rep. Row ends with k 3 times 2 sts crossed, k4, edge st.

12th row: as 4th.

13th row: as 9th.

14th row: as 4th.

15th row: as 7th.

16th row: as 4th.

17th row: as 5th.

18th row: as 4th.

19th row: as 3rd.

20th row: as 4th.

1st–20th rows: rep. continuously.

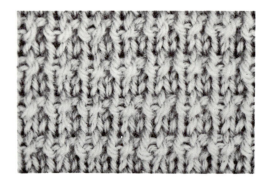

49 Knitting Pattern

Even number of sts.
1st row: edge st * thr.o., sl1 purlwise, k1. From * rep. Edge st.
2nd row: edge st * p1, k slipped st and thread-over of previous row tog. From * rep. Edge st.
3rd row: k.
4th row: p.
1st—4th rows: rep. continuously.

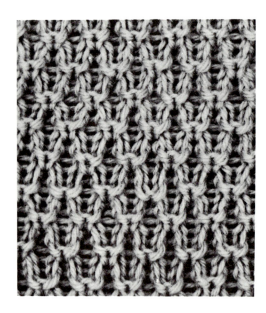

50 Knitting Pattern

Even number of sts.
1st—3rd rows: k.
4th row: p.
5th row: edge st * k.st, but with the right needle pick up the p link 3 rows below the following st, and k tog. with the st. From * rep. Edge st.
6th row: k.
7th row: k.
8th row: p.
9th row: edge st * pick up the p link 3 rows below the following st, with the right needle, and k tog. with this st, k1. From * rep. Edge st.
2nd—9th rows: rep. continuously.

51 Check Stitch

Number of sts to be divisible by 4, plus 2 edge sts.
1st row: edge st * k2, thr.o., k2, draw thread over, over the last 2 knitted sts. From * rep. Edge st.
2nd row: p.
3rd row: edge st * thr.o., k2, draw thread over, over the knitted sts, k2. From * rep. Edge st.
4th row: p.
1st—4th rows: rep. continuously.

52 Knitting Pattern

The pattern appears on the reverse side. Number of sts to be divisible by 4, plus 2 edge sts.

1st row: edge st * out of the next st k1, p1, k1 then p3 sts tog. From * rep. Edge st.

2nd row: p.

3rd row: edge st * p3 sts tog., out of the following st make 3 by k1, p1, k1. From * rep. Edge st.

1st—4th rows: rep. continuously.

53 Knitting Pattern

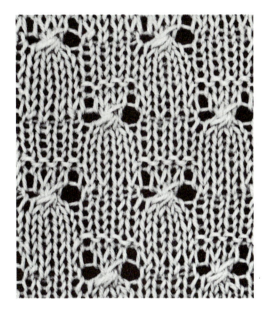

Number of sts to be divisible by 8, plus 2 edge sts.

1st row: k.

2nd row: p.

3rd row: k.

4th row: p.

5th row: k.

6th row: edge st * p4, p4 tog.; do not take the 4 sts from the needle but k them tog. once again. From * rep. Edge st.

7th row: edge st * pick up and k horizontal link, k2, pick up and k horizontal link, k4. From * rep. Edge st.

8th row: p.

9th row: edge st * p4, k4. From * rep. Edge st.

10th—13th rows: as 2nd—5th rows.

14th row: edge st * p4 sts tog. but do not take the sts off the needle, p them again tog., p4. From * rep. Edge st.

15th row: edge st * k4, pick up horizontal link and k, k2, pick up horizontal link and k. From * rep. Edge st.

16th row: p.

17th row: edge st * k4, p4. From * rep. Edge st.

18th row: p.

19th row: k.

20th row: p.

21st row: k.

6th—21st rows: rep. continuously.

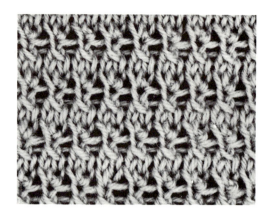

54 Knitting Pattern

Even number of sts.
1st row: k.
2nd row: p.
3rd row: edge st * k2 crossed tog. From *
rep. Edge st.
4th row: edge st * out of every st k1 and
p1. From * rep. Edge st.
1st—4th rows: rep. continuously.

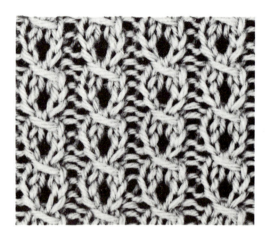

55 Knitting Pattern

Number of sts to be divisible by 4, plus 2
edge sts.
1st row: edge st * p1, sl1, k2, draw slipped
st over the 2 knitted sts. From * rep. Edge st.
2nd row: edge st * p1, thr.o., p1, k1. From *
rep. Edge st.
3rd row: edge st * p1, k the thread-over and
2 sts. From * rep. Edge st.
4th row: edge st * p3, k1. From * rep. Edge
st.
1st—4th rows: rep. continuously.

56 Knitting Pattern

Even number of sts.
1st row: edge st * cross 1st and 2nd sts
as follows: first k the 2nd st twisted, pull up
and draw over the 1st st, now k the 1st st.
From * rep. Edge st.
2nd row: edge st * cross the 1st and 2nd st
as follows: p the 2nd st and draw it over the
1st st, now p the 1st st. From * rep. Edge st.
3rd row: edge st, k1, then work the full row
crossed, as described in the 1st row. Row
ends with k1, edge st.
4th row: edge st, p1, then work the whole
row as described in 2nd row. Row ends with
p1, edge st.
1st—4th rows: rep. continuously.

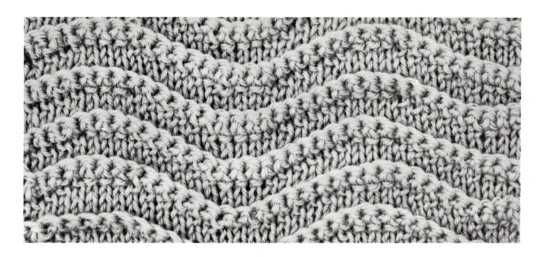

57 Knitting Pattern

Number of sts to be divisible by 18, plus 2 edge sts.

1st row: edge st * p4, k4, p1, k4, p1, k4. From * rep. Edge st.

2nd row: edge st * k1, p4, k4, p4, k1, p4. From * rep. Edge st.

3rd row: edge st, k5 * p1, k10, p1, k6. From * rep. Row ends with p1, k10, p1, k1, edge st.

4th row: edge st, p2 * k1, p8, k1, p8. From * rep. Row ends with k1, p1, k1, p6, edge st.

5th row: edge st, k7 * p1, k6, p1, k10. From * rep. Row ends with p1, k6, p1, k3, edge st.

6th row: edge st * p4, k1, p4, k1, p4, k4. From * rep. Edge st.

7th row: edge st * k4, p1, k4, p4, k4, p1. From * rep. Edge st.

8th row: edge st, p1 * k1, p10, k1, p6. From * rep. Row ends k1, p10, k1, p5, edge st.

9th row: edge st, k6 * p1, k8, p1, k8. From * rep. Row ends with p1, k8, p1, k2, edge st.

10th row: edge st, p3 * k1, p6, k1, p10. From * rep. Row ends with k1, p6, k1, p7, edge st.

1st–10th rows: rep. continuously.

Into the horizontal links of the p.sts on the right side work a Cr.st.

58 Knitting Pattern

1st row (backward row): k.

2nd–5th rows: 'smooth knitting' (i.e. forward row p, backward row k).

6th row (forward row): p, let the 3rd and every following 4th st drop 5 rows down, then pick up the 5 horizontal threads with the st, and k tog.

7th row (backward row): k.

8th–11th rows: 'smooth knitting'.

12th row (forward): p, let the 5th and every following 4th st drop to 5 rows down, then pick up the st and the 5 horizontal threads with the left needle, and k tog.

1st–12th rows: rep. continuously.

59 Knitting Pattern

The pattern appears on the reverse side. Number of sts divisible by 10, plus 7 sts (including the 2 edge sts).
1st row: edge st * k5, sl5 sts purlwise (yarn to the back). From * rep. Row ends with k5, edge st.
2nd row: k all sts.
3rd–7th rows: as in 1st and 2nd rows.
8th row: edge st, k7 * with the right needle pick up the 4 loose horizontal threads, and k tog. with the next st. K9. From * rep. Row ends: pick up the 4 loose horizontal threads and k tog. with the next st, k7, edge st.
9th row: edge st * sl5 sts purlwise (thread lies to the back of the work), k5. From * rep. Row ends with sl5 purlwise, edge st.
10th row: k.
11th–15th rows: as 9th and 10th rows.
16th row: edge st, k2 * pick up the 4 horizontal threads and k tog. with the next st. K9. From * rep. Row ends: pick up the 4 horizontal threads and k tog. with the next st, k2, edge st.
1st–16th rows: rep. continuously.

60 Knitting Pattern

Number of sts divisible by 4, plus 2 edge sts.
1st row: k.
2nd row: p.
3rd row: edge st * k2, sl2 purlwise (thread lies in front of sts). From * rep. Edge st.
4th row: edge st * sl2 purlwise (thread lies behind st), k2. From * rep. Edge st.
5th row: k.
6th row: p.
7th row: edge st * sl2 purlwise (thread in front of st), k2. From * rep. Edge st.
8th row: edge st * p2, sl2 purlwise (thread lies behind st). From * rep. Edge st.
1st–8th rows: rep. continuously.

61 Knitting Pattern

Number of sts divisible by 8.
1st row: edge st * k6, sl2 purlwise (thread in front of st). From * rep. Row ends with k6, edge st.
2nd row: edge st * p6, sl2 purlwise (thread behind st). From * rep. Row ends with p6 and edge st.
3rd row: as 1st.
4th row: p.
5th row: edge st, k2 * sl2 purlwise (thread in front of st), k6. From * rep. Row ends with sl2 purlwise (thread in front of st), k2, edge st.
6th row: edge st, p2 * sl2 purlwise (thread behind st), p6. From * rep. Row ends with sl2 purlwise (thread to the back), p2, edge st.
7th row: as 5th.
8th row: p.
1st–8th rows: rep. continuously.

62 Knitting Pattern

Number of sts divisible by 8.
1st row: edge st * p2, k3, p2, k1. From * rep. Row ends with p2, edge st.
2nd–4th rows: work sts as they appear (either k or p).
5th row: edge st * p2, k2 tog. and draw the slipped st over, p2, make 1 (pick up horizontal link and k in twisted form), k1, make 1. From * rep. Row ends with p2, edge st.
6th row: edge st, k2, p3, k2, p1, k2. From * rep. Edge st.
7th–10th rows: k sts as they appear (k or p).
11th row: edge st * p2, make 1, k1, make 1, p2, k3 tog. as described above. From * rep. Row ends with p2, edge st.
12th row: edge st, k2 * p1, k2, p3, k2, p3, k2. From * rep. Edge st.
13th–16th rows: k sts as they appear (k or p).
5th–16th rows: rep. continuously.

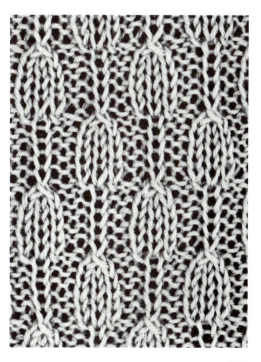

63 Knitting Pattern

Number of sts to be divisible by 4, plus 5.
1st–8th rows: 'smooth knitting', i.e. forward row k, backward p.
9th row: edge st * k3, let the following st drop 7 rows below, insert with a crochet hook from the front to the back, into the st, pick up topmost horizontal thread from the back and dr.thr. the st on the crochet hook; put the loop on the left needle and k. From * rep. Row ends with k3, edge st.
10th row: p.

11th–16th rows: 'smooth knitting'.
17th row: edge st, k1 * let the next st drop to 7 rows below; with a crochet hook insert from front to back into the st, from the back pick up the top horizontal link and dr.thr. the link on the crochet hook, put link on to the left needle and k. K3. From * rep. Row ends with a deep st, k1, edge st.
18th row: p.
19th–24th rows: 'smooth knitting'.
9th–24th rows: rep. continuously.

64 Knitting Pattern

Number of sts divisible by 6, plus 2 edge sts.
1st row: k.
2nd row: p.
3rd row: k.
4th row: p.
5th row: k.
6th row: edge st * p3, pick up 3 links below the next st with the right needle upwards, and k tog. Do not grip the st itself, let it drop. The next 2 sts are worked in the same way. From * rep. Edge st.
7th–11th rows: as 1st–5th.
12th row: edge st * pick up the 3 links below the next st from bottom to top with the right knitting needle and k tog. The st itself is not picked up, but dropped. The next 2 sts are knitted in the same way. P3. From * rep. Edge st.
1st–12th rows: rep. continuously.

65 Knitting Pattern

Number of sts divisible by 4, plus 3 (1 st and 2 edge sts).

1st row: edge st * thr.o., sl1 purlwise, k3. From * rep. Row ends with thr.o., sl1 purlwise, edge st.

2nd row: edge st * k tog. the thread-over of previous row and the slipped st. P3. From * rep. Row ends with k thread-over and slipped st of previous row tog. Edge st.

2nd and 5th rows: as 1st.

4th and 6th rows: as 2nd.

7th row: edge st, k2 * thr.o., sl1 purlwise, k3. From * rep. Row ends with thr.o., sl1 purlwise, k2, edge st.

8th row: edge st, p2 * k the next st tog. with the thread-over, p3. From * rep. Row ends with k next st with the thread-over tog., p2, edge st.

9th and 11th rows: as 7th.

10th and 12th rows: as 8th.

1st–12th rows: rep. continuously.

66 Knitting Pattern

Number of sts divisible by 12, plus 2.

1st row: (all sts are knitted), edge st * put 3 sts on a spare needle, leave in front of work, k the next 3 sts, now k the 3 sts from the spare needle. Put the next 3 sts on to the spare needle, and put *behind* the work, k the next 3 sts, then k the 3 from the spare needle. From * rep. Edge st.

2nd row: p.

3rd–6th rows: 'smooth knitting' (k forward rows, p backwards).

7th row: as 1st, but move the pattern as follows: edge st * put 3 sts on to spare needle and leave behind the work, k3, now k the 3 sts from the spare needle, again put 3 sts on the spare needle and leave in front of work, k3, now k the 3 from the spare needle. From * rep. Edge st.

8th row: p.

9th–12th rows: 'smooth knitting'.

1st–12th rows: rep. continuously.

Plait-cable Patterns

67   Knitting Pattern

Number of sts divisible by 11, plus 2.
1st row: edge st * k1, p2, k6, p2. From * rep.
Edge st.
2nd—4th rows: work sts as they appear.
5th row: edge st * k1, p2, sl the next 3 sts
on to spare needle, and leave in front of work,
k the next 3 sts (*see* left upper illustration),
then k sts on spare needle, p2. From * rep.
Edge st.
6th row: edge st * k2, p6, k2, p1. From * rep.
Edge st.
1st—6th rows: rep. continuously.

The 2nd illustration shows the working of the
plait, or cable.

The plait can be worked with 2, 4, 6 or 8 sts
and can be crossed in short or longer
intervals.

68   Knitting Pattern

Number of sts divisible by 3, plus 2 edge sts.
1st row: edge st * k2, p1. From * rep. Edge
st.
2nd row: edge st * k1, p2. From * rep. Edge
st.
3rd row: edge st * put 1 st on to spare
needle, k1, then k the st on spare needle, p1.
From * rep. Edge st.
4th row: as 2nd.
1st—4th rows: rep. continuously.

69 Knitting Pattern

Number of sts divisible by 7, plus 2 edge sts.
1st row: * purl 2, but following st on to spare needle and leave in front of work, k1 twisted, k st on spare needle, p2, k1. From * rep. Edge st.
2nd row: edge st * p1, k2, p2, k2. From * rep. Edge st.
3rd and 4th rows: work sts as they appear.
1st–4th rows: rep. continuously.

70 Knitting Pattern

Number of sts divisible by 12, plus 2 edge sts.
1st row: edge st * p2, k2, p1, k1, p2, k3. From * rep. Edge st.
2nd row: work sts as they appear.
3rd row: edge st * p2, put next st on to spare needle and leave in front of work, k2 twisted, k st on spare needle, p1, k next 2 sts crossed as previously described, p2, k3. From * rep. Edge st.
4th row: edge st * p3, k2, p2, k1, p2, k2. From * rep. Edge st.
1st–4th rows: rep. continuously.

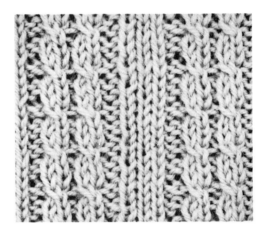

71 Knitting Pattern

Number of sts divisible by 5, plus 3 (1 st and 2 edge sts).
1st row: edge st * p1, k4. From * rep. Row ends with p1, edge st.
2nd row: work sts as they appear.
3rd row: edge st * p1, put 2 sts on to spare needle and leave in front of work, k next 2 sts tog., thr.o. twice, k sts on spare needle tog. From * rep. Row ends with p1, edge st.
4th row: work sts as they appear, out of the 2 thread-overs p1, k1.
5th–8th rows: as 1st and 2nd.
1st–8th rows: rep. continuously.

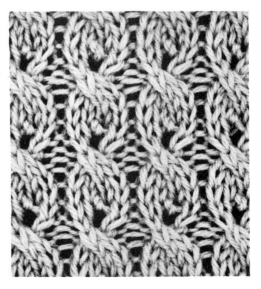

72　Knitting Pattern

Number of sts divisible by 7, plus 6 sts.
1st row: edge st * k1, p1, k4, p1. From * rep. Row ends with k1, p1, k2, edge st.
2nd row: work sts as they appear.
3rd row: edge st * k1, p1, k1, put 1 st on to a spare needle and leave in front of work, k2, put the sts of spare needle onto the right needle without knitting them (thread at the back of work), p1. From * rep. Row ends with k1, p1, k2, ed e st.
4th row: edge st, p2, k1, p1 * k1, p4, k1, p1. From * rep. Edge st.
5th row: edge st * k1, p1, sl2 sts on to spare needle and put to back of work, sl1 purlwise (thread to the back), k the 2 sts of spare needle, k1, p1. From * rep. Row ends with k1, p1, k2, edge st.
6th row: edge st, p2, k1, p1 * k1, p4, k1, p1. From * rep. Edge st.
3rd–6th rows: rep. continuously.

73　Knitting Pattern

Number of sts divisible by 6, plus　sts.
1st row: edge st, p2 * k4, p2. From * rep. Edge st.
2nd row: edge st, k2 * p4, k2. From * rep. Edge st.
3rd row: edge st, ρ2 * put 1 st on to spare needle, and leave in front of work, k1, k st of spare needle, put 1 st on to spare needle and put to back of work, k1, k st of spare needle, p2. From * rep. Edge st.
4th row: edge st, k2 * p4, k2. From * rep. Edge st.
5th row: edge st, p2 * sl1 st (thread behind the st), k2, sl1 st (thread behind the st), p2. From * rep. Edge st.
6th row: edge st, k2 * sl1 (thread in front of st), p2, sl1 (thread in front of st), k2. From * rep. Edge st.
3rd–6th rows: rep. continuously.

74 Knitting Pattern

Number of sts divisible by 17, plus 2 edge sts.

1st row: edge st * p1, k1 twisted, p3, k8, p3, k1 twisted. From * rep. Edge st.

2nd row: edge st * p1 twisted, k3, p8, k3, p1 twisted, k1. From * rep. Edge st.

3rd row: edge st * p1, k1 twisted, p3, sl next 2 sts on to spare needle, leave in front of work, k2, k the 2 sts of spare needle, sl next 2 sts on spare needle and put to back of work, k2, k the 2 sts of spare needle, p3, k1 twisted. From * rep. Edge st.

4th row: as 2nd.

1st–4th rows: rep. continuously.

Patterns with Crossed Stitches

75 Knitting Pattern

Number of sts divisible by 10, plus 2.

1st row: k.

2nd row: p.

3rd row: edge st * k6, miss 3 sts from the front and k the 4th st, then k the 1st, 2nd and 3rd sts, k6, drop the 4th st as already knitted. From * rep. Edge st.

4th row: p.

5th row: k.

6th row: p.

7th row: edge st, k1 * miss 3 sts from the front, and k the 4th st, then k the 1st, 2nd and 3rd sts, k6. From * rep. Row ends with miss 3 sts from the front and k the 4th st, then k the 1st, 2nd and 3rd of the missed sts, k5, edge st.

8th row: p.

1st–8th rows: rep. continuously.

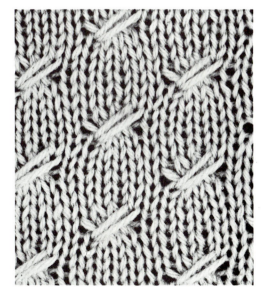

76 Knitting Pattern

Number of sts divisible by 8, plus 6 sts.
1st row: edge st * put 1 st on to spare needle and lay behind the work, k1, k spare needle st, 1 st on to spare needle and put in front of work, k1, k spare needle st, k4. From * rep. Row ends with sl1 on to spare needle, and put behind work, k1, k st of spare needle, sl1 st on to spare needle and put in front of work, k1, k st from spare needle, edge st.
2nd row: p.
3rd row: edge st * k4, sl1 st on to spare needle and put behind work, k1, k st from spare needle, sl1 st on to spare needle and leave in front of work, k1, k st from spare needle. From * rep. Row ends with k4, edge st.
4th row: p.
1st—4th rows: rep. continuously.

77 Knitting Pattern

Number of sts divisible by 10, plus 2 edge sts.
1st row: edge st * k6, sl next st on to spare needle and put behind work, k1, k spare needle st, next st sl on to spare needle and leave in front of work, k1, k spare needle st. From * rep. Edge st.
2nd and every backward row: p.
3rd row: edge st, k5 * sl st on to spare needle and behind work, k1, k spare needle st, k2, next st on to spare needle and in front of work, k1, k spare needle st, k4. From * rep. Row ends with next st on to spare needle and behind work, k1, k spare needle st, k3, edge st.
5th row: edge st, k1 * sl st on to spare needle and behind work, k1, k spare needle st, sl next st on to spare needle and leave in front of work, k1, k spare needle st, k6 sts. From * rep. Row ends with sl next st on to spare needle and put behind work, k1, k spare needle st, sl next st on to spare needle and leave in front of work, k1, k spare needle st, k5, edge st.
7th row: edge st * sl next st on to spare needle and put behind work, k1, k spare needle st, k2, next st on to spare needle and leave in front of work, k1, then k spare needle st, k4. From * rep. Edge st.
8th row: p.
1st—8th rows: rep. continuously.

78 Knitting Pattern

Number of sts divisible by 10, plus 2 edge sts.
1st row: edge st * k6, sl next st on to spare needle and put behind work, k1, k spare needle st, sl next st on to spare needle and put in front of work, k1, now k spare needle st. From * rep. Edge st.
2nd and every backward row: p.
3rd row: edge st * k6, sl next st on to spare needle and put in front of work, k1, k spare needle st, sl next st on to spare needle and put to the back of work, k1, k spare needle st. From * rep. Edge st.
5th–8th rows: as 1st–4th, but move the pattern.
1st–8th rows: rep. continuously.

79 Knitting Pattern

Number of sts divisible by 4, plus 2 edge sts.
1st row: edge st * miss the next st from the back and k the following st, then k the missed st. Miss the next st from the front and k the following st, then k the missed st. From * rep. Edge st.
2nd row: p.
3rd row: edge st * miss the next st from the front and k the following st, then k the missed st. Miss the next st from the back and k the following st, then k the missed st. From * rep. Edge st.
4th row: p.
1st–4th rows: rep. continuously.

Number of sts divisible by 12, plus 2 edge sts.
1st row: edge st * p2, k1, sl2 purlwise (thread to the back), k1, p2, sl1 purlwise (thread to the back), k2, sl1 purlwise. From * rep. Edge st.
2nd row: work sts as they appear; the slipped st again sl purlwise (thread in front of work).
3rd row: as 1st.
4th row: as 2nd.
5th row: edge st * p2, k next 2 sts crossed-wise (for this k the 2nd st from the front, then k the 1st st, after which take sts from the needle). Cross the next 2 sts from the back (i.e. first knit the 2nd st from the back, then the 1st st; now take both sts off the needle), p2, cross 2 sts from the back, next 2 sts from the front. From * rep. Edge st.

6th row: edge st * p4, k2. From * rep. Edge st.
7th row: edge st * p2, sl1 purlwise (thread to back), k2, sl1 purlwise (thread to back), p2, k1, sl2 purlwise, k1. From * rep. Edge st.
8th row: edge st * p1, sl2 purlwise (thread to the front), p1, k2. sl1 purlwise, p2, sl1 purlwise, k2. From * rep. Edge st.
9th row: as 7th.
10th row: as 8th.
11th row: edge st * p2 cross the next 2 sts from the back, and the following 2 from the front, p2, next 2 cross from the front and the following 2 from the back. From * rep. Edge st.
12th row: edge st * p4, k2. From * rep. Edge st.
1st–12th rows: rep. continuously.

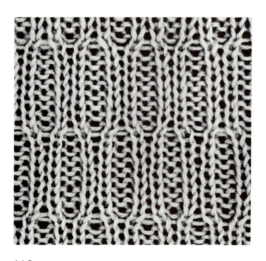

81 Knitting Pattern

Number of sts divisible by 4, plus 2 edge sts.
1st row: edge st * k2, p2. From * rep. Edge st.
2nd–8th rows: k sts as they appear.
9th row: edge st, p1 * the following k.st sl on to spare needle and leave in front of work; the next p.st, p, k st from spare needle. The 2 p.sts sl on to spare needle and put to the back of work, k the following st, p the sts from the spare needle. From * rep. Row ends: sl1 st on to spare needle, leave in front of work, p1, k st from spare needle, k1, edge st.
10th row: work sts as they appear.

11th row: edge st * p2, k2. From * rep. Edge st.

12th–18th rows: work sts as they appear.

19th row: edge st, k1 * sl next st purlwise on to spare needle and put behind work, k1, p st from spare needle, sl2 sts from spare needle and leave in front of work. P the next st and k the 2 sts from spare needle. From * rep. Row ends: sl next p.st on to spare needle and leave behind work, k next st, p st from spare needle, p1, edge st.

20th row: work sts as they appear.

1st–20th rows: rep. continuously.

82 Knitting Pattern

Number of sts divisible by 6, plus 2 edge sts.

1st row: edge st, k1 * p4, k2. From * rep. Row ends with p4, k1, edge st.

2nd row: edge st, p1 * k4, p2. From * rep. Row ends with k4, p1, edge st.

3rd row: edge st * sl1 st on to spare needle and leave in front of work, p1, k sts from spare needle, p2, sl1 st on to spare needle and leave behind work, k1. P st from spare needle. From * rep. Edge st.

4th row: edge st, k1 * sl1 purlwise (thread in front of st), k2. From * rep. Row ends with sl1 purlwise (thread in front of st), k1, edge st.

5th row: edge st, p1 * sl1 st on to spare needle and leave in front of work, p1, k st from spare needle, sl st on to spare needle and put behind work. K1, p st of spare needle, p2. From * rep. Row ends: first st on to spare needle and leave in front of work, p1, k st from spare needle, sl st on to spare needle and put behind work, k1, p st from spare needle, p1, edge st.

6th row: edge st, k2 * sl2 sts purlwise (thread in front of st), k4. From * rep. Row ends with sl2 sts purlwise, k2, edge st.

7th row: edge st, p2 * sl1 st on to spare needle and leave in front of work, k1, k st of spare needle, p4. From * rep. Row ends with sl1 st on to spare needle and leave in front of work, k1, k st of spare needle, p2, edge st.

8th row: edge st, k2 * sl2 sts purlwise (thread in front of st), k4. From * rep. Row ends with sl2 sts purlwise, k2, edge st.

9th row: edge st, p1 * sl1 st on to spare needle and put to back of work, k1, p st of spare needle, sl1 st to spare needle and leave in front of work, p1, k spare needle st, p2. From * rep. Row ends with sl1 st on to spare needle and leave in front of work. P1, k st of spare needle. P1, edge st.

10th row: edge st, k1 * sl1 purlwise (thread in front of st). K2. From * rep. Row ends with sl1 purlwise, k1, edge st.

11th row: edge st, sl1 st on to spare needle and put to back of work, k1, p spare needle st, p2, sl1 st on to spare needle and leave in front of work. P1, k st from spare needle. From * rep. Edge st.

12th row: edge st, sl1 st purlwise on to spare needle (thread to the front) * k4, sl2 purlwise (thread to the front). From * rep. Row ends with k4, sl1 purlwise, edge st.

13th row: edge st, k1 * p4, sl1 st on to spare needle and leave in front of work. K1, k st of spare needle. From * rep. Row ends with p4, k1, edge st.

14th row: edge st, sl1 purlwise (thread to the front) * k4, sl2 purlwise (thread to the front of work). From * rep. Row ends with k4, sl1 purlwise, edge st.

3rd–14th rows: rep. continuously.

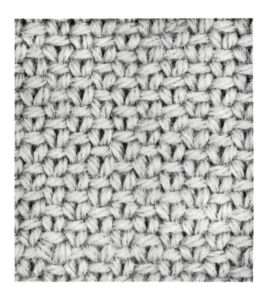

Weave and Plait Patterns

83   Knitting Pattern

Even number of sts.

1st row: edge st * k1, sl next st purlwise and put thread in front of work. From * rep. Edge st.

2nd row: edge st * p sl.st of previous row and sl the next st purlwise (thread to back of work). From * rep. Edge st.

Rep. the 2 rows continuously.

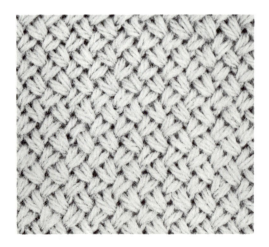

84   Knitting Pattern

Even number of sts.

1st row: edge st * cross next 2 sts as follows: sl1 st on to spare needle and leave in front of work, k the 2nd st, then the st from spare needle. From * rep. Edge st.

2nd row: edge st, p1 * cross the next 2 sts as follows: p the 2nd st, leave st on left needle, then p the 1st st and take both sts tog. from the needle. From * rep. Row ends with p1, edge st.

Work these 2 rows continuously. Practised hands can work this pattern without spare needle.

85 Knitting Pattern

Even number of sts.
1st row: edge st * cross the next 2 sts as follows: sl1 st on to spare needle and leave front of work, k 2nd st then k st from spare needle. From * rep. Edge st.
2nd row: p.
3rd row: edge st, k1 * sl next st on to spare needle and put behind work, k next st, now k st from spare needle and take both sts off needle. From * rep. Row ends with k1, edge st.
4th row: p.
1st–4th rows: rep. continuously.

86 Knitting Pattern

Any number of sts.
1st row: edge st * insert from the front to the back between the next and the next following st, thr.o. and bring yarn through, draw up and then k the 1st st. From * rep. Edge st.
2nd row: edge st * p the knitted st tog. with the thread-over. From * rep. Edge st.
1st and 2nd rows: rep. continuously.

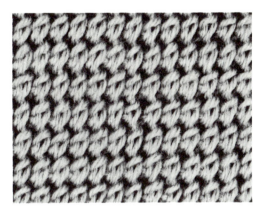

87 Knitting Pattern

Even number of sts.
1st row: k.
2nd row: p.
3rd row: edge st * draw the 2nd following st through the 1st st, and k, then k the 1st st. From * rep. Row ends with k1, edge st.
4th row: p.
5th row: edge st * draw the 2nd following st through the 1st st and k, then k the 1st st. From * rep. Edge st.
6th row: p.
3rd–6th rows: rep. continuously.

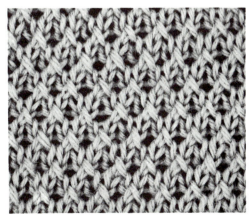

88 Knitting Pattern

Even number of sts.
1st row: k.
2nd row: edge st * sl1 (thread to back), k1. From * rep. Edge st.
3rd row: k.
4th row: edge st * k1, sl1 (thread to back). From * rep. Edge st.
1st–4th rows: rep. continuously.

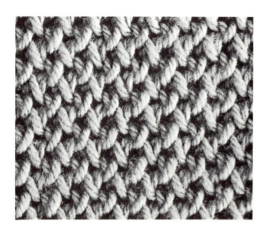

89 Knitting Pattern

Even number of sts.
This pattern should be worked quite loosely.
1st row: edge st * k the next-but-one st crossed (insert from the back without taking the 1st st off needle), draw up and over the 1st st, now k the 1st st. From * rep. Edge st.
2nd row: edge st * p the next-but-one st without taking 1st st off needle, draw over as in 1st row, and now p the 1st st. From * rep.
1st and 2nd rows: rep. continuously.

90 Knitting Pattern

Number of sts divisible by 6, plus 5 sts.
1st row: k.
2nd row: p.
3rd row: edge st * put 3 sts on to spare needle and leave in front of work, k the next 3 sts, then k the 3 sts from spare needle. From * rep. Row ends with k3, edge st.
4th row: p.
5th row: k.
6th row: p.
7th row: edge st, k3 * sl3 sts on to spare needle and put to back of work, k the following sts then k the 3 from spare needle. From * rep. Edge st.
8th row: p.
1st–8th rows: rep. continuously.

116

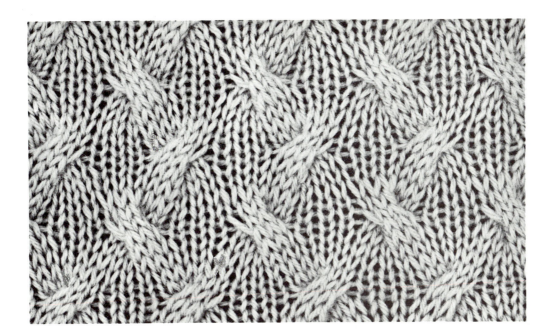

91 Knitting Pattern

Number of sts divisible by 9, plus sts.
1st row: edge st * k3, put next 3 sts on to spare needle and leave in front of work, k3, k sts from spare needle. From * rep. Edge st.
2nd row: p.

Vertical-stripe Patterns

3rd—6th rows: 'smooth knitting' (forward row k, backward row p).
7th row: edge st * put the next 3 sts on to spare needle, put to back of work, k3, k3 sts of spare needle. From * rep. Edge st.
8th row: p.
9th—12th ı ws: 'smooth knitting'.
1st—12th rows: rep. continuously.

92 Knitting Pattern

Even number of sts.
1st row: edge st * k1, p1. From * rep. Edge st.
2nd row: p.
1st—2nd rows: rep. continuously.

93 Knitting Pattern

Number of sts divisible by 7, plus 4 (2 sts, plus 2 edge sts).
1st row: edge st * p2, k2, p1, k2. From * rep. Row ends with p2, edge st.
2nd row: work sts as they appear.
3rd row: edge st * p2, k1, p1, k1, p1, k1. From * rep. Row ends with p2, edge st.
4th row: as 2nd.
1st–4th rows: rep. continuously.

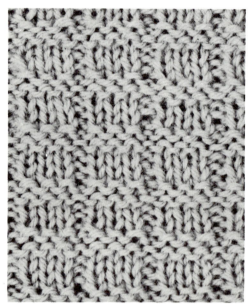

94 Knitting Pattern

Number of sts divisible by 4, plus 2 edge sts.
1st row: edge st * k3, p1. From * rep. Edge st.
2nd row: edge st * k1, p3. From * rep. Edge st.
3rd row: edge st * k3, p1. From * rep. Edge st.
4th row: k.
5th row: p.
6th row: edge st * k1, p3. From * rep. Edge st.
7th row: edge st * k3, p1. From * rep. Edge st.
8th row: edge st * k1, p3. From * rep. Edge st.
9th row: p.
10th row: k.
1st–10th rows: rep. continuously.

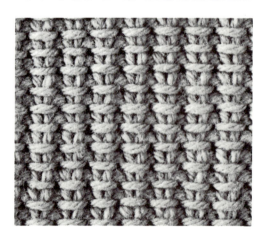

95 Knitting Pattern

The pattern appears on the wrong side. Even number of sts.
1st row: edge st * k1, sl1 purlwise (thread to the back). From * rep. Edge st.
2nd row: edge st * k1, sl1 purlwise (thread to the front). From * rep. Edge st.
1st and 2nd rows: rep. continuously.

96 Knitting Pattern

Pattern appears on the wrong side.
Number of sts divisible by 3, plus 4 sts.
1st row: edge st * k2, thr.o. and sl next st purlwise. From * rep. Edge st.
2nd row: edge st * k the slipped st with the thread-over, twisted tog., k2. From * rep. Edge st.
1st and 2nd rows: rep. continuously.

97 Knitting Pattern

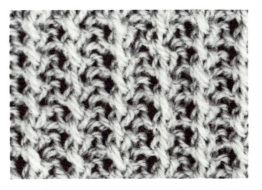

Number of sts divisible by 3.
1st row: edge st * p1, thr.o., k2 twisted tog. From * rep. Row ends with p1, edge st.
2nd row: edge st * k1, thr.o., p2 sts tog. From * rep. Row ends with k1, edge st.
1st and 2nd rows: rep. continuously.

98 Knitting Pattern

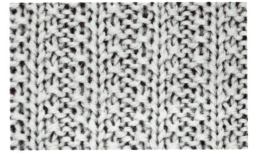

Number of sts divisible by 4, plus 1 st and 2 edge sts.
1st and all following rows: edge st * k2, p2. From * rep. Row ends with k2, p3, edge st.
2nd row: edge st * k2, p2. From * rep. Row ends with k2, p3, edge st.
These 2 rows are continuously repeated.

99 Knitting Pattern

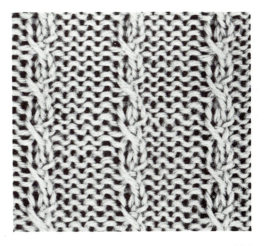

Number of sts divisible by 4, plus 2 edge sts.
1st row: edge st, p2 * k1, p5. From * rep. Row ends with k1, p3, edge st.
2nd row: edge st, k the knitted sts and sl the p.sts, thread to the front.
3rd row: edge st, p2 * out of the 2nd st, through the loop of the 1st st, k1 st. Then k the 1st st twisted. Let the sts slip off needle, p4. From * rep. Row ends: out of the following 2nd st, through the loop of the 3rd st, k1 twisted and let both sts slip off needle. P2, edge st.
4th row: work sts as they appear.
1st–4th rows: rep. continuously.

100   Knitting Pattern

Number of sts divisible by 6, plus 5.
1st row: k.
2nd row: p.
3rd row: k.
4th row: edge st * p3, k the following 3 tog., do not take off needle, but make 2 more sts out of them (p1, k1) then drop. From * rep. Row ends with p3, edge st.
1st–4th rows: rep. continuously.

101   Knitting Pattern

Even number of sts.
1st–4th rows: 'smooth knitting'.
5th row: * p1, sl1 purlwise (thread to front). From * rep.
6th row: * k1, sl1 purlwise (thread to back). From * rep.
1st–6th rows: rep. continuously.

102   Knitting Pattern

Number of sts divisible by 8, plus 2 sts.
1st row: edge st * k1, p2, sl1 purlwise (thread behind st), k2, draw the slipped st over the 2 knitted sts and k it twisted. P2. From * rep. Edge st.
2nd row: edge st * k2, p3, k2, p1. From * rep. Edge st.
Rep. these 2 rows.

103   Knitting Pattern

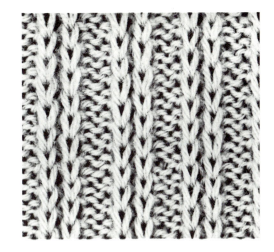

Number of sts divisible by 4.
1st row: edge st * p2, thr.o., sl1 purlwise, k1.
From * rep. Row ends with p2, edge st.
2nd row: edge st * k2, thr.o., sl1 purlwise, p tog. the next st with the thread-over of previous row. From * rep. Row ends with k2, edge st.
3rd row: edge st * p2, thr.o., sl1 purlwise, k the next st tog. with the thread-over of previous row. From * rep. Row ends with p2, edge st.
2nd and 3rd rows: rep. continuously.

104   Knitting Pattern

Number of sts divisible by 7, plus 5 sts.
1st row: edge st * p3, when knitting the next st thr.o. 3 times. The next 3 sts are knitted each with 3 thread-overs. From * rep. Row ends with p3, edge st.
2nd row: edge st * k3, sl the next 4 sts purlwise (thread to front), at the same time let the thread-overs of previous row drop. From * rep. Row ends with k3, edge st.
3rd row: edge st * p3, sl4 purlwise (thread to back). From * rep. Row ends with p3, edge st.
4th row: edge st * k3, sl4 purlwise (thread in front of st). From * rep. Row ends with k3, edge st.
1st–4th rows: rep. continuously.

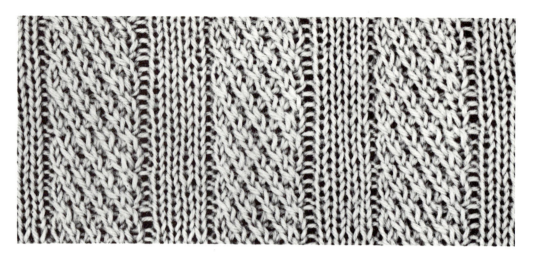

105 Knitting Pattern

Number of sts divisible by 14, plus 6 sts.
1st row: edge st * k4, p1. K the next-but-one st twisted from the back, then k the missed st and take both from needle. Rep. the crossing of sts 3 more times, p1. From * rep.

Row ends with k4, edge st.
2nd row: work sts as they appear.
3rd row: edge st * k4, p1, k1, cross the next 6 sts as described in 1st row. K1, p1. From * rep. Row ends with k4, edge st.
4th row: as 2nd.
1st–4th rows: rep. continuously.

106 Knitting Pattern

Number of sts divisible by 8, plus 2 edge sts.
1st row: edge st, k4 * p1, k7. From * rep. Row ends with p1, k3, edge st.
2nd row: edge st * p2, k3, p2, k1. From * rep. Edge st.
3rd row: edge st, k2 * p2, k1, p2, k3. From * rep. Row ends with p2, k1, p2, k1, edge st.
4th row: edge st, k2 * p3, k5. From * rep. Row ends with p3, k3, edge st.
5th row: edge st * k1, p1, k5, p1. From * rep. Edge st.
6th row: edge st * p7, k1. From * rep. Edge st.
1st–6th rows: rep. continuously.

107 Knitting Pattern

Number of sts divisible by 8, plus 1 st for the middle, and 2 edge sts. The middle st of the whole work is purled in forward, and knitted in backward rows.

1st row: edge st * k2, p2. From * rep. to the middle, p the middle st ** p2, k2. From ** rep. Edge st.

2nd row: edge st, k1 * p2. From * rep. to 3 sts before the middle, p2, the 3 middle sts., k ** p2, k2. From ** rep. Row ends with p2, k, edge st.

3rd row: edge st * p2, k2. From * rep. to the middle, p middle st ** k2, p2. From ** rep. Edge st.

4th row: edge st, p1 * k2, p2. From * rep. to 3 sts before the middle, then k2, p1. K the middle st, p1 ** k2, p2. From ** rep. Row ends with k2, p1, edge st.

1st–4th rows: rep. continuously.

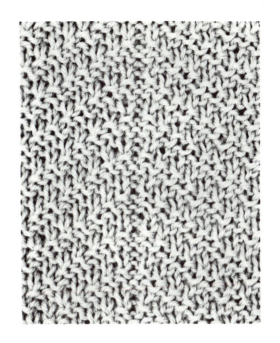

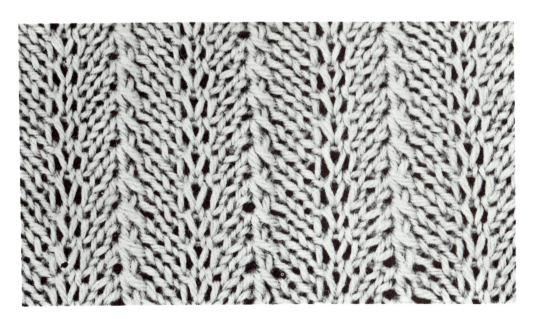

108 Knitting Pattern

Number of sts divisible by 8, plus 3 (1 st and 2 edge sts).

1st row: edge st, k2 tog. * k2, make 1 st (=pick up horizontal link and k twisted), k1, make 1, k2, k3 twisted. From * rep. Row ends with k2, make 1, k1, make 1, k2, k2 tog., edge st.

2nd row: p.

Rep. these 2 rows continuously.

Diagonal-stripe Patterns

109 Knitting Pattern

Number of sts divisible by 8, plus 2 edge sts.
1st row: edge st * k4, p4. From * rep. Edge st.
2nd row: edge st, p1 * k4, p4. From * rep. Row ends with k4, p3, edge st.
3rd row: edge st, k2 * p4, k4. From * rep. Row ends with p4, k2, edge st.
4th row: edge st, p3 * k4, p4. Row ends with k4, p1, edge st.
5th row: edge st * p4, k4. From * rep. Edge st.
6th row: edge st, k1 * p4, k4. From * rep. Row ends with p4, k3, edge st.
7th row: edge st, p2 * k4, p4. From * rep. Row ends with k4, p2, edge st.
8th row: edge st, k3 * p4, k4. From * rep. Row ends with p4, k1, edge st.
1st–8th rows: rep. continuously.

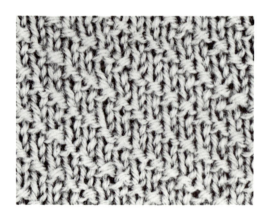

1. picture (front)

2. picture (back)

110 Knitting Pattern

Number of sts divisible by 4, plus 2 edge sts.
1st row: edge st * p1, k3. From * rep. Edge st.
2nd row (back): edge st, p2 * k1, p3. From

* rep. Row ends with k1, p1, edge st.
3rd row: edge st, k2 * p1, k3. From * rep. Row ends with p1, k1, edge st.
4th row: edge st * k1, p3. From * rep. Edge st.
1st–4th rows: rep. continuously. This pattern can be used on either side.

111   Knitting Pattern

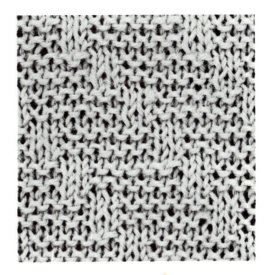

Number of sts divisible by 8, plus 2 edge sts.
1st and every forward row: k.
2nd row: edge st * k6, p2. From * rep. Edge st.
4th row: as 2nd.
6th row: edge st, k4 * p2, k6. From * rep. Row ends with p2, k2, edge st.
8th row: as 6th.
10th row: edge st, k2 * p2, k6. From * rep. Row ends with p2, k4, edge st.
12th row: as 10th.
14th row: edge st * p2, k6. From * rep. Edge st.
16th row: as 14th.
1st–16th rows: rep. continuously.

112   Knitting Pattern

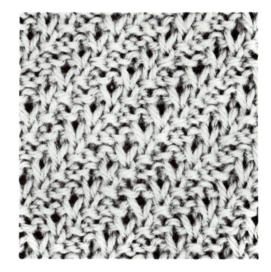

Number of sts divisible by 4, plus 2 edge sts.
1st row (backward row): edge st * k2, sl2 purlwise (thread to the front). From * rep. Edge st.
2nd row (forward row): edge st * k2, p2. From * rep. Edge st.
3rd row: edge st, sl1 purlwise (thread to front) * k2, sl2 purlwise (thread to front). From * rep. Row ends with k2, sl1 purlwise, edge st.
4th row: edge st, k1 * p2, k2. From * rep. Row ends with p2, k1, edge st.
5th row: edge st * sl2 purlwise (thread in front), k2. From * rep. Edge st.
6th row: edge st * p2, k2. From * rep. Edge st.
7th row: edge st, k1 * sl2 purlwise (thread in front), k2. From * rep. Row ends with sl2 purlwise (thread in front), k1, edge st.
8th row: edge st, p1 * k2, p2. From * rep. Row ends with k2, p1, edge st.
1st–8th rows: rep. continuously.

125

113 Knitting Pattern

Number of sts divisible by 20, plus 6 sts.
1st row: edge st, k2 * cross the next 2 sts
like this: sl1 st to spare needle and leave in
front of work, k the next st, then k the st from
spare needle. The following 14 sts (7 × 2)
cross in the same way, then k4. From * rep.
Row ends with k2, edge st.
2nd row: p.
Rep. these 2 rows continuously, but, in
every forward row move the pattern by 1 st to
the left. The 3rd row is like this: edge st, k3 *
cross the following 16 sts (8 × 2) as described
in 1st row. K4. From * rep. Row ends with k1,
edge st.

Holed Patterns

114 Knitting Pattern

Number of sts divisible by 8.
1st row: edge st * k6, thr.o., k2 tog. From *
rep. Row ends with k6, edge st.
2nd row: p all sts and thread-overs.
3rd row: k.
4th row: p.
5th row: edge st, k2 * thr.o., k2 tog., k6.
From * rep. Row ends with 1 thread-over,
k2 tog., k2, edge st.
6th row: as 2nd.
7th row: k.
8th row: p.
1st–8th rows: rep. continuously.
Chart: when working according to a chart,
begin and end with 1 edge st. K forward
rows continuously from * to * and once from
** to ∅. In backward rows p all sts and
thread-overs.
1st–8th rows: rep. continuously.
For explanation of diagram *see* p. 300.

Chart

r	r	r	r	r	r	r	r	r	r	r	r	r	r	
r	r	r	r	r	r	r	r	r	r	r	r	r	r	7. R
r	r	/	U	r	r	r	r	r	/	U	r	r	r	5. R
r	r	r	r	r	r	r	r	r	r	r	r	r	r	3. R
r	r	r	r	r	r	/	U	r	r	r	r	r	r	1. R

∅   **   *

126

115   Knitting Pattern

Number of sts divisible by 10, plus 2 edge sts.
1st row: edge st * thr.o., k2 tog., k8. From
* rep. Edge st.
2nd and every further backward row: p
all sts and thread-overs.
3rd row: edge st * k1, thr.o., k2 tog., k5,
sl1, k1 and draw the slipped st over, thr.o.
From * rep. Edge st.
5th row: edge st * k2, thr.o., k2 tog., k3,
sl1, k1 and draw slipped st over, thr.o., k1.
From * rep. Edge st.
7th row: edge st * k3, thr.o., k2 tog., k1,
sl1, k1 and draw the slipped st over, thr.o., k2.
From * rep. Edge st.
9th row: edge st * k4, thr.o., sl2 tog., k1 and
draw the slipped sts over, thr.o., k3. From *
rep. Edge st.
11th–16th rows: 'smooth knitting' (= k
forward, p backward rows).
1st–16th rows: rep. continuously.
Chart: when working to the chart forward
rows are worked continuously from * to **.
Backward rows p all sts and thread-overs.
1st–16th rows: rep. continuously.
For explanation of diagram, *see* p. 300.

Chart

r	r	r	r	r	r	r	r	r	r	15. R
r	r	r	r	r	r	r	r	r	r	13. R
r	r	r	r	r	r	r	r	r	r	11. R
r	r	r	U	■	U	r	r	r	r	9. R
r	r	U	⟍	r	╱	U	r	r	r	7. R
r	U	⟍	r	r	r	╱	U	r	r	5. R
U	⟍	r	r	r	r	r	╱	U	r	3. R
r	r	r	r	r	r	r	r	╱	U	1. R

★★   ★

116   Knitting Pattern

Number of sts divisible by 16, plus 2 edge sts.
1st row: edge st, k7 * thr.o., k2 tog., k14.
From * rep. Row ends with 1 thr.o., k2 tog., k7,
edge st.
2nd and every following backward row:
p all sts including thread-overs.
3rd row: edge st, k5 * thr.o., k2 tog., k2,
thr.o., k2 tog., k10. From * rep. Row ends with
thr.o., k2 tog., k2, thr.o., k2 tog., k5, edge
st.
5th row: edge st, k3 * thr.o., k2 tog., k6.
From * rep. Row ends with thr.o., k2 tog., k3,
edge st.
7th row: edge st, k1 * thr.o., k2 tog., k10,

thr.o., k2 tog., k2. From * rep. Row ends with
thr.o., k2 tog., k10, thr.o., k2 tog., k1, edge
st.
9th row: edge st, k15 * thr.o., k2 tog., k14.
From * rep. Row ends with thr.o., k2 tog., k15,
edge st.
11th row: as 7th.
13th row: as 5th.
15th row: as 3rd.
16th row: p all sts, inclusive of thread-
overs.
1st–16th rows: rep. continuously.

Illustration on next page.

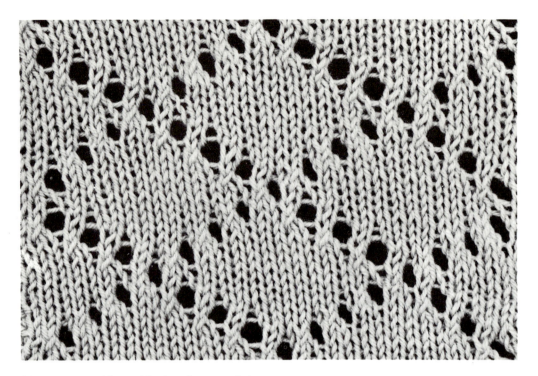

Chart: on working with the chart, work in forward rows once from ∅ to *, then continuously from * to **, and once from ** to ∅. In backward rows, p all sts and thread-overs.

1st–11th rows: rep. continuously.
For explanation of diagram: *see* p. 300.

Chart

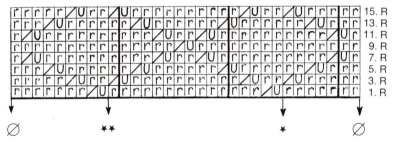

117 Knitting Pattern

Number of sts divisible by 11, plus 2 edge sts.
1st row: edge st * thr.o., sl1, k1 and draw slipped st over, thr.o., sl1, k1 and draw slipped st over, thr.o., sl1, k1 and draw slipped st over, thr.o., sl1, k1 and draw slipped st over, k3. From * rep. Edge st.

2nd and all backward rows: p all sts and thread-overs.

3rd row: edge st * thr.o., sl1, k1 and draw slipped st over, k9. From * rep. Edge st.

5th row: as 3rd.

7th row: edge st, thr.o., sl1, k1 and draw slipped st over * k3, thr.o., sl1, k1 and draw slipped st over, thr.o., sl1, k1 and draw slipped st over, thr.o., sl1, k1 and draw slipped st over, thr.o., sl1, k1 and draw slipped st over. From * rep. Row ends with k3, thr.o., sl1, k1 and draw slipped st over, thr.o., sl1, k1 and draw slipped st over, thr.o., sl1, k1 and draw slipped st over, edge st.

9th row: edge st, k5 * thr.o., sl1, k1 and draw slipped st over, k9. From * rep. Row ends with thr.o., sl1, k1 and draw slipped st over, k4, edge st.

11th row: as 9th.

13th row: edge st, k1, thr.o., sl1, k1 and draw slipped st over, thr.o., sl1, k1 and draw slipped st over, thr.o., sl1, k1 and draw slipped st over * k3, thr.o., sl1, k1 and draw slipped st over, thr.o., sl1, k1 and draw slipped st over, thr.o., sl1, k1 and draw slipped st over. From * rep. Row ends with k4, edge st.

15th row: edge st, k10 * thr.o., sl1, k1 and draw slipped st over, k9. From * rep. Row ends with thr.o., sl1, k1, and draw slipped st over, k10, edge st.

17th row: as 15th.

18th row: p all sts and thread-overs.

From here on continue pattern: *see* chart.

Chart: when using the chart, work in forward rows once from ⌀ to *, continuously from * to ** and once from ** to ⌀. In backward rows, p all sts, including thread-overs.

1st–66th rows: rep. continuously.

For explanation of diagram, *see* p. 300.

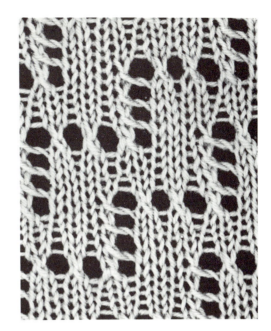

Chart

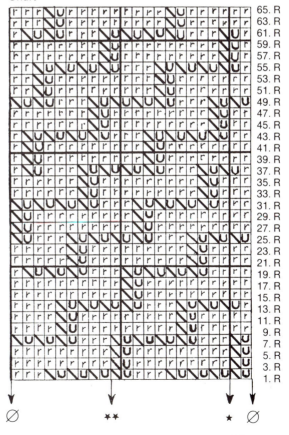

129

118 Knitting Pattern

Number of sts divisible by 8, plus 2 edge sts.
1st row: k.
2nd and every backward row: p all sts, including thread-overs.
3rd row: edge st * k6, thr.o., k2 tog. From * rep. Edge st.
5th row: edge st, k5 * thr.o., k2 tog., thr.o., k2 tog., k4. From * rep. Row ends with thr.o., k2 tog., k1, edge st.
7th row: as 3rd.
9th row: k all sts.
11th row: edge st, k2 * thr.o., k2 tog., k6. From * rep. Row ends with thr.o., k2 tog., k4, edge st.
13th row: edge st, k1 * thr.o., k2 tog., thr.o., k2 tog., k4. From * rep. Row ends with thr.o., k2 tog., thr.o., k2 tog., k3, edge st.
15th row: as 11th.
17th row: k all sts.
18th row: p.
3rd–18th rows: rep. continuously.

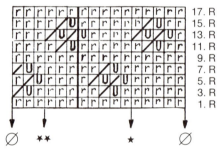

Chart

17. R
15. R
13. R
11. R
9. R
7. R
5. R
3. R
1. R

∅   ★★   ★   ∅

Chart: when using the chart, work in forward rows once from the beg. to *, then continuously from * to **, and once from ** to the end. In the backward rows, all thread-overs and sts are purled.
3rd–18th rows: rep. continuously.
For explanation of diagram, *see* p. 300.

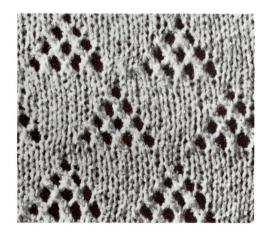

119 Knitting Pattern

Number of sts divisible by 12, plus 2 edge sts.
1st row: edge st * k4, thr.o., sl1, k1 and draw the slipped st over, thr.o., sl1, k1 and draw the slipped st over. Thr.o., sl1, k1 and draw the slipped st over. From * rep. Edge st.
2nd and all backward rows: p all sts and thread-overs.
3rd row: edge st, k5 * thr.o., sl1, k1 and draw the slipped st over. Thr.o., sl1, k1 and draw the slipped st over. Thr.o., sl1, k1 and draw the slipped st over. K6. From * rep. Row ends with thr.o., sl1, k1 and draw the slipped

st over. Thr.o., sl1, k1 and draw the slipped st over. Thr.o., sl1, k1 and draw the slipped st over. K1, edge st.

5th row: edge st, k6 * thr.o., sl1, k1 and draw the slipped st over, thr.o., sl1, k1 and draw the slipped st over. K8. From * rep. Row ends with thr.o., sl1, k1 and draw the slipped st over. Thr.o., sl1, k1 and draw the slipped st over. K2, edge st.

7th row: edge st, k7 * thr.o., sl1, k1 and draw the slipped st over. K10. From * rep. Row ends with thr.o., sl1, k1 and draw the slipped st over. K3, edge st.

8th row: p all sts and thread-overs.

9th–16th rows: as 1st–18th rows, but move the pattern so that the 9th row begins with edge st, then rep. 3 times the following: thr.o., 1 sl.st, k1 and draw the slipped st over, k4, etc.

1st–16th rows: rep. continuously.

Chart

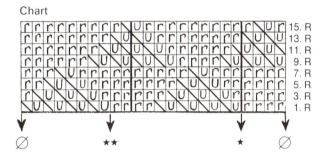

Chart: when using the chart work forward rows once from ⌀ to *, continuously from * to **, and once from ** to ⌀. P all sts and thread-overs in backward rows.

1st–16th rows: rep. continuously.

For explanation of chart, *see* p. 300.

120 Knitting Pattern

Number of sts divisible by 12, plus 2 edge sts.

1st row: edge st * k8, k2 tog., thr.o. twice, sl1, k1 and draw the slipped st over. From * rep. Edge st.

2nd and every subsequent backward row: p. The thread-overs are worked as follows: k1, p1.

3rd row: edge st, k6 * k2 tog., thr.o. twice, sl1, k1 and draw slipped st over, k2 tog., thr.o. twice, sl1, k1 and draw the slipped st over, k4. From * rep. Row ends with k2 tog., thr.o. twice, sl1, k1, and draw the slipped st over, k2 tog., thr.o. once, edge st.

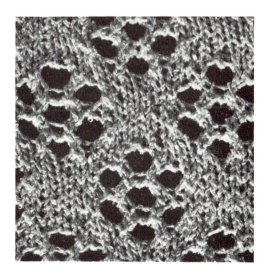

5th row: as 1st.
7th row: as 3rd.
9th row: as 1st.
11th row: edge st, k2 * k2 tog., thr.o. twice, sl1, k1 and draw the slipped st over, k8. From * rep. Row ends with k2 tog., thr.o. twice, sl1, k1 and draw the slipped st over, k6, edge st.

13th row: edge st * k2 tog., thr.o. twice, sl1, k1 and draw slipped st over, k2 tog., thr.o. twice, sl1, k1 and draw slipped st over. K4. From * rep. Edge st.
15th row: as 11th.
17th row: as 13th.
19th row: as 11th.
1st—20th rows: rep. continuously.

Chart

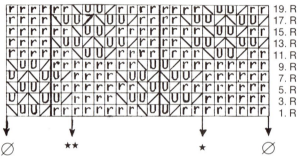

Chart: when working from the chart, work in forward rows once from ∅ to *, continuously from * to **, and once from ** to ∅. P all sts in backward rows, and work the double thread-overs with k1, p1.
1st—20th rows: rep. continuously.

For explanation of diagram, see p. 300.

121 Knitting Pattern

Number of sts divisible by 9, plus 4 sts (2 sts plus 2 edge sts).
1st row: k.
2nd row: p.
3rd row: edge st, k3 * sl1, k1 and draw the slipped st over, thr.o., k1, thr.o., k2 tog., k4. From * rep. Row ends with sl1, k1 and draw slipped st over, thr.o., k1, thr.o., k2 tog., k3, edge st.
4th and every subsequent backward row: p all sts and thread-overs.
5th row: edge st * k2, sl1, k1 and draw

slipped st over, thr.o., k3, thr.o., k2 tog. From * rep. Row ends with k2, edge st.

7th row: edge st, k4 * thr.o., k2 tog., k7. From * rep. Row ends with thr.o., k2 tog., k5, edge st.

9th row: edge st, k5 * thr.o., k2 tog., k7. From * rep. Row ends with thr.o., k2 tog., k4, edge st.

11th row: edge st, k6 * thr.o., k2 tog., k7. From * rep. Row ends with thr.o., k2 tog., k3, edge st.

13th row: edge st * k7, thr.o., k2 tog. From * rep. Row ends with k2, edge st.

14th row: p all sts and thread-overs.

1st–14th rows: rep. continuously.

Chart: when using chart, work in forward rows, once from ∅ to *, then continuously from * to ** and once from ** to ∅. P all sts and thread-overs in backward rows.

1st–14th rows: rep. continuously.

For explanation of diagram, *see* p. 300.

Chart

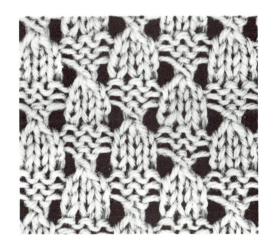

122   Knitting Pattern

Number of sts divisible by 6, plus 2 edge sts.

1st row: edge st * k3, p3. From * rep. Edge st.

2nd row: work all sts as they appear.

3rd row: as 1st.

4th row: edge st * p3, thr.o., sl1 purlwise, k2 twisted tog. and draw the slipped st over, thr.o. From * rep. Edge st.

5th row: edge st * p3, k3. From * rep. Edge st.

6th row: work all sts as they appear.

7th row: as 5th.

8th row: edge st * thr.o., sl1 purlwise, k2 twisted tog. and draw the slipped st over, thr.o., p3. From * rep. Edge st.

1st–8th rows: rep. continuously.

Chart: when using the chart, work continuously in forward rows from * to **, and in backward rows from ** to *.

1st–8th rows: rep. continuously.

For explanation of diagram, *see* p. 300.

Chart

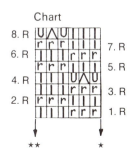

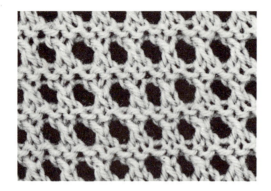

123 Knitting Pattern

Even number of sts.
1st row: edge st * thr.o., sl1, k1, and draw the slipped st over. From * rep. Edge st.
2nd row: p all sts, including thread-overs.
3rd row: p.
4th row: p.
1st—4th rows: rep. continuously.

124 Knitting Pattern

Even number of sts.
1st, 2nd and 3rd rows: k.
4th row: p.
5th row: edge st * thr.o., k2 tog. From * rep. Edge st.
6th row: p all sts and thread-overs.
1st—6th rows: rep. continuously.

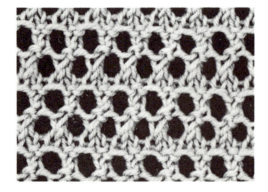

125 Knitting Pattern

Even number of sts.
1st row: k.
2nd row: edge st * k2 tog., thr.o. From * rep. Edge st.
3rd row: p.

4th row: edge st * thr.o., k2 tog. From * rep. Edge st.
5th row: p.
6th row: p.
1st—6th rows: rep. continuously.

126 Knitting Pattern

Number of sts divisible by 3, plus 2 edge sts.
1st row: edge st, k2 * thr.o., k3, draw the 1st of the 3 knitted sts over the 2 knitted sts. From * rep. Row ends with k1, edge st.
2nd row: p all sts, including thread-overs.
3rd row: edge st, k1 * k3, draw the 1st of the 3 knitted sts over the following 2 knitted sts, thr.o. From * rep. Row ends with k2, edge st.
4th row: p all sts and thread-overs.
1st—4th rows: rep. continuously.

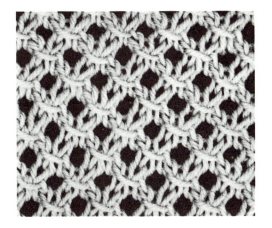

127 Knitting Pattern

Even number of sts.
1st row: k1 * thr.o., sl1, k1 twisted and draw slipped st over. From * rep. Row ends with k1.
2nd row: p2 * thr.o., sl1, p1 and draw the slipped st over. From * rep.
1st and 2nd rows: rep. continuously.

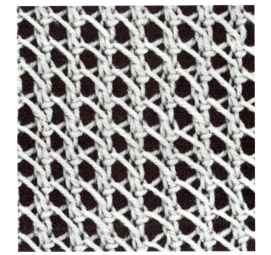

128 Knitting Pattern

Number of sts divisible by 3, plus 2 edge sts.
1st row: k.
2nd row: edge st * sl1, k2 and draw the slipped st over the 2 knitted sts, thr.o. From * rep. Edge st.
3rd row: k.
4th row: edge st, k1 * thr.o., sl1, k2 and draw the slipped st over. From * rep. Row ends with thr.o., sl1, k1 and draw the slipped st over, edge st.
1st—4th rows: rep. continuously.

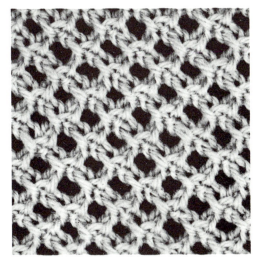

129 Knitting Pattern

Number of sts divisible by 6, plus 7 (5 sts plus 2 edge sts).

1st row: p.

2nd row: k.

3rd row: edge st, p5 * thr.o., k1, thr.o., p5. From * rep. Edge st.

4th row: edge st * k5, p3. From * rep. Row ends with k5, edge st.

5th row: edge st * p5, k3. From * rep. Row ends with p5, edge st.

6th row: edge st * k5, p3 tog. From * rep. Row ends with k5, edge st.

7th row: p.

8th row: k.

9th row: edge st, p2 * thr.o., k1, thr.o., p5. From * rep. Row ends with thr.o., k1, thr.o., p2, edge st.

10th row: edge st, k2 * p3, k5. From * rep. Row ends with p3, k2, edge st.

11th row: edge st, p2 * k3, p5. From * rep. Row ends with k3, p2, edge st.

12th row: edge st, k2 * p3 tog., k5. From * rep. Row ends with p3 tog., k2, edge st.

1st–12th rows: rep. continuously.

130 Knitting Pattern

Number of sts divisible by 6, plus 2 edge sts.

1st row: edge st, k1, k2 tog. * thr.o., k1, thr.o., sl1, k1 and draw slipped st over, k1, k2 tog. From * rep. Row ends with thr.o., k1, thr.o., sl1, k1, and draw the slipped st over, edge st.

2nd and every subsequent backward row: p all sts and thread-overs.

3rd, 5th, 7th, 9th and 11th rows: as 1st.

13th row: edge st * k1, thr.o., sl1, k1 and draw slipped st over, k1, k2 tog., thr.o. From * rep. Edge st.

15th, 17th, 19th, 21st and 23rd rows: as 13th.

1st–24th rows: rep. continuously.

Chart: when working according to the chart, in forward rows work once from ∅ to *, continuously from * to **, and then once from ** to ∅. In backward rows all sts and thread-overs are purled.

1st–24th rows: rep. continuously.
For explanation of diagram, *see* p. 300.

For explanation of diagram, *see* p. 300.

Chart

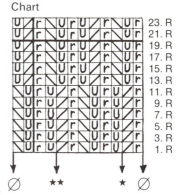

131 Knitting Pattern

Number of sts divisible by 4, plus 2 edge sts.
1st row: edge st * p1, k2, p1. From * rep. Edge st.
2nd row: edge st * k1, p2, k1. From * rep. Edge st.
3rd row: edge st * k2 tog., thr.o. twice, sl1, k1 and draw the slipped st over. From * rep. Edge st.
4th row: edge st * p1, k the 1st thread-over twisted, k the 2nd thread-over, p1. From * rep. Edge st.
5th row: edge st * k1, p2, k1. From * rep. Edge st.
6th row: edge st * p1, k2, p1. From * rep. Edge st.
7th row: edge st, thr.o. * sl1, k1 and draw slipped st over, k2 tog., thr.o. twice. From * rep. Row ends with thr.o., edge st.
8th row: edge st, k thread-over * p2, k 1st thread-over twisted, k 2nd thread-over. From * rep. Row ends with p2, k thread-over, edge st.

1st–8th rows: rep. continuously.

Chart: if working to the chart, in forward rows work continuously from * to **, in backward rows from ** to *.

1st to 8th rows: rep. continuously.
For explanation of diagram, *see* p. 300.

For explanation of diagram, *see* p. 300.

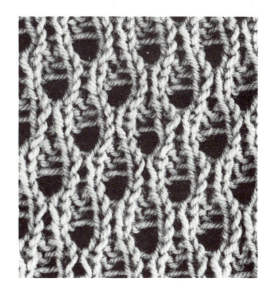

Chart

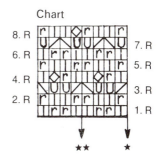

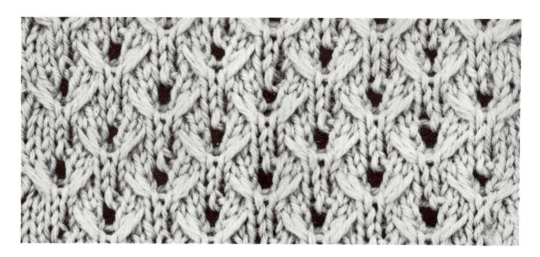

132 Knitting Pattern

Number of sts divisible by 6, plus 2 edge sts.
1st row: edge st, k6, sl2 purlwise (thread to back of st), k6. From * rep. Edge st.
2nd row: p, sl the slipped st again purlwise, but thread in *front* of st.
3rd row: edge st, k4 * put the next 2 sts on to spare needle and leave behind work, k the slipped st, then k the 2 sts from spare needle tog., and thr.o. Put 2nd slipped st on to spare needle and leave in front of work, k2 tog. k the st from spare needle, k2. From * rep. Row ends: put 2 sts on to spare needle and leave behind work, k the 1st slipped st then k the 2 sts from spare needle tog. Thr.o. Put the 2nd slipped st on to spare needle and leave in front of work, k2 tog. K st from spare needle, k4, edge st.
4th row: p. Out of every thread-over, p1 and k1.

5th row: edge st, k2 * sl2 purlwise (thread behind work), k6. From * rep. Row ends with sl2 purlwise (thread to back), k2, edge st.
6th row: p, sl the slipped sts again purlwise (thread in front of work).
7th row: edge st * put the next 2 sts on to spare needle and leave behind work. K the 1st slipped st, then k the 2 sts from spare needle tog., thr.o., put 2nd slipped st on to spare needle, and leave in front of work. K2 tog., then k st from spare needle, k2. From * rep. Row ends: put 2 sts on to spare needle and leave behind work, k 1st slipped st, then k sts from spare needle tog., thr.o., put 2nd slipped st on to spare needle and leave in front of work, k2 tog., then k spare needle st, edge st.
8th row: p. out of every thread-over p1 and k1.

1st–8th rows: rep. continuously.

Chart

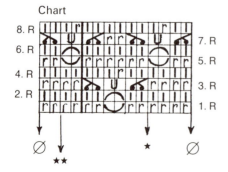

Chart: when using chart, work in forward rows once from ∅ to *, continuously from * to **, and once from ** to ∅. In backward rows once from ∅ to **, continuously from ** to *, and once from * to ∅. In 4th and 8th rows work out of the thread-over, 1 p and 1 k.st.
1st–8th rows: rep. continuously.
For explanation of diagram, *see* p. 300.

133 Knitting Pattern

Number of sts divisible by 14.

1st row: edge st * k4 twisted, k2 tog., thr.o. twice, sl1, k1 and draw slipped st over, k4 twisted, k2. From * rep. Row ends: k4 twisted, k2 tog., thr.o. twice, sl1, k1 and draw slipped st over, k4 twisted, edge st.

2nd row: edge st, p3 * p2 twisted tog., thr.o. twice, drop thread-overs from 1st row from needle, p2 tog., p8. From * rep. Row ends with p2, twisted tog., thr.o. twice, drop thread-overs from 1st row from needle, p2 twisted tog., p3, edge st.

3rd row: edge st, k2 * k2 tog., thr.o. twice, let thread-overs of 2nd row drop off needle, sl1, k1 and draw slipped st over, k6. From * rep. Row ends with k2 tog., thr.o. twice, drop thread-overs of 2nd row, sl1, k1 and draw slipped st over, k2, edge st.

4th row: edge st, p1 * p2 twisted tog., thr.o. twice, drop thread-overs of 3rd row, p2 tog., p4. From * rep. Row ends with p2 twisted tog., thr.o. twice, drop thread-overs of 3rd row, p2 twisted tog., p1, edge st.

5th row: edge st * k2 tog., thr.o. twice, drop thread-overs of 4th row, sl1, k1 and draw slipped st over, k2. From * rep. Row ends with k2 tog., thr.o. twice and drop thread-overs of 4th row, sl1, k1 and draw slipped st over, edge st.

6th row: edge st, p1 * thr.o. 4 times, drop thread-overs of 5th row, k tog. the 5 threads of previous rows, 1st purl- then knit-wise, thr.o. 4 times, p4. From * rep. Row ends with thr.o. 4 times, drop the thread-overs of 5th row, first p then k tog. the 5 threads of previous rows, thr.o. 4 times, p1, edge st.

7th row: edge st, k1 * out of the thread-overs k4 twisted sts, k2, k4 twisted, k2 tog., thr.o. twice, sl1, k1 and draw slipped st over. From * rep. Row ends with k4 twisted, k2, k4 twisted, k1, edge st.

8th row: edge st, thr.o. twice * p2 tog., p8, p2 twisted tog., thr.o. twice and drop the thread-overs of 7th row. From * rep. Row ends with p2 tog., p8, p2 twisted tog., thr.o. twice, edge st.

9th row: edge st * thr.o. twice, drop thread-overs of 8th row, sl1, k1 and draw slipped st over, k6, k2 tog. From * rep. Row ends with thr.o. twice, drop thread-overs of 8th row, edge st.

10th row: edge st * thr.o. twice, drop thread-overs of 9th row, p2 tog., p4, p2 twisted tog. From * rep. Row ends with thr.o.

twice, drop thread-overs of 9th row, edge st.
11th row: edge st * thr.o. twice, drop thread-overs of 10th row, sl1, k1 and draw slipped st over, k2, k2 tog. From * rep. Row ends with thr.o. twice, drop thread-overs of 10th row, edge st.
12th row: edge st * drop thread-overs of 11th row, first p, then k the 5 threads of previous

rows tog., thr.o. 4 times p4, thr.o. 4 times. From * rep. Row ends: first p, then k, the 5 threads of previous rows tog., edge st.
1st–12th rows: rep. continuously, but, the following patterns start:
1st row: k the edge st with the 2 1st sts tog., then as 1st row, and at the end of needle again k 2 sts with the edge st tog.

Chart

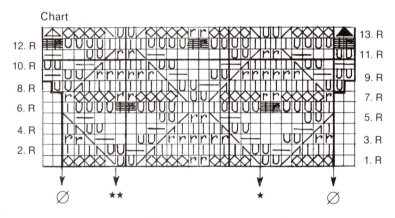

Chart: when using chart, work in forward rows once from ⌀ to *, continuously from * to **, and once from ** to ⌀. In backward rows, work once from ⌀ to **, continuously from ** to *, and once from * to ⌀. The empty squares have no significance.
2nd–13th rows: rep. continuously.
For explanation of diagram, *see* p. 300.

134 Knitting Pattern

Number of sts divisible by 8, plus 2 edge sts.
1st row: edge st, k2 tog. * thr.o., k1 twisted, thr.o., k2 twisted tog., k5. From * rep. Row ends with thr.o., k1 twisted tog., thr.o., k2 twisted tog., k3, edge st.
2nd row: edge st, p2 * p2 twisted tog., p7. From * rep. Row ends with p2 twisted tog., p5, edge st.
3rd row: edge st, k2 * thr.o., k1 twisted, thr.o., k2, k2 twisted tog., k3. From * rep. Row ends with thr.o., k1 twisted, thr.o., k2, k2 twisted tog., k1, edge st.
4th row: edge st * p2 twisted tog., p7. From * rep. Edge st.
5th row: edge st, k2, k1 twisted, thr.o. * k4, k2 twisted tog., k1, thr.o., k1 twisted, thr.o. From * rep. Row ends with k5, edge st.

6th row: edge st, p8 * p2 twisted tog., p7. From * rep. Row ends with p2 twisted tog., p8, edge st.

7th row: edge st, k7 * k2 tog., thr.o., k1 twisted, thr.o., k5. From * rep. Row ends with k2 tog., thr.o., k1 twisted, thr.o., k7, edge st.

8th row: edge st, p10 * p2 tog., p7. From * rep. Row ends with p2 tog., p6, edge st.

9th row: edge st, k5 * k2 tog., k2, thr.o., k1 twisted, thr.o., k3. From * rep. Row ends with

k2 tog., thr.o., k2, edge st.

10th row: edge st, p3 * p2 tog., p7. From * rep. Row ends with p2 tog., p4, edge st.

11th row: edge st, k2, thr.o., k1 * k2 tog., k4, thr.o., k1 twisted, thr.o., k1. From * rep. Row ends with k2 tog., thr.o., k3, edge st.

12th row: edge st, p4 * p2 tog., p7. From * rep. Row ends with p2 tog., p3, edge st.

1st–12th rows: rep. continuously.

Chart: when using chart, in forward rows once from ∅ to *, and continuously from * to **, and once from ** to ∅. In backward rows, once from ∅ to **, continuously from ** to *, and once from * to ∅. The empty squares on the chart have no significance.
1st–12th rows: rep. continuously.
For explanation of diagram, *see* p. 300.

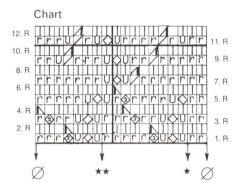

Chart

135 Knitting Pattern

Number of sts divisible by 5, plus 2 edge sts.
1st row: k.
2nd row: p.
3rd row: edge st * out of the following st make 4, like this: k1, p1, k1, p1, then k4. From * rep. Edge st.
4th row: p.
5th row: edge st * k4, k next 4 sts tog. From * rep. Edge st.
6th row: p.
7th row: edge st * k4, out of the following st make 4 as described in 3rd row. From * rep. Edge st.
8th row: p.
9th row: edge st * k4 sts tog., k4. From * rep. Edge st.
10th row: p.
3rd–10th rows: rep. continuously.

136 Openwork Pattern

Number of sts divisible by 4.
1st–4th rows: 'smooth knitting'.
5th row: edge st * thr.o., k2 tog., k2. From *
rep. Row ends with thr.o., k2 tog., edge st.
6th row: p, including all thread-overs.
7th and 8th rows: 'smooth knitting'.
9th row: edge st, k2 * thr.o., k2 tog., k2.
From * rep. Edge st.
10th row: p, including thread-overs.
3rd–10th rows: rep. continuously.

137 Knitting Pattern

Number of sts divisible by 10, plus 3 (1 st
and 2 edge sts).
1st row: edge st * k1 twisted, p1, thr.o., p1,
thr.o., p1, k1 twisted, p1, k1, twisted, p1,
k1 twisted, p1. From * rep. Row ends with k1
twisted, edge st.
2nd row: edge st, p1, twisted * k1, p1 twisted,
k1, p1, twisted, k1, p1 twisted, k1, p3, k1,
p1 twisted. From * rep. Edge st.
3rd row: edge st * k1 twisted, p1, thr.o.,
(thread behind work), k2 tog. and draw slipped
st over, thr.o., p1, k1 twisted, p1, k1 twisted,
p1, k1 twisted, p1. From * rep. Row ends with
k1 twisted, edge st.
4th row: as 2nd.
5th row: as 3rd.
6th row: as 2nd.
7th row: as 3rd.

8th row: as 2nd.

9th row: edge st * k1 twisted, p1, sl1 (thread to the back), k2 tog. and draw slipped st over, p1, k1 twisted, p1, k1 twisted, p1, k1 twisted, p1. From * rep. Row ends with k1 twisted, edge st.

10th row: edge st, p1 twisted * k1, p1 twisted, k1, p1 twisted, k1, p1 twisted, k1, p1, k1, p1 twisted. From * rep. Edge st.

11th row: edge st * k1 twisted, p1, k1 twisted, p1, k1 twisted, p1, k1 twisted, thr.o. once, p1, thr.o. once, k1 twisted, p1. From * rep. Row ends with k1 twisted, edge st.

12th row: edge st, p1 twisted * k1, p1 twisted, p3, p1 twisted, k1, p1 twisted, k1, p1 twisted, k1, p1 twisted. From * rep. Edge st.

13th row: edge st * k1 twisted, p1, k1 twisted, p1, k1 twisted, p1, k1 twisted, thr.o.

once, sl1, k2 tog. and draw slipped st over, thr.o., k1 twisted, p1. From * rep. Row ends with k1 twisted, edge st.

14th row: as 12th.

15th row: as 13th.

16th row: as 12th.

17th row: as 13th.

18th row: as 12th.

19th row: edge st * k1 twisted, p1, k1 twisted, p1, k1 twisted, p1, k1 twisted, sl1, k2 tog. and draw slipped st over, k1 twisted, p1. From * rep. Row ends with k1 twisted, edge st.

20th row: edge st, p1 twisted * k1, p1 twisted, k1, p1 twisted, k1, p1 twisted, k1, p1 twisted, k1, p1 twisted. From * rep. Edge st.

1st–20th rows: rep. continuously.

Chart

Chart: when using the chart, work, in forward rows continuously from * to **, and once from ** to ⌀. In backward rows, work once from ⌀ to **, then continuously from ** to *.

1st–20th rows: rep. continuously.

For explanation of diagram, *see* p. 300.

138 Knitting Pattern

Number of sts divisible by 8, plus 6 sts and 2 edge sts.

1st row: edge st * p2, k2, p2, k1, thr.o., k1. From * rep. Row ends with p2, k2, p2, edge st.

2nd and every backward row: work sts as they appear, and p thread-overs.

3rd row: edge st * p2, k2, p2, k3. From * rep. Row ends with p2, k2, p2, edge st.

5th row: as 3rd.

7th row: edge st * p2, k1, thr.o., k1, p2, k1, let 1 st drop (the st will drop to the thread-over of 1st row), k1. From * rep. Row ends

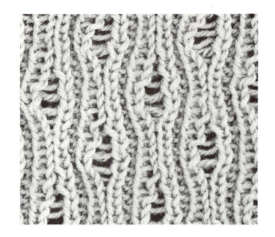

with p2, k1, thr.o., k1, p2, edge st.
9th row: edge st * p2, k3, p2, k2. From *
rep. Row ends with p2, k3, p2, edge st.
11th row: as 9th.
13th row: edge st * p2, k1, let 1 st drop
(it will drop to thread-over of 7th row), k1,
p2, k1, thr.o., k1. From * rep. Row ends with
p2, k1, let 1 st drop, k1, p2, edge st.
14th row: work sts as they appear, but p the
thread-overs.

Chart

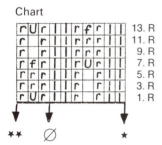

						13. R
						11. R
						9. R
						7. R
						5. R
						3. R
						1. R

** ⌀ *

Chart: when using the chart, forward rows
are continuously worked from * to **, and
once from * to ⌀. In backward rows, sts are
worked as they appear, thread-overs p. The
empty squares have no significance.
For explanation of diagram, *see* p. 300.

139 Knitting Pattern

Number of sts divisible by 14, plus 2 edge sts.
1st row: edge st * k2, thr.o., k1, thr.o., k2,
p3, p3 tog., p3. From * rep. Edge st.
2nd and every backward row: work sts
as they appear. P thread-overs.
3rd row: edge st * k2, thr.o., k3, thr.o., k2,
p2, p3 tog., p2. From * rep. Edge st.
5th row: edge st * k2, thr.o., k5, thr.o., k2, p1,
p3 tog., p1. From * rep. Edge st.

7th row: edge st * k2, thr.o., k7, thr.o., k2,
p3 tog. From * rep. Edge st.
9th row: edge st * k2, p3, p3 tog., p3, k2,
thr.o., k1, thr.o. From * rep. Edge st.
11th row: edge st * k2, p2, p3 tog., p2, k2,
thr.o., k3, thr.o. From * rep. Edge st.
13th row: edge st * k2, p1, p3 tog., p1, k2,
thr.o., k5, thr.o. From * rep. Edge st.
15th row: edge st * k2, p3 tog., k2, thr.o., k7,
thr.o. From * rep. Edge st.
1st–16th rows: rep. continuously.

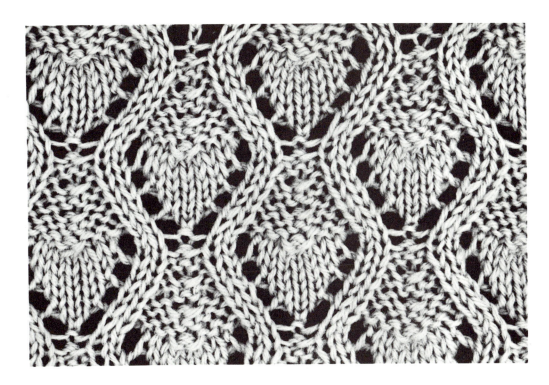

Chart: when using chart, work forward rows from * to **, backward rows work sts as they appear, p thread-overs.

1st–16th rows: rep. continuously.

For explanation of diagram, *see* p. 300.

Chart

U	r	r	r	r	r	r	U	r	r	3	r	r	15. R
U	r	r	r	r	r	U	r	r		3		r	r	13. R
U	r	r	r	U	r	r			3			r	r	11. R
U	r	U	r	r				3				r	r	9. R
3	r	r	U	r	r	r	r	r	r	U	r	r	7. R
3		r	r	U	r	r	r	r	r	U	r	r	5. R
3			r	r	U	r	r	r	r	U	r	r	3. R
3				r	r	U	r	U	r	r	1. R

★★   ★

140 Knitting Pattern

Number of sts divisible by 6, plus 2 edge sts.

1st row: curled.

2nd–6th rows: as 1st.

7th row: edge st * k1, thr.o. 3 times. From * rep. Edge st.

8th row: edge st * sl the next 6 sts on to the right needle, let the thread-overs of previous row drop (this makes long sts). Draw the 1st 2 slipped sts with the left needle over the last 3 slipped sts. Leave the 1st sts on the left needle and transfer back, also the other 3 sts. Now k the 6 sts. From * rep.

3rd–8th rows: rep. continuously.

141 Knitting Pattern

Number of sts divisible by 6, plus 4.
1st row: k.
2nd row: edge st, k1 * k1 and out thread twice around needle. From * rep. Row ends with k1, edge st.
3rd row: edge st, k1 * put next 6 sts on to the right needle, when doing so, let thread-overs drop; with the left needle draw the 1st 3 sts over the last 3 sts. The remaining 3 sts put back on to the left needle, and out of each st k1, and k1 twisted. From * rep. Row ends with k1, edge st.
4th row: k.
1st—4th rows: rep. continuously.

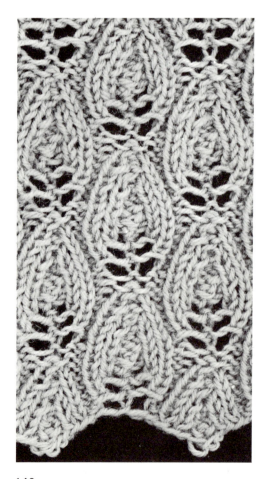

142 Knitting Pattern

The pattern appears on the reverse side. Number of sts divisible by 14, plus 2 edge sts.
1st row: edge st * k2, thr.o., k1, thr.o., k2, p2, k1, k3 tog., k1, p2. From * rep. Edge st.
2nd and every further alternate row: work sts as they appear but p the thread-overs.
3rd row: edge st * k2, p1, thr.o., k1, thr.o., p1, k2, p2, k3 tog., p2. From * rep. Edge st.
5th row: edge st * k2, p2, thr.o., k1, thr.o., p2, k2, p1, k3 tog., p1. From * rep. Edge st.
7th row: edge st * k2, p2, k1, thr.o., k1, thr.o., k1, p2, k2, k3 tog. From * rep. Edge st.
9th row: edge st * k2, p2, k1, k3 tog., k1, p2, k2, thr.o., k1, thr.o. From * rep. Edge st.
11th row: edge st * k2, p2, k3 tog., p2, k2, p1, thr.o., k1, thr.o., p1. From * rep. Edge st.
13th row: edge st * k2, p1, k3 tog., p1, k2, p2, thr.o., k1, thr.o., p2. From * rep. Edge st.
15th row: edge st * k2, k3 tog., k2, p2, k1, thr.o., k1, thr.o., k1, p2. From * rep. Edge st.
1st—16th rows: rep. continuously.

Chart: when using chart, work the odd rows
continuously from * to **. In the even rows,
k sts as they appear, but p thread-overs.
1st–16th rows: rep. continuously.
For explanation of diagram, *see* p. 300.

For explanation of diagram, *see* p. 300.

Chart

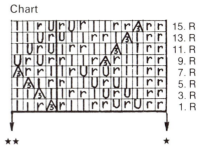

143   Knitting Pattern

Number of sts divisible by 13 plus 2 edge sts.
1st row: p.
2nd row: k.
3rd row: edge st * k2 tog., k4, thr.o., k1,
thr.o., k4, k2 tog. From * rep. Edge st.
4th row: edge st * p2 tog., p3, thr.o., p3,
thr.o., p3, p2 tog. From * rep. Edge st.
5th row: edge st * k2 tog., k2, thr.o., k2, k2
tog. From * rep. Edge st.
6th row: edge st * p2 tog., p1, thr.o., p7,
thr.o., p1, p2 tog. From * rep. Edge st.
7th row: edge st * k2 tog., thr.o., k9, thr.o.,
k2 tog. From * rep. Edge st.
8th row: p, including thread-overs.
1st–8th rows: rep. continuously.
The casting-on row of this pattern does not
form a straight, but a zig-zag line.

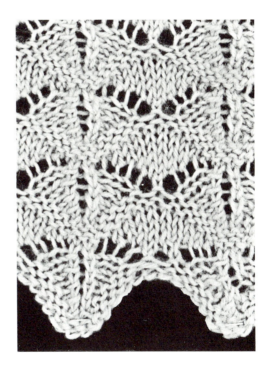

Chart: when using chart, work forward rows
continuously from * to **, backward rows
from ** to *.
1st–8th rows: rep. continuously.
For explanation of diagram, *see* p. 300.

For explanation of diagram, *see* p. 300.

Chart

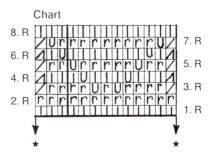

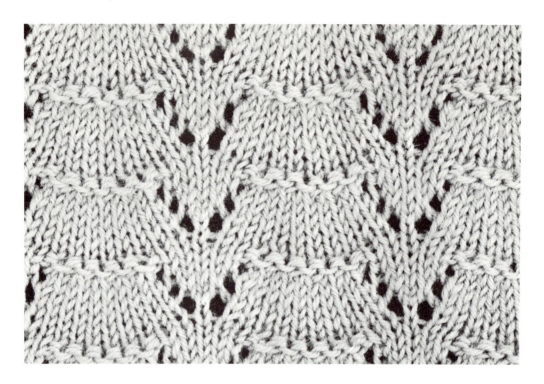

144 Knitting Pattern

Number of sts divisible by 11, plus 1 st (the number of sts changes in every row).
1st row: k1, thr.o. * k10, thr.o., k1, thr.o. From * rep. Row ends with k10, thr.o., k1.
2nd and all subsequent backward rows: p (including thread-overs).

3rd row: k2, thr.o. * k10, thr.o., k3, thr.o. From * rep. Row ends with k10, thr.o., k3.
5th row: k3, thr.o. * k10, thr.o., k5, thr.o. From * rep. Row ends with k10, thr.o., k3.
7th row: k3 * p 6 times 2 tog., k5. From * rep. Row ends with p 6 times 2 tog., k3.
8th row: p.
1st–8th rows: rep. continuously.

Chart

Chart: when using chart, in forward rows work once from ∅ to *, continuously from * to **, and once from ** to ∅. In backward rows p all sts and thread-overs.
For explanation of diagram, *see* p. 300.

145 Knitting Pattern

Number of sts divisible by 12, plus 2 sts.
1st row: edge st * p1, k2 tog., k3, thr.o., k1, thr.o., k3, k2 twisted tog. From * rep. Edge st.
2nd row: edge st * p2 tog., p2, thr.o., p3, thr.o., p2, p2 tog., k1. From * rep. Edge st.
3rd row: edge st * p1, k2 tog., k1, thr.o., k5, thr.o., k1, k2 twisted tog. From * rep. Edge st.
4th row: edge st * p2 tog., thr.o., p7, thr.o., p2 tog., k1. From * rep. Edge st.
5th row: edge st, k2 tog. * thr.o., k9, thr.o., k3 tog. From * rep. Row ends with thr.o., k9, thr.o., k the last st tog. with the edge st.
6th row: edge st * thr.o., p3, p2 tog., k1, p2 tog., p3, thr.o., p1. From * rep. Edge st.

7th row: edge st, k2 * thr.o., k2, k2 twisted tog., p1, k2 tog., k2, thr.o., k3. From * rep. Row ends with thr.o., k2, k2 twisted tog., p1, k2 tog., k2, thr.o., k1, edge st.
8th row: edge st, p2 * thr.o., p1, p2 tog., k1, p2 tog., p1, thr.o., p5. From * rep. Row ends with thr.o., p1, p2 tog., k1, p2 tog., p1, thr.o., p3, edge st.
9th row: edge st, k4 * thr.o., k2 twisted tog., p1, k2 tog., thr.o., k7. From * rep. Row ends with thr.o., k2 twisted tog., p1, k2 tog., thr.o., k3, edge st.
10th row: edge st, p4 * thr.o., p3 tog., thr.o., p9. From * rep. Row ends with thr.o., p3 tog., thr.o., p5, edge st.
1st–10th rows: rep. continuously.

Chart

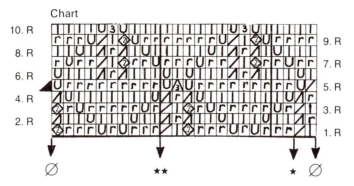

Chart: when using chart, work in forward rows once from ⌀ to ★, repeatedly from ★ to ★★, and once from ★★ to ⌀. In backward rows, once from ⌀ to ★★, repeatedly from ★★ to ★ and once from ★ to ⌀. For explanation of diagram, *see* p. 300.

146 Knitting Pattern

Number of sts divisible by 18, plus 3.
1st row: edge st, k2 tog., k4, thr.o., k1 ★ k6, thr.o., k4, sl1, k2 tog. and draw the slipped st over, k4, thr.o., k1. From ★ rep. Row ends with k6, thr.o., k4, sl1. K1 and draw the slipped st over, edge st.
2nd row: edge st, p5, k2, p5 ★ k2, p9, k2, p5. From ★ rep. Row ends with k2, p5, edge st.
3rd row: edge st, k2 tog., k3, thr.o., k2 ★ k7, thr.o., k3, sl1, k2 tog. and draw slipped st over, k3, thr.o., k2. From ★ rep. Row ends with k7, thr.o., k3, sl1, k1 and draw slipped st over, edge st.
4th row: edge st, p4, k3, p5 ★ k3, p7, k3, p5. From ★ rep. Row ends with k3, p4, edge st.
5th row: edge st, k2 tog., k2, thr.o., k3 ★ k8, thr.o., k2, sl1, k2 tog. and draw slipped st over,

k2, thr.o., k3. From ★ rep. Row ends with k8, thr.o., k2, sl1, k1 and draw slipped st over, edge st.
6th row: edge st, p3, k4, p5 ★ k4, p5, k4, p5. From ★ rep. Row ends with k4, p3, edge st.
7th row: edge st, k2 tog., k1, thr.o., k4 ★ k9, thr.o., k1, sl1, k2 tog. and draw slipped st over, k1, thr.o., k4. From ★ rep. Row ends with k9, thr.o., k1, sl1, k1 and draw slipped st over, edge st.
8th row: edge st, p2, k5, p5 ★ k5, p3, k5, p5. From ★ rep. Row ends with k5, p2, edge st.
9th row: edge st, k2 tog., thr.o., k5 ★ k10, thr.o., sl1, k2 tog. and draw slipped st over, thr.o., k5. From ★ rep. Row ends with k10, thr.o., sl1, k1 and draw slipped st over, edge st.
10th row: edge st, p1, k6, p5 ★ k6, p1, k6, p5. From ★ rep. Row ends with k6, p1, edge st.
1st–10th rows: rep. continuously.

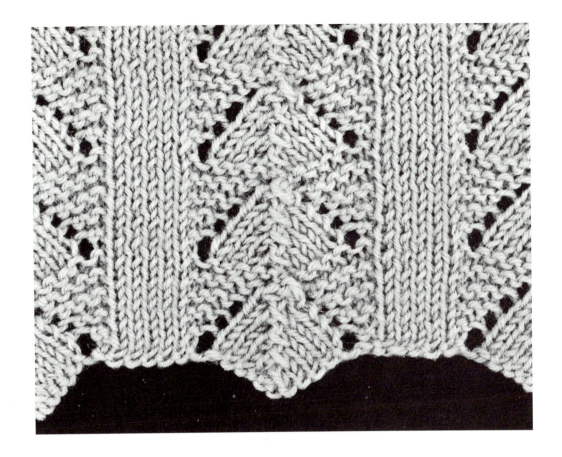

Chart: when using chart, in forward rows work once from ∅ to *, repeatedly from * to **, and once from ** to ∅. In backward rows, once from ∅ to **, repeatedly from ** to *, and once from * to **.

For explanation of diagram, *see* p. 300.

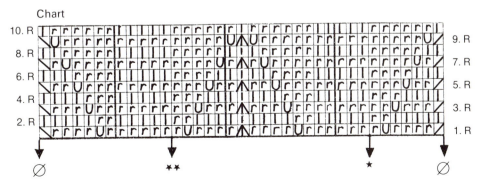

151

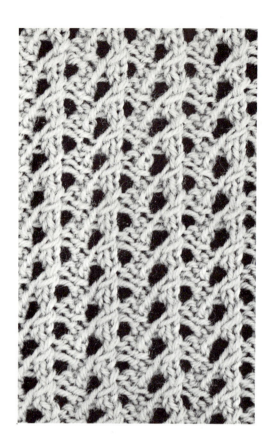

Open Stripes

147 Knitting Pattern

Number of sts divisible by 4, plus 2 edge sts.
1st row: edge st * k2, p2 tog., thr.o. From *
rep. Edge st.
2nd row: edge st * k2 (including thread-over),
p2. From * rep. Edge st.
3rd row: edge st * k2 tog., thr.o., p2. From *
rep. Edge st.
4th row: edge st * k2, p2. From * rep. Edge
st.
1st–4th rows: rep. continuously.

148 Curly Knit with Drop-stitch Row

Number of sts as desired.
1st–10th rows: curly knit (k backward and
forward row).
11th row: edge st * k1, thr.o. From * rep.
Edge st.
12th row: k (let the thread-overs drop).
1st–12th rows: rep. continuously.

149　Knitting with Needles of Different Sizes

With this, one can achieve without difficulty a very attractive pattern. * Begin with needles appropriate to the strength of the wool, and k 3 rows, change to needles twice the size and k 1 row. From * rep. With the smaller needles, more or fewer rows may be knitted, according to choice.

150　Knitting Pattern

Number of sts divisible by 10, plus 6.
1st row: * k6, thr.o., k1, thr.o. twice, k1, thr.o. 3 times, k1, thr.o. twice, k1, thr.o. From * rep. Row ends with k6.
2nd row: k all sts and let the thread-overs drop.
3rd row: k.
4th row: k.
5th row: * k1, thr.o., k1, thr.o. twice, k1, thr.o. 3 times, k1, thr.o. twice, k1, thr.o., k5. From * rep. Row ends with k1, thr.o., k1, thr.o. twice, k1, thr.o. 3 times, k1, thr.o. twice, k1, thr.o., k1.
6th row: as 2nd.
7th row: k.
8th row: k.
1st–18th rows: rep. continuously.

151　Knitting Pattern

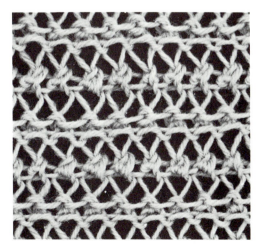

Even number of sts.
1st row: k.
2nd row: edge st * k2 tog., thr.o. From * rep. Edge st.
3rd row: k, and let the thread-overs of previous row drop.
4th row: out of every st k1 and p1.
2nd–4th rows: rep. continuously.

152 Knitting Pattern

Even number of sts.
1st row: edge st * k2 tog., thr.o. From * rep. Edge st.
2nd and every subsequent backward row: p, also the thread-overs.
3rd row: edge st * thr.o., k2 tog. From * rep. Edge st.
5th row: edge st, k1 * thr.o., k2 tog. From * rep. Row ends with k1, edge st.
1st–6th rows: rep. continuously.

Chart

Chart: when using chart, work in forward rows once from ∅ to *, repeatedly from * to **, and once from ** to ∅. In backward rows p all sts and thread-overs.
1st–6th rows: rep. continuously.
For explanation of diagram, *see* p. 300.

153 Knitting Pattern

Number of sts divisible by 4, plus 2 edge sts.
1st row (backward row): edge st * p2, thr.o. From * rep. Row ends with p2, edge st.
2nd row (forward): edge st, k1 * sl1 purlwise (thread behind st), k the thread-over, and the next st, then draw slipped st over. From * rep. Row ends with k1, edge st.
3rd row: edge st * p1, thr.o., p1. From * rep. Edge st.
4th row: edge st * sl next st purlwise (thread to back), k the thread-over and the following st, then draw slipped st over. From * rep. Edge st.
1st–4th rows: rep. continuously.

154 Knitting Pattern

Number of sts divisible by 9, plus 2 edge sts.
1st row: edge st * k7, thr.o., sl1, k1 and draw slipped st over. From * rep. Edge st.
2nd and all subsequent backward rows: p all sts and thread-overs.
3rd row: edge st, k8 * thr.o., sl1, k1 and draw

slipped st over, k7. From * rep. Row ends with k1, edge st.
5th row: edge st * thr.o., sl1, k1 and draw slipped st over, k7. From * rep. Edge st.
7th row: edge st, k1, then continue as described from * in 5th row, but row ends with thr.o., sl1, k1 and draw slipped st over, k6, edge st.

9th row: edge st, k2, then continue as from * in 5th row: row ends with thr.o., sl1, k1 and draw slipped st over, k6, edge st.

11th row: edge st, k3, then continue as in 5th row from *. Row ends with thr.o., k2 tog. by drawing over, k4, edge st.

13th row: edge st, k4, continue as in 5th row from *. Row ends with thr.o., k2 tog. by drawing 1 over, k3, edge st.

15th row: edge st, k5, continue as in 5th row from *. Row ends with thr.o., k2 tog. by drawing 1 over, k2, edge st.

17th row: edge st, k6, continue as in 5th row from *. Row ends with thr.o., k2 tog. by drawing over, k1, edge st.

18th row: p all sts and thread-overs.

1st—18th rows: rep. continuously.

Chart: when using chart, in forward rows work once from ∅ to *, repeatedly from * to **, and once from ** to ∅. Backward rows: all sts and thread-overs are purled.

1st—18th rows: rep. continuously.

For explanation of chart, *see* p. 300.

Chart

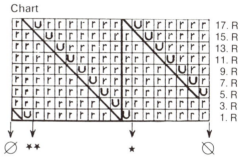

155   Knitting Pattern

Number of sts divisible by 8, plus 2 edge sts.

1st row: edge st * thr.o., sl1, k1 and draw slipped st over, k6. From * rep. Edge st.

2nd and every subsequent even row: p.

3rd row: edge st, k1 * thr.o., sl1, k1 and draw slipped st over, k6. From * rep. Row ends with thr.o., sl1, k1 and draw slipped st over, k5, edge st.

5th row: edge st, k2 * thr.o., sl1, k1 and draw slipped st over, k2, out of the next st make 6 as follows: k1, k1 twisted, k1, k1 twisted, k1, k1 twisted. Draw all sts one after another over the last loop, k3. From * rep. Row ends with thr.o., sl1, k1 and draw slipped st over, k2, out of the following st work a nap as described before, k1, edge st.

7th row: edge st, k3 * thr.o., sl1, k1 and draw slipped st over, k6. From * rep. Row ends

with thr.o., sl1, k1 and draw slipped st over, k3, edge st.

9th row: edge st, k4 * thr.o., sl1, k1 and draw slipped st over, k6. From * rep. Row ends with thr.o., sl1, k1 and draw slipped st over, k2, edge st.

11th row: edge st, k5 * thr.o., sl1, k1 and draw slipped st over, k6. From * rep. Row ends

Chart

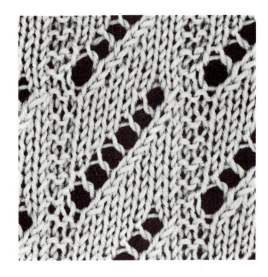

with thr.o., sl1, k1 and draw slipped st over, k1, edge st.

13th row: edge st * k2, out of the next st make 6 sts as follows: k1, k1 twisted, k1, k1 twisted, k1, k1 twisted: draw all sts one after another over the last loop, k3, thr.o., sl1, k1 and draw slipped st over. From * rep.

15th row: edge st, k7 * thr.o., sl1, k1 and draw slipped st over, k6. From * rep. At the end of the needle, after the thread-over, k the last st tog. with the edge st.

16th row: p.

1st–16th rows: rep. continuously.

Chart: when using chart, work in forward rows once from ∅ to *, repeatedly from * to ** and once from ** to ∅. P all thread-overs and sts in backward rows.

1st–16th rows: rep. continuously.
For explanation of diagram, *see* p. 300.

156 Knitting Pattern

Number of sts divisible by 9, plus 4 sts.

1st row: edge st * p2, k5, k2 tog., thr.o. From * rep. This row and all odd rows end with p2, edge st.

2nd and all further even rows: p.

3rd row: edge st * p2, k4, k2 tog., thr.o., k1. From * rep.

5th row: edge st * p2, k2, k2 tog., thr.o., k2. From * rep.

7th row: edge st * p2, k2, k2 tog., thr.o., k3. From * rep.

9th row: edge st * p2, k1, k2 tog., thr.o., k4. From * rep.

11th row: edge st * p2, k2 tog., thr.o., k5. From * rep.

1st–12th rows: rep. continuously.

Chart: when using chart, in forward rows work repeatedly from * to ** and once from ** to ∅, and in backwards p all sts and thread-overs.

1st–12th rows: rep. continuously.
For explanation of diagram, *see* p. 300.

Chart

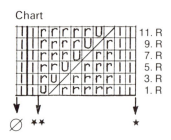

157   Knitting Pattern

Even number of sts.
1st row: edge st * thr.o., sl1, k1 and draw slipped st over. From * rep. Edge st.
Rep. this row continuously.

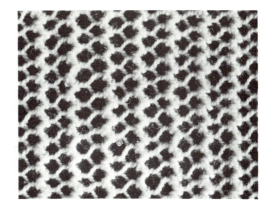

158   Knitting Pattern

Number of sts divisible by 7, plus 2 sts.
1st row: edge st * k1, p2, k1, thr.o., k2 twisted tog., thr.o., k2 twisted tog. From * rep. Edge st.
2nd row: edge st * thr.o., k next st tog. with the thread-over of previous row, k1, p1, k1. From * rep. Edge st.
1st and 2nd rows: rep. continuously.

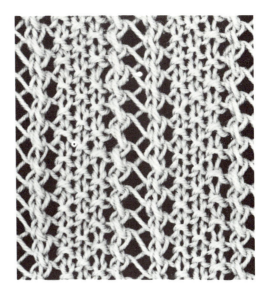

159   Knitting Pattern

Number of sts divisible by 8, plus 2 edge sts.
1st row: edge st * p4, k2 tog., thr.o., k2. From * rep. Edge st.
2nd row: edge st * p2 tog., thr.o., p2, k4. From * rep. Edge st.
1st and 2nd rows: rep. continuously.

160   Knitting Pattern

Number of sts divisible by 3, plus 2 edge sts.
1st row: edge st, k2 tog., thr.o. * k1, sl1, k1 and draw slipped st over, thr.o. From * rep. Row ends with k1, edge st.
2nd row: edge st, p following st with the thread-over * thr.o., p1, p following st tog. with the thread-over. From * rep. Row ends with thr.o., p1, edge st.
3rd row: edge st, sl1, k the thread-over and draw slipped st over * thr.o., k1, sl1, k the thread-over and draw slipped st over. From * rep. Row ends with thr.o., k1 edge st.
2nd and 3rd rows: rep. continuously.

Chart

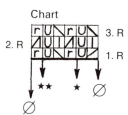

Chart: when using chart, forward rows are worked once from ∅ to *, repeatedly from * to ** and once from ** to ∅. In backward rows, once from ∅ to **, repeatedly from ** to * and once from * to ∅.
For explanation of diagram, *see* p. 300.

161   Knitting Pattern

Number of sts divisible by 8, plus 1 st.
1st row: p1 * k2, thr.o., k2 twisted tog., p1. From * rep.
2nd row: k1 * p thread-over of previous row, thr.o., p2 tog. From * rep.
3rd row: p1, k1, k thread-over of previous row, thr.o., k2 twisted tog., p1. From * rep.
4th row: as 2nd.
3rd and 4th rows: rep. continuously.

Chart

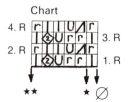

Chart: when using the chart, forward rows are worked once from ∅ to * and repeatedly from * to **. In backward rows, repeatedly from ** to * and once from * to ∅.
For explanation of diagram, *see* p. 300.

162 Knitting Pattern

Number of sts divisible by 6, plus 2 edge sts.
1st row: edge st * thr.o., k2, k2 tog., k2.
From * rep. Edge st.
2nd row: p all sts and thread-overs.
3rd row: edge st * k2, k2 tog., k2, thr.o. From
* rep. Edge st.
4th row: as 2nd.
1st—4th rows: rep. continuously.

Chart: working from the chart, in forward
rows work repeatedly from * to **. In backward rows p all sts, including thread-overs.
For explanation of diagram, *see* p. 300.

Chart

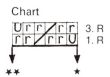

163 Knitting Pattern

Number of sts divisible by 14, plus 9 (7 sts
and 2 edge sts).
1st row: edge st * k8, thr.o., sl1, k2, draw
slipped st over, thr.o., sl1, k2, draw slipped st
over. From * rep. Row ends with k7, edge st.
2nd row: p.
3rd row: edge st, k7 * sl1, k2, draw slipped st
over, thr.o., k2 and draw slipped st over, thr.o.,
k8. From * rep. Edge st.
4th row: p.
1st—4th rows: rep. continuously.

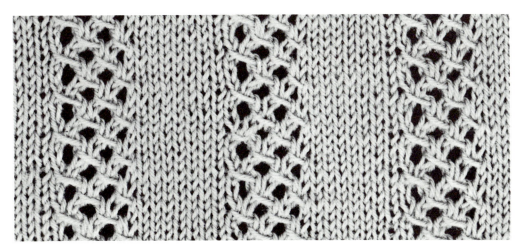

Chart

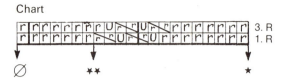

3. R
1. R

∅   ★★   ★

Chart: when using chart, in forward rows work repeatedly from ★ to ★★ and once from ★ to ∅. In backward rows p all sts and thread-overs.
1st–4th rows: rep. continuously.
For explanation of diagram, *see* p. 300.

164   Knitting Pattern

Even number of sts.
1st row: edge st ★ thr.o., k2 tog. From ★ rep. Edge st.
2nd row: p all sts and thread-overs.
3rd row: edge st ★ k2 tog., thr.o. From ★ rep. Edge st.
4th row: p all sts and thread-overs.
1st–4th rows: rep. continuously.

165   Knitting Pattern

Number of sts divisible by 4, plus 2 edge sts.
1st row: edge st ★ thr.o., sl1 purlwise (thread to back of st), p2 tog. and draw slipped st over, thr.o., k1. From ★ rep. Edge st.
2nd row: p.
1st and 2nd rows: rep. continuously.

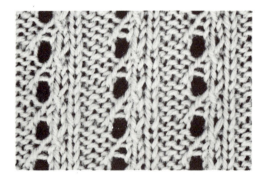

166   Knitting Pattern

Number of sts divisible by 6, plus 2 edge sts.
1st row: edge st ★ k3, p3. From ★ rep. Edge st.
2nd and 3rd rows: k sts as they appear.
4th row: edge st ★ k1, sl1, k1 and draw slipped st over, thr.o., p3. From ★ rep. Edge st.
1st–4th rows: rep. continuously.

167 Knitting Pattern

Number of sts divisible by 4.
1st row: edge st, p2 * thr.o., sl1, k1 and draw slipped st over, p2. From * rep. Edge st.
2nd row: edge st * k2, p2. From * rep. Row ends with k2, edge st.
3rd row: edge st, p2 * k2 tog., thr.o., p2. From * rep. Edge st.
4th row: as 2nd.
1st–4th rows: rep. continuously.

168 Knitting Pattern

Number of sts divisible by 13, plus 5.
1st row: edge st, p3 * k1, p1, k1, p3, k2 tog., thr.o., k2 tog., thr.o., p3. From * rep. Edge st.
2nd and all following backward rows: edge st * k3, p4, k3, p3. From * rep. Row ends with k3, edge st.
3rd row: edge st, p3 * k1, p1, k1, p3, thr.o., k2 tog., thr.o., k2 tog., p3. From * rep. Edge st.
5th row: as 1st.
7th row: as 3rd.
9th row: as 1st.
11th row: edge st, p3 * put next st on to spare needle and leave in front of the sts on the left needle, k the 2nd, and then the 1st st, slide both sts from needle, k st from spare needle, p3, thr.o., k2 tog., thr.o., k2 tog., p3. From * rep. Edge st.
1st–12th rows: rep. continuously.

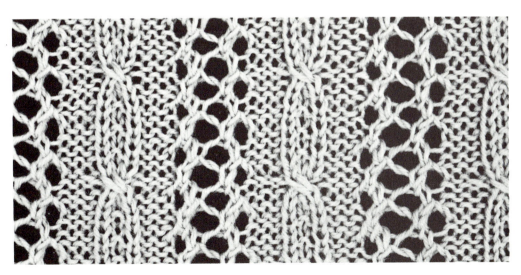

Chart

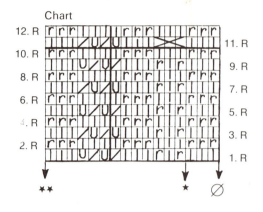

12. R
11. R
10. R
9. R
8. R
7. R
6. R
5. R
4. R
3. R
2. R
1. R

** ★ ∅

Chart: when using chart, in forward rows work once from ∅ to ★, then repeatedly from ★ to ★★. In backward rows work repeatedly from ★★ to ★, and once from ★ to ∅.
1st–12th rows: rep. continuously.
For explanation of diagram, *see* p. 300.

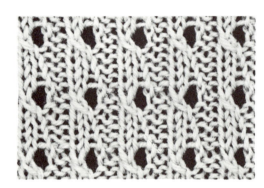

169 Knitting Pattern

Number of sts divisible by 4, plus 2 edge sts.
1st–4th rows: edge st ★ k2, p2. From ★ rep. Edge st.
5th row: edge st ★ thr.o., sl1, k1 and draw slipped st over, p2. From ★ rep. Edge st.
6th row: k sts as they appear, p the thread-overs.
1st–6th rows: rep. continuously.

170 Knitting Pattern

Number of sts divisible by 8, plus 7 sts and 2 edge sts (the number of sts changes in every row).
1st row: edge st ★ p7, k1, thr.o. From ★ rep. Row ends with p7, edge st.
2nd row: edge st ★ k7, thr.o., p2. From ★ rep. Row ends with k7, edge st.
3rd row: edge st ★ p7, k3, thr.o. From ★ rep. Edge st. Row ends with p7, edge st.
4th row: edge st ★ k7, thr.o., p4. From ★ rep. Row ends with k7, edge st.
5th row: edge st ★ p7, k5, thr.o. From ★ rep.

162

Row ends with k7, edge st.

6th row: edge st * k7, p2 tog., p4. From * rep. Row ends with k7, edge st.

7th row: edge st * p7, k3, k2 tog. From * rep. Row ends with p7, edge st.

8th row: edge st * k7, p2 tog., p2. From *

rep. Row ends with k7, edge st.

9th row: edge st * p7, k1, k2 tog. From * rep. Row ends with p7, edge st.

10th row: edge st * k7, p2 tog. From * rep. Row ends with k7, edge st.

1st–10th rows: rep. continuously.

Chart

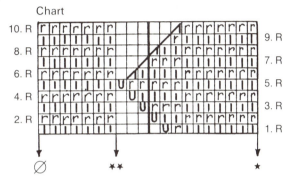

Chart: when using chart, in forward rows work repeatedly from * to ** and once from ** to ⌀. In backward rows work once from ⌀ to **, then repeatedly from ** to *.

Up to the 5th row, the number of sts increases, and from there to the 10th row it decreases.

1st–10th rows: rep. continuously.

For explanation of diagram, *see* p. 300.

171 Knitting Pattern

Number of sts divisible by 13, plus 6 sts.

1st row: edge st, k3 * k2 tog., thr.o., k2 tog.,

thr.o., k3, thr.o., k2 tog., thr.o., k2 tog., k2. From * rep. Row ends with k1, edge st.

2nd row: p all sts and thread-overs.

3rd row: edge st * k4, k2, tog., thr.o., k2

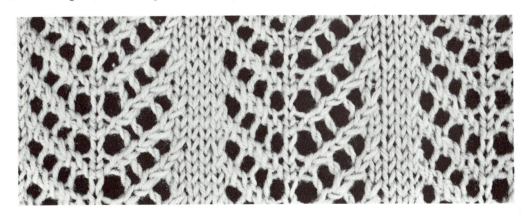

Chart

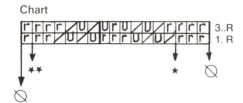

tog., thr.o., k1, thr.o., k2 tog., thr.o., k2 tog. From * rep. Row ends with k4, edge st.
4th row: p all sts and thread-overs.
1st–4th rows: rep. continuously.

Chart: when using chart, in forward rows work once from ∅ to *, repeatedly from * to ** and once from * to ∅. In backward rows p all sts, including thread-overs.
1st–4th rows: rep. continuously.
For explanation of diagram, *see* p. 300.

172   Knitting Pattern

Number of sts divisible by 11, plus 3.
1st row: edge st, k1 * thr.o., k1, p1, k1, p2, out of the next st make 5 (k1, p1, k1, p1, k1), p2, k1, p1, k1. From * rep. Edge st.
2nd row: work sts as they appear, k the thread-overs, p the 1st and 5th of the increased sts, and k the 3 inbetween.
3rd row: edge st, k1 * thr.o., insert into the next 2 sts as if to k tog., but only put on to the right needle, then sl back again on to the left needle so that the 2nd st is to the front. K the 2 sts with the 3rd st twisted tog., k1, p2, k1, p1, out of the next st make 3 (k1, p1, k1), p1, k1, p2, k1, k2 tog. From * rep. Edge st.
4th row: work sts as they appear, k all

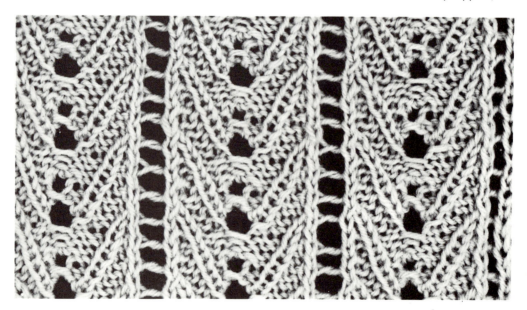

thread-overs and the 3 increased sts.

5th row: edge st, k1 * thr.o., k3 tog. as described in 3rd row, p2, k1, p5, k1, p2, k2 tog. From * rep. Edge st.

6th row: work sts as they appear and k thread-overs.

7th row: edge st, k1 * thr.o., k3 tog. as described in 3rd row, p1, k1, p2. Out of the next st make 5, p2, k1, p1, k2 tog. From * rep. Edge st.

8th row: as 2nd.

3rd–8th rows: rep. continuously.

Chart

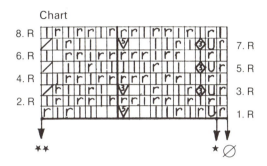

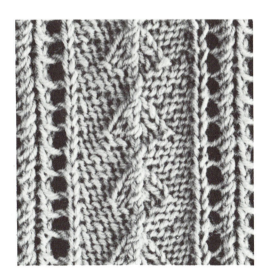

4th row: edge st * k the thread-over twisted, k3, p5, k3, k thread-over twisted, p6 (also the thread-over). From * rep. Edge st.

5th row: edge st * k1, thr.o., k2 twisted tog., k2 tog., thr.o., k1, thr.o., p4, k1, k3 tog., k1, p4, thr.o. From * rep. Edge st.

(handwritten index card overlay):

...net Pattern divisable by 13
+ 6

1 Edge Stitch

1st row K3 *
2 tog. y.o. K2 tog. y.o.
K3 y.o. K2 tog y.o. K2
Repeat from * Row ends with
K1 edge stitch.

2nd row Purl all stitches
& y.o overs.

Row 3 1 Edge Stitch.
K4. K2 tog. y.o. K2 tog
y.o. K1. y.o. K2 tog y.o.
K2 tog Repeat from.

4 Row. Purl as Row 2.

ow: edge st * k thread-overs twisted, B, k4, k thread-overs twisted, p6. From Edge st.
row: edge st * k1, thr.o., k2 twisted tog., og., thr.o., k1, thr.o., p5, k3 tog., p5, thr.o. From * rep. Edge st.

8th row: edge st * k thread-over twisted, k5, p1, k5, k thread-over twisted, p6. From * rep. Edge st.

3rd–8th rows: rep. continuously. The casting-on row forms a scalloped line.

Chart

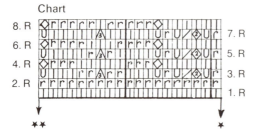

8. R
6. R
4. R
2. R

7. R
5. R
3. R
1. R

** *

Chart: when using chart, work in forward rows repeatedly from * to ** and in backward rows repeatedly from ** to *.
3rd–8th rows: rep. continuously.
For explanation of diagram, *see* p. 300.

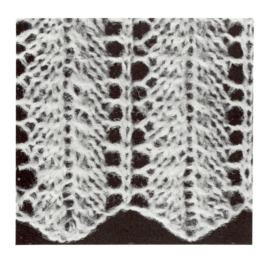

174 Knitting Pattern

Number of sts divisible by 9, plus 2 edge sts.
1st row: edge st, k2 tog., k2 * thr.o., k1, thr.o., k2, sl1, k1 and draw slipped st over, k2 tog., k2. From * rep. The row ends with thr.o., k1, thr.o., k2, sl1, and draw slipped st over, edge st.
2nd row: p all sts and thread-overs.
1st and 2nd rows: rep. continuously.

175 Knitting Pattern

Number of sts divisible by 18 plus 2 edge sts.
1st row: edge st, k 3 times 2 sts tog. * k1, thr.o., rep. 5 times (i.e. 6 times in all), k2 tog. 6 times. From * rep. At the beginning and end of row always k 3 times 2 sts tog., or 3 times k1, thr.o., so that one achieves a nice edge.
2nd row: p all sts and thread-overs.
3rd and 4th rows: k.
1st–4th rows: rep. continuously.

166

176 Knitting Pattern

Numb... divisible by 6, plus 5.
1... st * p3, thr.o., sl1, k2, and draw
... thr.o. From * rep. The row
... ge st.
... st, k3, p3 alternately. Row
... e st.
s: work as they appear.
... p. continuously.

... forward rows
... once from
... ce from

NIZA

... Number of sts divisible by ... 5 sts
and 2 edge sts.
1st row: edge st * k5, thr.o., sl1, k2 tog. and
draw slipped st over, thr.o., p2, thr.o., sl1,

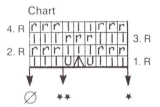

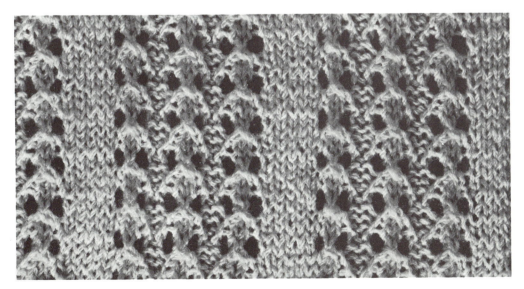

k2 tog. and draw slipped st over, thr.o. From * rep. Row ends with k5, edge st.
2nd row: edge st, p5 * p3, k2, p3, k2, p8. From * rep. Edge st.

3rd row: edge st, k5 * k3, p2, k3, p2, k8. From * rep. Edge st.
4th row: as 2nd.
1st–4th rows: rep. continuously.

Chart

Chart: when using chart, in forward rows work continuously from * to **, and once from ** to ⌀. In backward rows work once from ⌀ to **, then repeatedly from ** to *.
1st–4th rows: rep. continuously.
For explanation of diagram, *see* p. 300.

178   Openwork Stripe Pattern

This is 11 sts wide.
1st row: thr.o., sl1, k2 tog. and draw slipped st over, thr.o., k5, thr.o., sl1, k2 tog. and draw slipped st over, thr.o.
2nd and every subsequent backward row: p all sts and thread-overs.

3rd row: as 1st.
5th row: k3, thr.o., sl1, k1 and draw slipped st over, k1, k2 tog., thr.o., k3.
7th row: thr.o., sl1, k2 tog. and draw slipped st over, thr.o., k1, thr.o., sl1, k2 tog. and draw slipped st over, thr.o., k1, thr.o., sl1, k2 tog. and draw slipped st over.
8th row: p all sts and thread-overs.
1st–8th rows: rep. continuously.

Sts between the open-stripe pattern can be purled, plain-knitted or, as in illustration, curly-knitted. Width of stripes between patterns according to choice.

Chart: when using chart, p all sts and thread-overs.

1st–8th rows: rep. continuously.

For explanation of diagram, *see* p. 300.

For explanation of diagram, *see* p. 300.

Chart

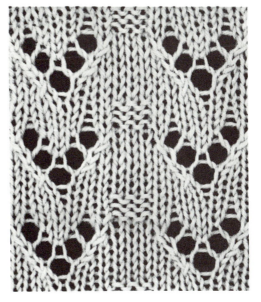

179 Knitting Pattern

Number of sts divisible by 10, plus 5.

1st row: edge st, k6 * thr.o., k2 tog., k8. From * rep. Row ends with thr.o., k2 tog., k5, edge st.

2nd row: p all sts and thread-overs.

3rd row: edge st, k4 * k2 tog., thr.o., k1, thr.o., sl1, k1 and draw slipped st over, k5. From * rep. Row ends with k2 tog., thr.o., k1, thr.o., sl1, k1 and draw slipped st over, k4, edge st.

4th row: p all sts and thread-overs.

5th row: edge st * k3, k2 tog., thr.o., k3, thr.o., sl1, k1 and draw slipped st over. From * rep. Row ends with k3, edge st.

6th row: p all sts and thread-overs.

7th row: edge st * p3, k7. From * rep. Row ends with p3, edge st.

8th row: work sts as they appear.

9th row: as 7th.

10th row: p.

1st–10th rows: rep. continuously.

Chart: when using chart, in forward rows work once from ⌀ to *, repeatedly from * to ** and once from ** to ⌀.

1st–10th rows: rep. continuously.

For explanation of diagram, *see* p. 300.

For explanation of diagram, *see* p. 300.

Chart

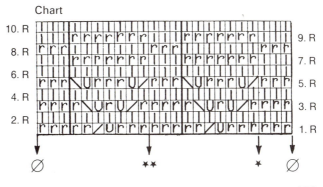

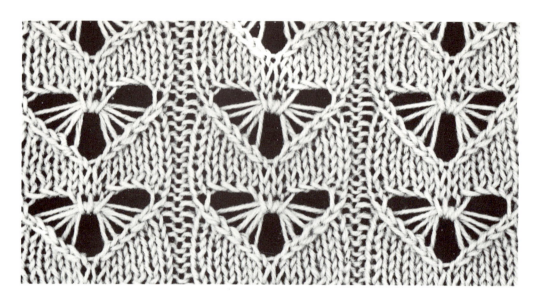

180   Knitting Pattern

Number of sts divisible by 14, plus 4.

1st row: edge st * p2, k4, k2 tog., thr.o. twice, sl1, k1 and draw slipped st over, k4. From * rep. Row ends with p2, edge st.

2nd row: edge st, k2 * p3, p2 twisted tog., thr.o. twice, sl the double thread-over of previous row as 1 thread-over, p2 tog., p3, k2. From * rep.

3rd row: edge st * p2, k2, k2 tog., thr.o. twice, sl purlwise the thread-overs of the 1st and 2nd rows as 2 thread-overs, sl1, k1 and draw slipped st over, k2. From * rep. Row ends with p2, edge st.

4th row: edge st, k2 * p1, p2 twisted tog., thr.o. twice and sl the 3 thread-overs of previous row purlwise, p2 tog., p1, k2. From * rep. Edge st.

5th row: edge st * p2, k2 tog., thr.o. twice, sl the 4 thread-overs of previous rows purlwise, sl1, k1 and draw the slipped st over. From * rep. Row ends with p2, edge st.

6th row: edge st, k2 * p1, thr.o. 4 times, k the 5 threads of previous rows tog. with p1 and k1, then thr.o. 4 times, p1, k2. From * rep.

7th row: edge st * p2, k1, out of the 4 thread-overs k4 twisted sts, k2, k4 twisted sts out of the next thread-over, k1. From * rep. Row ends with p2, edge st.

8th row: edge st, k2 * p12, k2. From * rep. Edge st.

9th row: edge st * p2, k12. From * rep. Row ends with p2, edge st.

10th row: as 8th.

1st–10th rows: rep. continuously.

Chart

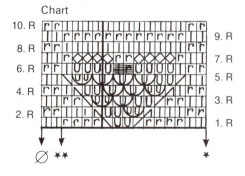

Chart: when using chart, in forward rows work repeatedly from * to ** and once from ** to ∅. In backward rows work once from ∅ to ** and continually from ** to *.

1st–10th rows: rep. continuously.

For explanation of diagram, *see* p. 300.

181   Knitting Pattern

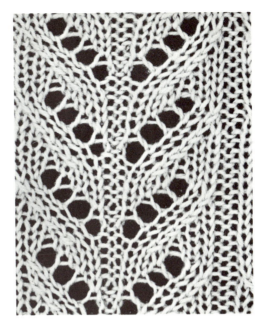

Number of sts divisible by 16, plus 4.

1st row: edge st * p2, k3, k2 tog., k1, thr.o., p2, thr.o., k1, sl1, k1 and draw slipped st over, k3. From * rep. Row ends with p2, edge st.

2nd and all following backward rows: k2, p6 alternately. Row ends with k2, edge st.

3rd row: edge st * p2, k2, k2 tog., k1, thr.o., k1, p2, k1, thr.o., k1, sl1, k1 and draw slipped st over, k2. From * rep. Row ends with p2, edge st.

5th row: edge st * p2, k1, k2 tog., k1, thr.o., k2, p2, k2, thr.o., k1, sl1, k1 and draw slipped st over, k1. From * rep. Row ends with p2, edge st.

7th row: edge st * p2, k2 tog., k1, thr.o., k3, p2, k3, thr.o., k1, sl1, k1 and draw slipped st over. From * rep. Row ends with p2, edge st.

1st–8th rows: rep. continuously.

Chart: when using chart, in forward rows work continuously from * to **, and once from ** to ∅. In backward rows work once from ∅ to ** and continuously from ** to *.

1st–8th rows: rep. continuously.

For explanation of diagram, *see* p. 300.

Chart

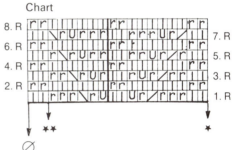

182   Knitting Pattern

Number of sts divisible by 10, plus 3.

1st row: edge st * p1, k2 tog., thr.o. twice, sl1, k1 and draw slipped st over, p1, plait the next 4 sts (p 1st and 2nd sts on spare needle, leave in front of work, k 3rd and 4th sts, then k the 2 from spare needle). From * rep. Row ends with p1, edge st.

2nd row: edge st, k1 * p2 tog., thr.o., p2, k1, p1, out of the 2 thread-overs, k1 and p1 st, p1, k1. From * rep. Edge st.

3rd row: edge st * p1, k4, p1, k2 tog., thr.o., k2. From * rep. Row ends with p1, edge st.

4th row: edge st, k1 * p2 tog., thr.o., p2, k1, p4, k1. From * rep. Edge st.

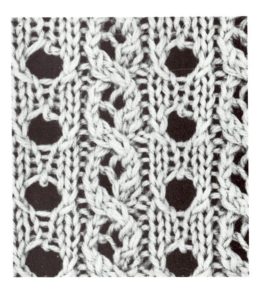

171

Chart

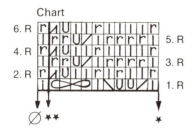

6. R
4. R
2. R
5. R
3. R
1. R

∅ ⋆⋆ ⋆

5th and 6th rows: as 3rd and 4th.
1st–6th rows: rep. continuously.

Chart: when using chart, in forward rows work repeatedly from ⋆ to ⋆⋆ and once from ⋆⋆ to ∅. In backward rows once from ∅ to ⋆⋆ and repeatedly from ⋆⋆ to ⋆.
1st–6th rows: rep. continuously.
For explanation of diagram, *see* p. 300.

183 Knitting Pattern

Number of sts divisible by 12, plus 4.
1st row: edge st ⋆ p2, plait 4 sts (put the 1st 2 sts on to spare needle, leave in front of work, k the next 2 sts, then k the 2 sts from spare needle). From ⋆ rep. This row and all subsequent forward rows end with p2, edge st.
2nd row: edge st, k2 ⋆ p2 tog., thr.o., p2, k2, p4, k2. From ⋆ rep. Edge st.
3rd row: edge st ⋆ p2, k4, p2, k2 tog., thr.o., k2. From ⋆ rep.
4th row: as 2nd.
5th row: edge st ⋆ p2, plait 4 sts (as in 1st row), p2, k2 tog., thr.o., k2. From ⋆ rep.
6th row: as 2nd.
7th row: as 3rd.
8th row: as 2nd.
9th row: as 1st.
10th row: edge st, k2 ⋆ p4, k2, p2 tog., thr.o., p2, k2. From ⋆ rep.
11th row: edge st ⋆ p2, k2 tog., thr.o., k2, p2, k4. From ⋆ rep.
12th row: as 10th.
13th row: edge st ⋆ p2, k2 tog., thr.o., k2, p2, plait 4 sts. From ⋆ rep.
14th row: as 10th.
15th row: as 11th.
16th row: as 10th.
1st–16th rows: rep. continuously.

Chart

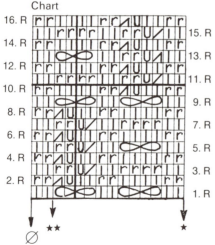

16. R
14. R
12. R
10. R
8. R
6. R
4. R
2. R
15. R
13. R
11. R
9. R
7. R
5. R
3. R
1. R

∅ ⋆⋆ ⋆

Chart: when using chart, in forward rows work repeatedly from ⋆ to ⋆⋆ and once from ⋆⋆ to ∅. In backward rows, once from ∅ to ⋆⋆ and repeatedly from ⋆⋆ to ⋆.
1st–16th rows: rep. continuously.
For explanation of diagram, *see* p. 300.

Lace Patterns

184 Knitting Pattern

Even number of sts.
1st row: edge st * thr.o., sl1, k1 and draw slipped st over. From * rep. Edge st.
2nd row: p all sts and thread-overs.
3rd row: edge st * sl1, k1 and draw slipped st over, thr.o. From * rep. Edge st.
4th row: as 2nd.
1st–4th rows: rep. continuously.

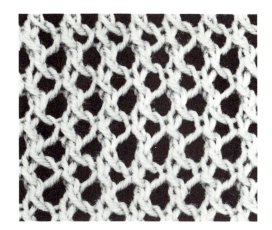

185 Knitting Pattern

Number of sts divisible by 6, plus 2 edge sts.
1st row: edge st * thr.o., sl1, k2 tog. and draw slipped st over, thr.o., k3. From * rep. Edge st.
2nd row: p all sts and thread-overs.
3rd row: edge st * k3, thr.o., sl1, k2 tog. and draw slipped st over, thr.o. From * rep. Edge st.
4th row: p all sts and thread-overs.
1st–4th rows: rep. continuously.

Chart: when using chart, in forward rows work once from ∅ to *, repeatedly from * to ** and once from ** to ∅. In backward rows, work once from ∅ to **, repeatedly from ** to * and once from * to ∅.
1st–6th rows: rep. continuously.
For explanation of diagram, *see* p. 300.

Chart

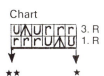

186 Knitting Pattern

Number of sts divisible by 6, plus 6 sts (4 sts and 2 edge sts).
1st row: edge st * k4, k2 tog., thr.o. From * rep. Row ends with k4, edge st.
2nd row: edge st, p5 * thr.o., p2 tog., p4. From * rep. Row ends with thr.o., p2 tog., p3, edge st.
3rd row: edge st, p2 * k2 tog., thr.o., k4. From * rep. Row ends with k2 tog., thr.o., edge st.
4th row: edge st * p4, p2 tog., thr.o. From * rep. Row ends with p4, edge st.

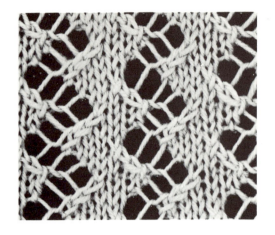

5th row: edge st, k5 * thr.o., sl1, k1 and draw slipped st over, k4. From * rep. Row ends with thr.o., sl1, k1 and draw slipped st over, k3, edge st.

6th row: edge st, p2 * p2 tog., thr.o., p4. From * rep. Row ends with p2 tog., thr.o., edge st.

1st–6th rows: rep. continuously.

Chart

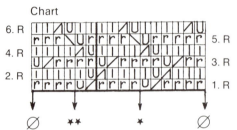

Chart: when using chart, in forward rows work once from ∅ to *, repeatedly from * to **, and once from ** to ∅. In backward rows, once from ∅ to **, repeatedly from ** to * and once from * to ∅.

1st–6th rows: rep. continuously.

For explanation of diagram, *see* p. 300.

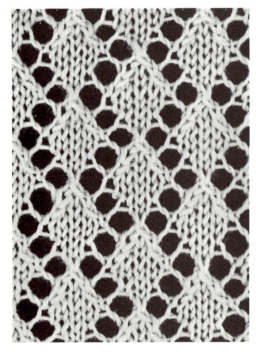

187 Knitting Pattern

Number of sts divisible by 8, plus 2 edge sts.

1st row: edge st * k5, thr.o., sl1, k2 tog. and draw slipped st over, thr.o. From * rep. Edge st.

2nd and every further backward row: p all sts and thread-overs.

3rd row: edge st * thr.o., sl1, k1 and draw slipped st over, k1, k2 tog., thr.o., k3. From * rep. Edge st.

5th row: edge st, k1 * thr.o., sl1, k2 tog., and draw slipped st over, thr.o., k5. From * rep. Row ends with thr.o., sl1, k2 tog. and draw slipped st over, thr.o., k4, edge st.

7th row: edge st, k4 * thr.o., sl1, k1 and draw slipped st over, k1, k2 tog., thr.o., k3. From * rep. Row ends with thr.o., sl1, k1 and draw slipped st over, k2, edge st.

8th row: p all sts and thread-overs.

1st–8th rows: rep. continuously.

Chart: when using chart, in forward rows work once from ⌀ to *, repeatedly from * to ** and once from ** to ⌀. In backward rows all sts and thread-overs are purled.

1st–8th rows: rep. continuously.
For explanation of chart, *see* p. 300.

Chart

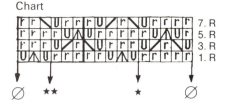

188 Knitting Pattern

Number of sts divisible by 6, plus 2 edge sts.
1st row: edge st * thr.o., k3, thr.o., sl1, k2 tog. and draw slipped st over. From * rep. Edge st.
2nd and every further back row: p all sts and thread-overs.
3rd row: edge st * thr.o., sl1, k1 and draw slipped st over, k1, k2 tog., thr.o., k1. From * rep. Edge st.
5th row: edge st, k1 * thr.o., sl1, k2 tog. and draw slipped st over, thr.o., k3. From * rep. Row ends with thr.o., sl1, k2 tog. and draw slipped st over, thr.o., k2, edge st.
7th row: edge st * k2 tog., thr.o., k1, thr.o., sl1, k1 and draw slipped st over, k1. From * rep. Edge st.
9th row: edge st, k4 * thr.o., sl1, k2 tog. and draw slipped st over, thr.o., k3. From * rep. Row ends with thr.o., sl1, k1 and draw slipped st over, edge st.
10th row: p all sts and thread-overs.
3rd–10th rows: rep. continuously.

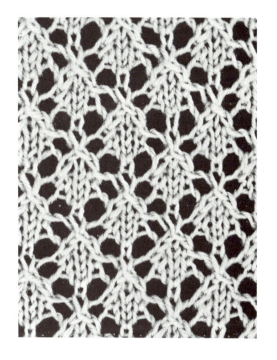

Chart: when using chart, in forward rows work once from ⌀ to *, repeatedly from * to ** and once from ** to ⌀. In backward rows all sts and thread-overs are purled.
3rd–10th rows: rep. continuously.
For explanation of chart, *see* p. 300.

Chart

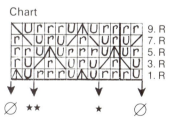

189 Knitting Pattern

Number of sts divisible by 10, plus 2 edge sts.
1st row: edge st, k3 * thr.o., sl1, k2 tog., and draw slipped st over, thr.o., k7. From * rep. Row ends with thr.o., sl1, k2 tog. and draw

slipped st over, k4, edge st.
2nd and every further back row: p all sts and thread-overs.
3rd row: edge st, k2 tog., k2 * thr.o., k1, thr.o., k2, sl1, k1 and draw slipped st over, k1, k2 tog., k2. From * rep. Row ends with

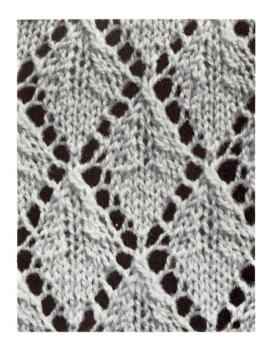

5th row: edge st * k2 tog., k1, thr.o., k3, thr.o., k1, sl1, k1 and draw slipped st over, k1. From * rep. Edge st.

7th row: edge st, k2 tog. * thr.o., k5, thr.o., sl1, k1 and draw slipped st over, k1, k2 tog. From * rep. Row ends with thr.o., k5, thr.o., sl1, k1 and draw slipped st over, k1, edge st.

9th row: edge st, k1, thr.o. * k7, thr.o., sl1, k2 tog. and draw slipped st over, thr.o. From * rep. Row ends with k7, thr.o., sl1, k1 and draw slipped st over, edge st.

11th row: edge st, k1 * thr.o., k2, sl1, k1 and draw slipped st over, k1, k2 tog., k2, thr.o., k1. From * rep. Edge st.

13th row: edge st, k2 tog. * thr.o., k1, sl1, k1 and draw slipped st over, k1, k2 tog., k1, thr.o., k3. From * rep. Row ends with thr.o., k1, sl1, k1 and draw slipped st over, k1. k2 tog., k1, thr.o., k2, edge st.

15th row: edge st, k2 * thr.o., sl1, k1 and draw slipped st over, k1, k2 tog., thr.o., k5. From * rep. Row ends with thr.o., sl1, k1 and draw slipped st over, k1, k2 tog., thr.o., k3, edge st.

16th row: p all sts and thread-overs.

1st–16th rows: rep. continuously.

thr.o., k1, thr.o., k2, sl1, k1 and draw slipped st over, k1, edge st.

Chart

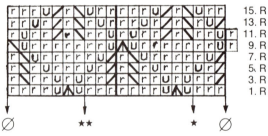

Chart: when using chart, in forward rows work once from ∅ to *, repeatedly from * to ** and once from ** to ∅. In backward rows, p all sts including thread-overs. In 9th and 11th rows is 1 extra st, which is decreased in 13th row.

1st–16th rows: rep. continuously.

For explanation of chart, *see* p. 300.

190 Knitting Pattern

Number of sts divisible by 10, plus 5.

1st row: edge st, p4 * k2 tog., thr.o., k1, thr.o., sl1, k1 and draw slipped st over, p5. From * rep. Row ends with k2 tog., thr.o., k1, thr.o., sl1, k1 and draw slipped st over, p4, edge st.

2nd and all subsequent backward rows: work all sts as they appear, but p thread-overs.

3rd row: edge st, p3 * k2 tog., thr.o., k3, thr.o., sl1, k1 and draw slipped st over, p3. From * rep. Edge st.

5th row: edge st, p2 * k2 tog., thr.o., k5, thr.o., sl1, k1 and draw slipped st over, p1. From * rep. Row ends with p1 and edge st.

7th row: edge st * thr.o., sl1, k2 tog. and draw slipped st over, thr.o., k7. From * rep. Row ends with thr.o., sl1, k2 tog. and draw slipped st over, thr.o., edge st.

9th row: edge st, k2 * thr.o., sl1, k1 and draw slipped st over, p5, k2 tog., thr.o., k1. From * rep. Row ends with k1, edge st.

11th row: edge st, k3 * thr.o., sl1, k1 and draw slipped st over, p3, k2 tog., thr.o., k3. From * rep. Edge st.

13th row: edge st, k4 * thr.o., sl1, k1 and draw slipped st over, p1, k2 tog., thr.o., k5. From * rep. Row ends with thr.o., sl1, k1 and draw slipped st over, p1, k2 tog., thr.o., k4; edge st.

15th row: edge st, k5 * thr.o., sl1, k2 tog. and draw slipped st over, thr.o., k7. From * rep. Row ends with thr.o., sl1, k2 tog. and draw slipped st over, thr.o., k5, edge st.

1st–16th rows: rep. continuously.

Chart: when using chart, in forward rows work once from ∅ to *, repeatedly from * to ** and once from ** to ∅. In backward rows work sts as they appear, but p thread-overs.

1st–16th rows: rep. continuously. For explanation of chart, *see* p. 300.

Chart

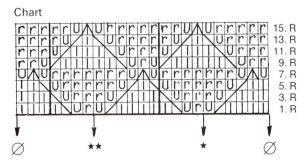

177

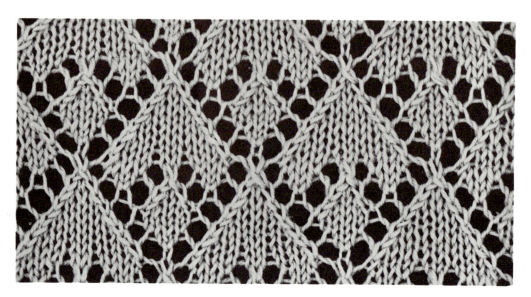

191 Knitting Pattern

Number of sts divisible by 12, plus 2 edge sts.
1st row: edge st * k1, thr.o., sl1, k1 and draw slipped st over, k7, k2 tog., thr.o. From * rep. Edge st.
2nd and all further backward rows: p all sts and thread-overs.
3rd row: edge st * k2, thr.o., sl1, k1 and draw slipped st over, k5, k2 tog., thr.o., k1. From * rep. Edge st.
5th row: edge st * k3, thr.o., sl1, k1 and draw slipped st over, k3, k2 tog., thr.o., k2. From * rep. Edge st.
7th row: edge st * k1, k2 tog., thr.o., k1, thr.o., sl1, k1 and draw slipped st over, k1, k2 tog., thr.o., k1, thr.o., sl1, k1 and draw slipped st over. From * rep. Edge st.

9th row: edge st, k2 tog. * thr.o., k3, thr.o., sl1, k2 tog. and draw slipped st over, thr.o., k3, thr.o., sl1, k2 tog. and draw slipped st over. From * rep. Row ends with thr.o., k3, thr.o., sl1, k2 tog. and draw slipped st over, thr.o., k4, edge st.
11th row: edge st * k4, k2 tog., thr.o., k1, thr.o., sl1, k1 and draw slipped st over, k3. From * rep. Edge st.
13th row: edge st * k3, k2 tog., thr.o., k3, thr.o., sl1, k1 and draw slipped st over, k2. From * rep. Edge st.
15th row: edge st * k2, k2 tog., thr.o., k5, thr.o., sl1, k1 and draw slipped st over, k1. From * rep. Edge st.
17th row: as 7th.
19th row: as 9th.
1st–20th rows: rep. continuously.

Chart

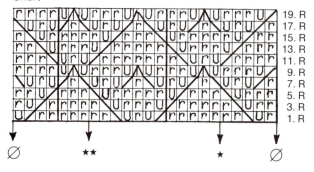

19. R
17. R
15. R
13. R
11. R
9. R
7. R
5. R
3. R
1. R

∅   ★★   ★   ∅

Chart: when using chart, in forward rows work once from ∅ to *, repeatedly from * to **, and once from ** to ∅. In backward rows all sts and thread-overs are purled.
1st–20th rows: rep. continuously. For explanation of chart, *see* p. 300.

192 Knitting Pattern

Number of sts divisible by 8, plus 2 edge sts.
1st row: edge st * thr.o., k2 twisted tog., k1, k2 tog., thr.o., k3. From * rep. Edge st.
2nd and all backward rows: p all sts and thread-overs.
3rd row: edge st, k4 * thr.o., k2 twisted tog., k1, k2 tog., thr.o., k3. From * rep. Row ends with thr.o., k2 twisted tog., k2, edge st.
5th row: edge st * k5, thr.o., sl1, k2 tog. and draw slipped st over, thr.o. From * rep. Edge st.
7th row: edge st * k2 tog., thr.o., k1, thr.o., k2 twisted tog., k3. From * rep. Edge st.
9th row: k edge st and next st tog. * thr.o., k3, thr.o., k2 twisted tog., k1, k2 tog. From * rep. Row ends with thr.o., k3, thr.o., k2 twisted tog., k2, edge st.
11th row: edge st * thr.o., k2 twisted tog., k1, k2 tog., thr.o. From * rep. Edge st.
13th row: edge st, k1 * thr.o., sl1, k2 tog. and draw slipped st over, thr.o., k5. From * rep. Row ends with thr.o., sl1, k2 tog. and draw slipped st over, thr.o., k4, edge st.

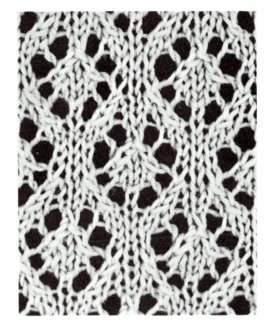

15th row: edge st, k4 * k2 twisted tog., k3. From * rep. Row ends with k2 tog., thr.o., k2, edge st.
1st–16th rows: rep. continuously.

Chart: when using chart, in forward rows work once from ∅ to *, repeatedly from * to ** and once from ** to ∅. In backward rows p all sts and thread-overs.
1st–16th rows: rep. continuously.
For explanation of chart, *see* p. 300.

Chart

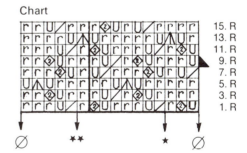

193 Knitting Pattern

Number of sts divisible by 12, plus 2 edge sts.
1st row: k.
2nd and all subsequent backward rows: p all sts and thread-overs.
3rd row: edge st * k1, thr.o., sl1, k1 and draw slipped st over, k7, k2 tog., thr.o. From * rep. Edge st.
5th row: edge st * k1, thr.o., k1, sl1, k1 and draw slipped st over, k5, k2 tog., k1, thr.o. From * rep. Edge st.
7th row: edge st * k1, thr.o., k2, sl1, k1 and draw slipped st over, k3, k2 tog., k2, thr.o. From * rep. Edge st.

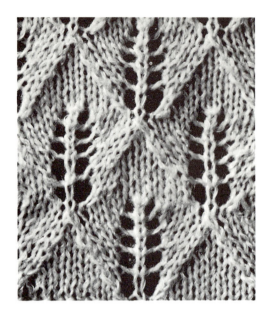

9th row: edge st * k1, thr.o., k3, sl1, k1 and draw slipped st over, k1, k2 tog., k3, thr.o. From * rep. Edge st.

11th row: edge st * k1, thr.o., k4, sl1, k2 tog., and draw slipped st over, k4, thr.o. From

* rep. Edge st.

13th row: edge st, k4, k2 tog. * thr.o., k1, thr.o., sl1, k1 and draw slipped st over, k7, k2 tog. From * rep. Row ends with thr.o., k1, thr.o., sl1, k1 and draw slipped st over, k3, edge st.

15th row: edge st, k3, k2 tog., k1 * thr.o., k1, thr.o., k1, sl1, k1 and draw slipped st over, k5, k2 tog., k1. From * rep. Row ends with thr.o., k1, thr.o., k1, sl1, k1 and draw slipped st over, k2, edge st.

17th row: edge st, k2, k2 tog., k2 * thr.o., k1, thr.o., k2, sl1, k1 and draw slipped st over, k3, k2 tog., k2. From * rep. Row ends with thr.o., k1, thr.o., k2, sl1, k1 and draw slipped st over, k1, edge st.

19th row: edge st, k1, k2 tog., k3 * thr.o., k1, thr.o., k3, sl1, k1 and draw slipped st over, k1, k2 tog., k3. From * rep. Row ends with thr.o., k1, thr.o., k3, sl1, k1 and draw slipped st over, edge st.

21st row: edge st, k2 tog., k4 * thr.o., k1, thr.o., k4, sl1, k2 tog. and draw slipped st over, k4. From * rep. Row ends with thr.o., k1, thr.o., k4, sl next st, and in the next row, with the edge st p the 2 tog.

3rd–22nd rows: rep. continuously.

Chart

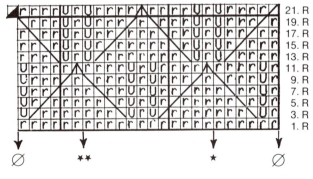

Chart: when using chart, in forward rows work once from ∅ to *, repeatedly from * to **, and once from ** to ∅. In backward rows p all sts and thread-overs.

3rd–22nd rows: rep. continuously.

For explanation of diagram, *see* p. 300.

194 Knitting Pattern

Number of sts divisible by 8, plus 2 edge sts.
1st row: edge st * k1, k2 tog., thr.o., k1, thr.o., k2 tog., thr.o., k2 tog. From * rep. Edge st.
2nd and all subsequent backward rows: p.
3rd row: edge st, k3 * thr.o., k2 tog., thr.o., k2 tog., k4. From * rep. Row ends with thr.o., k2 tog., thr.o., k2 tog., k1, edge st.
5th row: edge st * thr.o., k2 tog., k2. From * rep. Edge st.
7th row: edge st * k1, thr.o., k2 tog., k3, k2 tog., thr.o. From * rep. Edge st.
9th row: edge st * thr.o., k2 tog., thr.o., k2 tog., k1, k2 tog., thr.o., k1. From * rep. Edge st.
11th row: edge st, k1 * thr.o., k2 tog., k4, thr.o., k2 tog. From * rep. Row ends with thr.o., k2 tog., k5, edge st.
13th row: as 5th.
15th row: edge st, k2 * k2 tog., thr.o., k1, thr.o., k2 tog., k3. From * rep. Row ends with k2 tog., thr.o., k1, thr.o., k2 tog., k1, edge st.
16th row: p, including thread-overs.
1st–16th rows: rep. continuously.

Chart: when using chart, in forward rows work once from ⌀ to *, repeatedly from * to ** and once from ** to ⌀. In backward rows p all sts and thread-overs.
1st–16th rows: rep. continuously.
For explanation of chart, *see* p. 300.

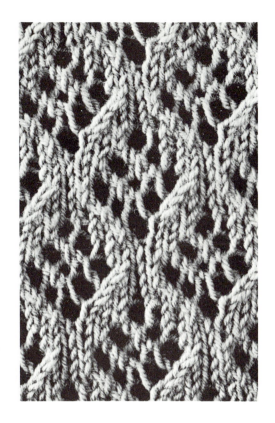

Chart

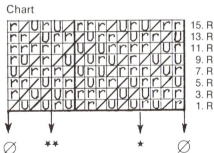

195 Knitting Pattern

Number of sts divisible by 6, plus 4 sts.
1st row: edge st, k7 * thr.o., k2 tog., k1, thr.o., sl1, k1 and draw slipped st over, k1. From * rep. End row with thr.o., k2 tog., k5, edge st.

2nd and all subsequent backward rows: k5, then p all sts, k the last 5 sts, edge st.
3rd row: edge st, k8 * k2 tog., thr.o., k1, thr.o., sl1, k1 and draw slipped st over, k1. From * repeat. Row ends with k6, edge st.
5th row: edge st, k6 * thr.o., sl1, k2 tog. and draw slipped st over, thr.o., k3. From * rep.

Row ends with thr.o., k2 tog., k6, edge st.

7th row: edge st, k7 * thr.o., sl1, k1 and draw slipped st over, k1, thr.o., k2 tog., k1. From * rep. Row ends with thr.o., sl1, k1 and draw slipped st over, k5, edge st.

9th row: edge st, k5 * k2 tog., thr.o., k1, thr.o., sl1, k1 and draw slipped st over, k1. From * rep. Row ends with k2 tog., thr.o., k7, edge st.

11th row: edge st, k9 * thr.o., sl1, k2 tog. and draw slipped st over, thr.o., k3. From * rep. Row ends with k5, edge st.

12th row: edge st, k5, then p all sts and end row with k5, edge st.

1st–12th rows: rep. continuously.

Chart

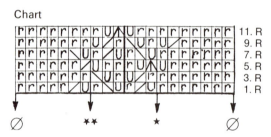

Chart: when using chart, in forward rows work once from ⌀ to *, repeatedly from * to ** and once from ** to ⌀. In backward rows k the 1st and last 5 sts, and p the remainder, including thread-overs.

1st–12th rows: rep. continuously.

For explanation of chart, *see* p. 300.

196   Knitting Pattern

Number of sts divisible by 7, plus 6 sts.

1st row: edge st * put the next 2 sts on spare needle and leave behind work, k2, k sts from spare needle, thr.o., k3 tog., thr.o. From * rep. Row ends with sl2 sts on to spare needle and put behind work, k2, k spare needle sts, edge st.

2nd and every further backward row: p.

3rd row: edge st * k2, thr.o., k2, thr.o., k3 tog., thr.o. From * rep. Row ends with k2, thr.o., k2, edge st.

5th row: edge st * k2, thr.o., k1, thr.o., k2, k3 tog. From * rep. Row ends with k2, thr.o., k1, thr.o., k2, edge st.

7th row: edge st, k2 * thr.o., k3 tog., thr.o., put the next 2 sts on to spare needle and

182

leave in front of work, then k the next 2 sts tog., k1, k sts from spare needle. From * rep. Row ends with thr.o., k3 tog., thr.o., k2, edge st.

9th row: edge st * k2, thr.o., k3 tog., thr.o., k2, thr.o. From * rep. Row ends with k2, thr.o., k3 tog., thr.o., k2, edge st.

11th row: edge st * k2, k3 tog., k2, thr.o., k1, thr.o. From * rep. Row ends with k2, k3 tog., k2, edge st.

13th row: edge st * put next 3 sts on to spare needle and leave behind work, k2, k 1st 2 sts on spare needle tog., k the 3rd st, thr.o., k3 tog., thr.o. From * rep. Row ends with k5 sts crossed as described at the beg. of the row, edge st.

14th row: p.

3rd–14th rows: rep. continuously.

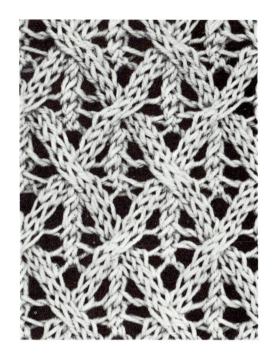

Chart

Chart: when using chart, in forward rows, work once from ⌀ to *, repeatedly from * to ** and once from ** to ⌀. In backward rows, p all sts and thread-overs.

The empty squares have no significance.

3rd–14th rows: rep. continuously.

For explanation of chart, see p. 300.

197   Knitting Pattern

Number of sts divisible by 14, plus 9.

1st row: edge st * k1, k2 tog., thr.o., k1, thr.o., k2 tog., k1, thr.o., k2 tog., k1, sl1 purlwise (thread lies behind st), k1, k2 tog., thr.o. From * rep. Row ends with k1, k2 tog., thr.o., k1, thr.o., k2 tog., k1, edge st.

2nd and every further backward row: p all sts and thread-overs *except* slipped sts of previous row. These again sl purlwise (this time thread *in front* of st).

3rd row: edge st * k2 tog., thr.o., k3, thr.o., k2 tog., k1, thr.o., k2 tog., sl1 purlwise (thread to the back) and thereby pick up horizontal thread, lying behind the st of the last-but-one

183

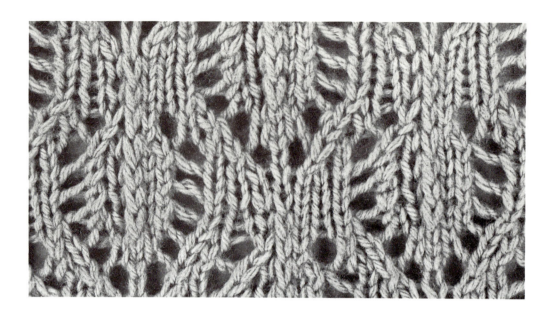

row, and dr.thr. the slipped st, k2 tog., k1. From * rep. Row ends with k2 tog., thr.o., k3, thr.o., k2 tog., edge st.

5th row: edge st, k1 * thr.o., k2, sl1 purlwise (thread to the back), k2, thr.o., k2 tog., k2, sl1 purlwise (thread to the back), k2, thr.o., k2 tog., k2, sl1 purlwise (thread to the back) thereby picking up the horizontal thread lying behind the st of the last-but-one row, and dr.thr. the slipped st, k2, k2 tog. From * rep. Row ends with thr.o., k2, sl1 purlwise (thread to back), k2, thr.o., k1, edge st.

7th row: edge st, k1 * thr.o., k2 tog., k1, sl1 purlwise (thread to back) thereby pick up horizontal thread lying behind st of the last-but-one row, and dr.thr. the slipped st, k1, k2 tog., thr.o., k3, sl1 purlwise (thread to back) and work as previously described, k3. From * rep. Row ends with thr.o., k2 tog., k1, sl1 purlwise and pick up horizontal threads (work as before), k1, k2 tog., thr.o., k1, edge st.

9th row: edge st, k1 * thr.o., k2 tog., k1, sl1 purlwise (thread to back) pick up horizontal threads and work as described, k1, k2 tog., thr.o., k3, sl1 purlwise, pick up horizontal thread and work as before, then put st back on to left needle and k it, k3. From * rep. Row ends with thr.o., k2 tog., k1, sl1 purlwise,

pick up horizontal thread as before and dr.thr. slipped st, k1, k2 tog., thr.o., k1, edge st.

11th row: edge st * k1, thr.o., k2 tog., k1, sl1 purlwise (thread to back), pick up horizontal thread as before and dr.thr. slipped st, k1, k2 tog., thr.o., k1, k2 tog., thr.o., k1, thr.o., k2 tog. From * rep. Row ends with k1, thr.o., k2 tog., k1, sl1 purlwise (thread to back), pick up horizontal thread as before and dr.thr. slipped st, k1, k2 tog., thr.o., k1, edge st.

13th row: edge st * k2 tog., thr.o., k2 tog., sl1 purlwise (thread to back), pick up horizontal thread as before and dr.thr. slipped st, k2 tog., thr.o., k2 tog., k1, thr.o., k3, thr.o., k1. From * rep. Row ends with k2 tog., thr.o., k2 tog., sl1 purlwise (thread to back), pick up horizontal thread as before and dr.thr. slipped st, k2 tog., thr.o., k2 tog., edge st.

15th row: edge st, k3 * sl1 purlwise (thread to back), pick up horizontal thread as before and dr.thr. slipped st, k2, k2 tog., thr.o., k2, sl1 purlwise (thread to back), k2, thr.o., k2 tog., k2. From * rep. Row ends with sl1 purlwise (thread to back), pick up horizontal thread as before and dr.thr. slipped st, k3, edge st.

17th row: edge st * k3, sl1 purlwise (thread to back), pick up horizontal thread as before

184

and dr.thr. slipped st, k3, thr.o., k2 tog., k1, sl1 purlwise (thread to back), pick up horizontal thread as before and dr.thr. slipped st, k1, k2 tog., thr.o. From * rep. Row ends with k3, sl1 purlwise (thread to back), pick up horizontal thread as before and dr.thr. slipped st, k3, edge st.

19th row: edge st, k3 * sl st purlwise, pick up horizontal thread as before and dr.thr. slipped st, then put st back on to left needle and k it, k3, thr.o., k2 tog., k1, sl1 purlwise (thread to back), pick up horizontal thread as before and dr.thr. slipped st, k1, k2 tog., thr.o., k3. From * rep. Row ends with sl st purlwise, pick up horizontal thread as before and dr.thr. slipped st, then put st back on to left needle and k it, k3, edge st.

21st row: edge st * k1, k2 tog., thr.o., k1, thr.o., k2 tog., k1, thr.o., k2 tog., k1, sl1 purlwise (thread to back), pick up horizontal thread as before and dr.thr. slipped st, k1, k2

tog., thr.o. From * rep. Row ends with k1, k2 tog., thr.o., k1, thr.o., k2 tog., k1, edge st.
22nd row: as 2nd.
3rd—22nd rows: rep. continuously.

Chart: when using chart, in forward rows work once from ∅ to *, repeatedly from * to ** and once from ** to ∅. The empty squares have no significance. 2nd and every other backward row, p all sts and thread-overs, but the slipped sts again sl purlwise, but this time with thread to the *front*.
3rd—22nd rows: rep. continuously.
For explanation of chart, *see* p. 300.

Chart

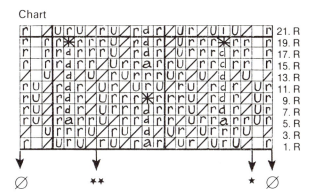

198 Knitting Pattern

Number of sts divisible by 7, plus 5 (3 sts and 2 edge sts).
1st row: edge st * k5, thr.o., sl1, k1 and draw slipped st over. From * rep. Row ends with k3, edge st.

2nd and all other backward rows: p.
3rd row: edge st, k3 * k2 tog., thr.o., k1, thr.o., sl1, k1 and draw slipped st over, k2. From * rep. Edge st.
5th row: edge st, k2 * k2 tog., thr.o., k3, thr.o., sl1, k1 and draw slipped st over. From * rep. Row ends with k1, edge st.

185

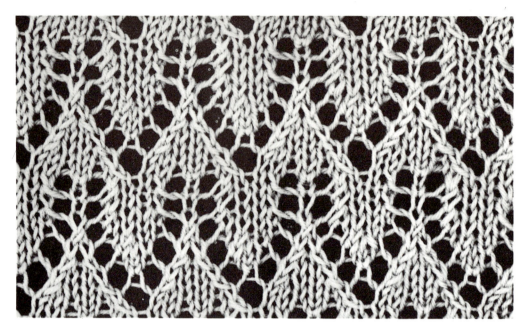

7th row: edge st, k1 * k2 tog., thr.o., k2, k2 tog., k1, thr.o. From * rep. Row ends with k2, edge st.

9th row: edge st, k2 * thr.o., sl1, k1 and draw slipped st over, k2, k2 tog., thr.o., k1. From * rep. Row ends with k1, edge st.

11th row: as 9th.

1st–12th rows: rep. continuously.

Chart

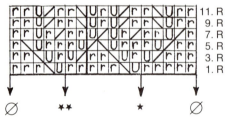

Chart: when using chart, in forward rows work once from ∅ to *, repeatedly from * to ** and once from ** to ∅. All sts and thread-overs are purled in backward rows.

1st–12th rows: rep. continuously.

For explanation of chart, *see* p. 300.

199   Knitting Pattern

Number of sts divisible by 8, plus 2 edge sts.

1st row: edge st * thr.o., k2, k3 tog. (sl1, k2 tog. and draw slipped st over), k2, thr.o., k1. From * rep. Edge st.

2nd row: p all sts and thread-overs.

3rd row: edge st * k1, thr.o., k1, k3 tog. (as in 1st row), k1, thr.o., k2. From * rep. Edge st.

4th row: p.

5th row: edge st * k2, thr.o., k3 tog. (as in 1st row), thr.o., k3. From * rep. Edge st.
6th row: p.
1st–6th rows: rep. continuously.

Chart

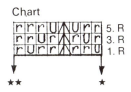

Chart: when using chart, in forward rows work continuously from * to **. In backward rows all sts and thread-overs are purled. For explanation of chart, *see* p. 300.

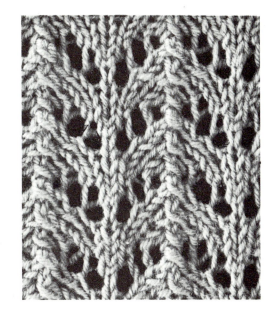

200   Knitting Pattern

Number of sts divisible by 13, plus 4 sts (2 sts and 2 edge sts).
1st row: edge st * p2, thr.o., k4, sl1, k2 tog. and draw slipped st over, k4, thr.o. From * rep. Row ends with p2, edge st.
2nd and every further backward row: work sts as they appear, and p thread-overs.
3rd row: edge st * p2, k1, thr.o., k2, sl1, k2 tog. and draw slipped st over, k3, thr.o., k1. From * rep. Row ends with p2, edge st.
5th row: edge st * p2, k2, thr.o., k2, sl1, k2 tog. and draw slipped st over, k2, thr.o., k2. From * rep. Row ends with p2, edge st.
7th row: edge st * p2, k3, thr.o., k1, sl1, k2 tog. and draw slipped st over, k1, thr.o., k3. From * rep. Row ends with p2, edge st.
9th row: edge st * p2, k4, thr.o., sl1, k2 tog. and draw slipped st over, thr.o., k4. From * rep. Row ends with p2, edge st.
1st–10th rows: rep. continuously.

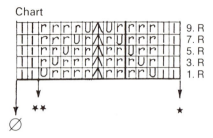

Chart: when using chart, in forward rows, work repeatedly from * to **, once from ** to ⊘. In backward rows work sts as they appear and p the thread-overs.
For explanation of chart, *see* p. 300.

201   Knitting Pattern

Number of sts divisible by 8, plus 2 edge sts.
1st row: edge st * thr.o., sl1, k1 and draw slipped st over, k5, k1 twisted. From * rep. Edge st.
2nd row: edge st * p1 twisted, p4, p2 twisted tog., thr.o., p1. From * rep. Edge st.
3rd row: edge st * thr.o., k2, sl1, k1 and draw slipped st over, k3, k1 twisted. From * rep. Edge st.
4th row: edge st * p1 twisted, p2, p2 twisted tog., p3, thr.o. From * rep. Edge st.
5th row: edge st * thr.o., k4, sl1, k1 and draw slipped st over, k1, k1 twisted. From * rep. Edge st.

6th row: edge st * p1 twisted, p2 twisted tog., p5, thr.o. From * rep. Edge st.
7th row: edge st * thr.o., k6, sl1, k1 and draw slipped st over. From * rep. Edge st.
8th row: edge st * thr.o., p1 twisted, p2 twisted tog. From * rep. Edge st.
9th row: edge st * sl1, k1 and draw slipped st over, k4, k1 twisted, thr.o., k1. From * rep. Edge st.
10th row: edge st * p2, thr.o., p1 twisted, p3, p2 twisted tog. From * rep. Edge st.
11th row: edge st * sl1, k1 and draw slipped st over, k2, k1 twisted, thr.o., k3. From * rep. Edge st.
12th row: edge st * p4, thr.o., p1 twisted, p1, p2 twisted tog. From * rep. Edge st.

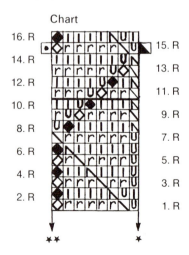

13th row: edge st * sl1, k1 and draw slipped st over, k1 twisted, thr.o., k5. From * rep. Edge st.
14th row: edge st * p6, thr.o., p2 twisted tog. From * rep. Edge st.
15th row: k edge st tog. with following st * thr.o., sl1, k1 and draw slipped st over, k5, k1 twisted. From * rep. Row ends with thr.o., sl1, k1 and draw slipped st over, k5, k1 twisted, out of the connecting link, edge st.
16th row: as 2nd.

3rd–16th rows: rep. continuously.

Chart: when using chart, in forward rows work repeatedly from * to **, and in backward rows repeatedly from ** to *. In the 15th row the edge st is knitted tog. with the following st, and at the end of the row, pick up the connecting link before the edge st, and k twisted.
3rd–16th rows: rep. continuously.
For explanation of chart, *see* p. 300.

202   Knitting Pattern

Number of sts divisible by 11, plus 7.
1st row: edge st * k1, thr.o., k2, sl1, k2 tog. and draw slipped st over, k5. From * rep. Row ends with k1, thr.o., k2, sl1, k1 and draw slipped st over, edge st.
2nd and every further backward row: p all sts and thread-overs.
3rd row: edge st, k2 * thr.o., k1, sl1, k2 tog. and draw slipped st over, k4, thr.o., k3. From * rep. Row ends with thr.o., k1, sl1, k1 and draw slipped st over, edge st.
5th row: edge st, k3 * thr.o., sl1, k2 tog. and draw slipped st over, k3, thr.o., k5. From * rep. Row ends with thr.o., sl1, k1 and draw slipped st over, edge st.
7th row: edge st, thr.o., k3 * sl1, k2 tog. and draw slipped st over, k2, thr.o., k1, thr.o., k5. From * rep. Row ends with sl1, k1 and draw slipped st over, edge st.
9th row: edge st, thr.o., k3 * sl1, k2 tog. and draw slipped st over, k1, thr.o., k3, thr.o., k4. From * rep. Row ends with sl1, k1 and draw slipped st over, edge st.
11th row: edge st * thr.o., k3, sl1, k2 tog. and draw slipped st over, thr.o., k5. From * rep. Row ends with thr.o., k3, sl1, k1 and draw slipped st over, edge st.
1st–12th rows: rep. continuously.

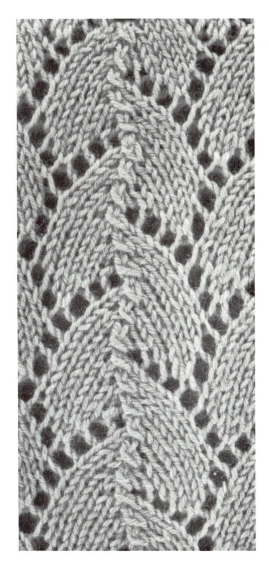

Chart

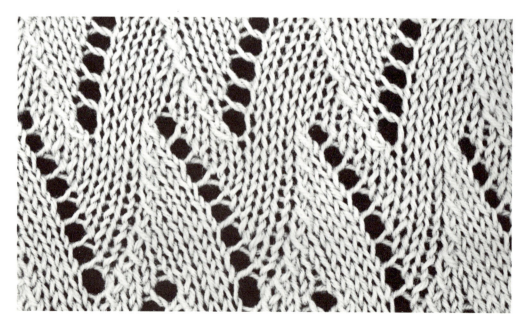

N	r	r	U	r	r	r	r	U	r	r	11. R

Chart: when using chart, in forward rows work continuously from * to ** and once from ∅ to * and from ** to ∅. In backward rows p all sts and thread-overs.

1st–12th rows: rep. continuously.
For explanation of diagram, *see* p. 300.

203 Knitting Pattern

Number of sts divisible by 9, plus 2 edge sts.
1st row: edge st * thr.o., sl1, k1 and draw slipped st over, k7. From * rep. Edge st.
2nd and all following backward rows: p all sts and thread-overs.
3rd row: edge st * thr.o., k1, sl1, k1 and draw slipped st over, k6. From * rep. Edge st.
5th row: edge st * thr.o., k2, sl1, k1, and draw slipped st over, k5. From * rep. Edge st.

7th row: * thr.o., k3, sl1, k1 and draw slipped st over, k4. From * rep. Edge st.
9th row: edge st * thr.o., k4, sl1, k1 and draw slipped st over, k3. From * rep. Edge st.
11th row: edge st * thr.o., k5, sl1, k1 and draw slipped st over, k2. From * rep. Edge st.
13th row: edge st * thr.o., k6, sl1, k1 and draw slipped st over, k1. From * rep. Edge st.
15th row: edge st * thr.o., k2, sl1, k1 and draw slipped st over, k3, sl1, k1 and draw slipped st over. From * rep. Edge st.
17th row: edge st * k2, sl1, k1 and draw

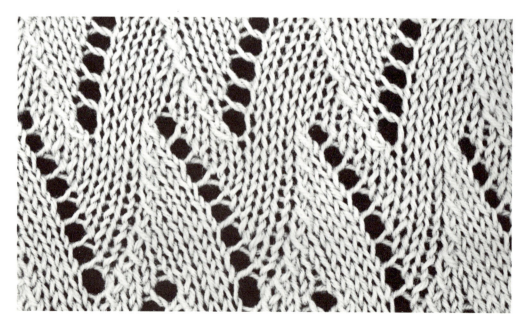

190

slipped st over, k1, thr.o., k4. From * rep. Edge st.

19th row: edge st * k1, sl1, k1 and draw slipped st over, k2, thr.o., k4. From * rep. Edge st.

21st row: edge st * sl1, k1 and draw slipped st over, k3, thr.o., k4. From * rep. Edge st.

23rd row: edge st, sl1, k1 and draw slipped st over, k3, thr.o., k3, sl1, k1 and draw slipped st over * k4, thr.o., k3, sl1, k1 and draw slipped st over. From * rep. Row ends with k4, thr.o., k4, edge st.

25th row: edge st, sl1, k1 and draw slipped st over, k3, thr.o., k2, sl1, k1 and draw slipped st over, k1 * k4, thr.o., k2, sl1, k1 and draw slipped st over, k1. From * rep. Row ends with k4, thr.o., k4, edge st.

27th row: edge st, sl1, k1 and draw slipped st over, k3, thr.o., k1, sl1, k1 and draw slipped st over, k2 * k4, thr.o., k1, sl1, k1 and draw slipped st over, k2. From * rep. Row ends with k4, thr.o., k4, edge st.

29th row: edge st, k1, sl1, k1 and draw slipped st over, k2, thr.o., sl1, k1 and draw slipped st over, k3 * thr.o., sl1, k1 and draw slipped st over, k2, thr.o., sl1, k1 and draw slipped st over, k3. From * rep. Row ends

with thr.o., sl1, k1 and draw slipped st over, k2, thr.o., k4, edge st.

30th row: p all sts and thread-overs.

3rd—30th rows: rep. continuously.

Chart

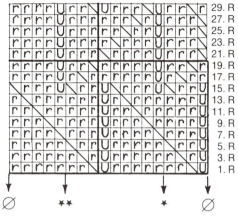

Chart: when using chart, in forward rows work once from ∅ to *, repeatedly from * to **, and once from ** to ∅. In backward rows all sts and thread-overs are purled.

3rd—30th rows: rep. continuously.

For explanation of diagram, *see* p. 300.

204 Knitting Pattern

Number of sts divisible by 10, plus 7.

1st row: edge st * k1, thr.o., k1, sl1, k2 tog. and draw slipped st over, k1, thr.o., k1, p3. From * rep. Row ends with k1, thr.o., k1, sl1, k2 and draw slipped st over, thr.o., edge st.

2nd and every following backward row: work sts as they appear, and p the thread-overs.

3rd, 5th and 7th rows: as 1st.

9th row: edge st, k1 * k1, p3, k1, thr.o., k1, sl1, k2 tog. and draw slipped st over, k1, thr.o. From * rep. Row ends with k1, p3, edge st.

11th, 13th and 15th rows: as 9th.

Chart

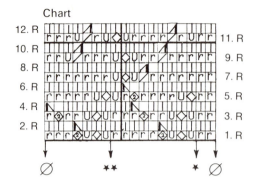

16th row: work sts as they appear, p thread-overs.
1st–16th rows: rep. continuously.

Chart: when using chart, in forward rows work once from ⌀ to *, repeatedly from * to ** and once from ** to ⌀. In backward rows work all sts as they appear, and p thread-overs.
1st–16th rows: rep. continuously.
For explanation of diagram, see p. 300.

205 Knitting Pattern

11 sts are needed for this pattern.
1st row: thr.o., k1, thr.o., sl1, k1 and draw slipped st over, k5, k2 tog., thr.o., k1, thr.o.
2nd and all further backward rows: p all sts and thread-overs.
3rd row: thr.o., k3, thr.o., sl1, k1 and draw slipped st over, k3, k2 tog., thr.o., k3, thr.o.
5th row: thr.o., sl1, k1 and draw slipped st over, k1, k2 tog., thr.o., sl1, k1 and draw slipped st over, k1, k2 tog., thr.o., sl1, k1 and draw slipped st over, k1, k2 tog., thr.o.
7th row: thr.o., sl1, k1 and draw slipped st over, k1, k2 tog., thr.o., k3 tog. (sl1, k2 tog. and draw slipped st over), thr.o., sl1, k1 and draw slipped st over, k1, k2 tog., thr.o.
9th row: thr.o., sl1, k1 and draw slipped st over, k1, k2 tog., thr.o., k1, thr.o., sl1, k1 and draw slipped st over, k1, k2 tog., thr.o.
11th row: as 9th.
1st–12th rows: rep. continuously.

Chart

Chart: when using chart, in forward rows work according to chart. In backward rows p all sts and thread-overs. The empty squares have no significance.
1st–12th rows: rep. continuously.
For explanation of diagram, see p. 300.

206 Knitting Pattern

Number of sts divisible by 15, plus 4.
1st row: edge st * p2, k2, k2 tog., thr.o., k2 tog., thr.o., k1, thr.o., sl1, k1 and draw slipped st over, thr.o., sl1, k1, draw slipped st over, k2. From * rep. Row ends with p2, edge st.
2nd and all following backward rows: edge st, k2 * p13, k2. From * rep. Edge st.
3rd row: edge st * p2, k1, k2 tog., thr.o., k2 tog., thr.o., k3, thr.o., sl1, k1 and draw slipped st over, thr.o., sl1, k1 and draw slipped st over, k1. From * rep. Row ends with p2, edge st.
5th row: edge st * p2, k2 tog., thr.o., k2 tog., thr.o., k5, thr.o., sl1, k1, draw slipped st over, thr.o., sl1 and draw slipped st over. From * rep. Row ends with p2, edge st.
7th row: edge st * p2, k2, thr.o., sl1, k1 and draw slipped st over, thr.o., sl1, k1, draw slipped st over, k1, k2 tog., thr.o., k2 tog., thr.o., k2. From * rep. Row ends with p2, edge st.

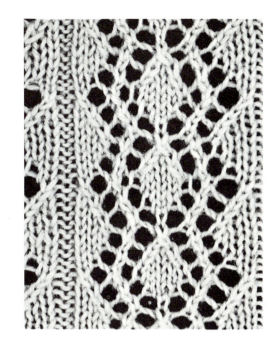

Chart

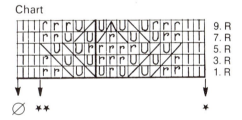

Chart: when using chart, in forward rows work repeatedly from * to ** and once from ** to ∅. In backward rows work sts as they appear, and p thread-overs.
1st–10th rows: rep. continuously.
For explanation of chart, *see* p. 300.

207 Knitting Pattern

Number of sts divisible by 17, plus 8 sts.
1st row: edge st * p1, k2, thr.o., k2 twisted tog., p1, thr.o., k1, thr.o., k3 twisted tog., k3, k3 tog., thr.o., k1, thr.o. From * rep. Row ends with p1, k2, thr.o., k2 twisted tog., p1, edge st.

2nd row: edge st * k1, p2, thr.o., k2 tog., k1, p11. From * rep. Row ends with k1, p2, thr.o., k2 tog., k1, edge st.
3rd row: edge st * p1, k2, thr.o., k2 twisted tog., p1, thr.o., k3, thr.o., sl1, k1 and draw slipped st over, k1, k2 tog., thr.o., k3, thr.o. From * rep. Row ends with p1, k2, thr.o., k2 twisted tog., p1, edge st.

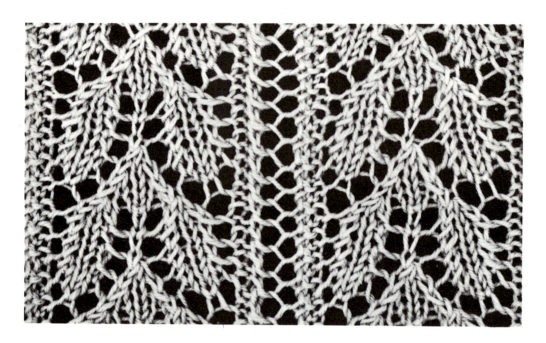

4th row: edge st * k1, p2, thr.o., k2 tog., k1, p13. From * rep. Row ends with k1, p2, thr.o., k2 tog., k1, edge st.

5th row: edge st, p1, k2, thr.o., k2 twisted tog., p1, thr.o., sl1, k1 and draw slipped st over, k1, k2 tog., thr.o., k3 tog., thr.o. sl1, k1, draw slipped st over, k1, k2 tog., thr.o. From * rep. Row ends with p1, k2, thr.o., k2 twisted tog., p1, edge st.

6th row: as 2nd.

7th row: edge st * p1, k2, thr.o., k2 twisted tog., p1, thr.o., sl1, k1, draw slipped st over, k1, k2 tog., thr.o., k1, thr.o., sl1, k1, draw slipped st over, k1, k2 tog., thr.o. From * rep. Row ends with p1, k2, thr.o., k2 twisted tog., p1, edge st.

8th and 10th rows: as 2nd.

9th row: as 7th.

1st–10th rows: rep. continuously.

Chart

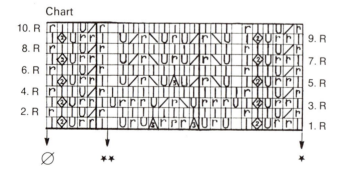

Chart: when using chart, in forward rows work repeatedly from * to ** and once from ** to ∅. In backward rows, work once from ∅ to ** and continuously from ** to *.

1st–10th rows: rep. continuously.
For explanation of diagram, *see* p. 300.
The empty squares in the chart have no significance.

194

Multi-coloured Knitting Patterns

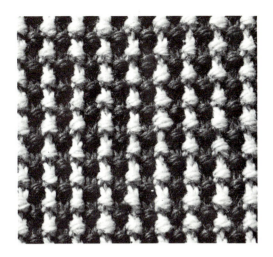

208   Bi-coloured Pearl Pattern

The pattern appears on the reverse side.
Even number of sts.

1st row: (1st colour) k.
2nd row: (2nd colour) edge st * k1, sl next st purlwise (thread behind st). From * rep. Edge st.
3rd row: (2nd colour) k the knitted sts of previous row, again sl the slipped sts of previous row purlwise, but with the thread to the front.
4th row: (1st colour) k sts in 1st colour twisted. The remaining sts sl purlwise (thread to back).
5th row: (1st colour) as 3rd.
6th row: (2nd colour) k sts in 2nd colour, the other sts sl purlwise (thread to back).
3rd–6th rows: rep. continuously.

209   Knitting Pattern

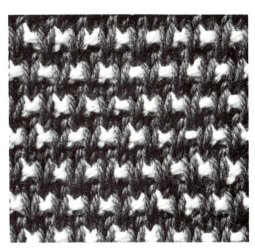

Even number of sts.
1st row: (1st colour) k.
2nd row: (2nd colour) p.
3rd row: (2nd colour) edge st * k1, sl1 purlwise (thread to back). From * rep. Edge st.
4th row: (2nd colour) edge st * sl1 purlwise (thread to front), k1. From * rep. Edge st.
5th row: (1st colour) k.
6th row: (1st colour) p.
7th row: (2nd colour) edge st * sl1 purlwise (thread behind st), k1. From * rep. Edge st.
8th row: (2nd colour) edge st * k1, sl1 purlwise (thread to front). From * rep. Edge st.
1st–8th rows: rep. continuously.

210 Knitting Pattern

Even number of sts.
1st and 2nd rows: (1st colour) 'curled'
(k forward and backward rows).
3rd row: (2nd colour) edge st * k1, sl1
purlwise (thread to back). From * rep. Edge
st.
4th row: (2nd colour) edge st * the slipped
st of previous row again sl purlwise (thread
in front of st), k1. From * rep. Edge st.
5th and 6th rows: (1st colour) 'curled'.
7th row: (2nd colour) edge st * sl st purlwise (thread to back), k1. From * rep. Edge
st.
8th row: (2nd colour) edge st * k1, the
slipped st of previous row again sl purlwise
(thread to front). From * rep. Edge st.
1st–8th rows: rep. continuously.

211 Knitting Pattern

Even number of sts.
1st row: (1st colour) edge st * k1, thr.o., sl1
purlwise. From * rep. Edge st.
2nd row: (1st colour) edge st * k slipped
st with the thread-over of previous row tog.,
p1. From * rep. Edge st.
3rd row: (2nd colour) as 1st.
4th row: (2nd colour) as 2nd.
1st–4th rows: rep. continuously.

212 Knitting Pattern

Work with needles pointed at both ends.
Even number of sts.
1st row: (forward row, 2nd colour) edge st *
k1, sl1 purlwise (thread in front). From * rep.
Edge st.
2nd row: (forward row, 1st colour) k.
3rd row: (backward row, 2nd colour) edge
st * p1, sl1 purlwise (thread to back). From *
rep. Edge st.
4th row: (backward row, 1st colour) p.
1st–4th rows: rep. continuously.

213 Bi-colour Star-stitch

Number of sts divisible by 3.
1st row: (1st colour) edge st, k1 ★ sl1,
thr.o., sl1, k1 and draw 1st slipped st over the
following 3 sts. From ★ rep. Edge st.
2nd row: (1st colour) p.
3rd row: (2nd colour) edge st, k3 ★ sl1,
thr.o., sl1, k1, draw 1st slipped st over the
following 3 sts. From ★ rep. Row ends with
k1, edge st.
4th row: (2nd colour) p.
1st–4th rows: rep. continuously

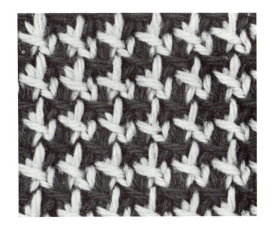

214 Tweed Pattern

Even number of sts.
The bi-coloured tweed pattern is knitted in
forward, and purled in backward rows, to
cast-on, use 1 of the colours. After the 1st
row, k alternately 1 st light, 1 st dark. Hold the
2 coloured threads together around your
finger so with every st the length of thread is
evened out. In the 2nd and following rows
k the dark sts of previous row in light and the
light sts, dark.

215 Knitting Pattern

Number of sts divisible by 4, plus 1 st.
1st and 2nd rows: (1st colour) 'curled'.
3rd row: (2nd colour) edge st ★ k3, sl1
purlwise (thread behind st). From ★ rep. Row
ends with k3, edge st.
4th row: (2nd colour) edge st ★ k3, sl1
purlwise (thread in front). From ★ rep. Row
ends with k3, edge st.
5th row: (1st colour) edge st, k1 ★ sl1
purlwise (thread behind st), k3. From ★ rep.
Row ends with sl1 purlwise, k1, edge st.
6th row: (1st colour) edge st, k1 ★ sl1 purlwise (thread in front), k3. From ★ rep. Row
ends with sl1 purlwise, k1, edge st.
3rd–6th rows: rep. continuously.

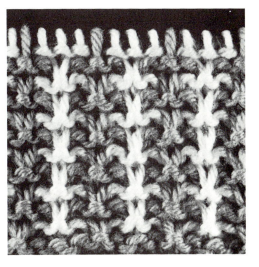

216   Knitting Pattern

Pattern may be used either side. Number of sts divisible by 4, plus 3.

K all forward rows: p backward rows.

1st–4th rows: light.
5th–8th rows: dark.
9th row: (light) * k2, let the 4th st down over the dark st, pick up the 1st light st and the 4 dark threads on to needle and k them as

1 st tog. From * rep. Row ends with k3.
10th–12th rows: light.
13th row: (dark) k1 * let the next st down over all the light sts, pick up the 1st dark st and all 4 light threads, and k tog. as 1 st, k3. From * rep. The row ends with: let the next st down over all the light sts, pick up the 1st dark st and all 4 light threads, k tog. as 1 st, k1.
14th–16th rows: dark.
9th–16th rows: rep. continuously.

217   Knitting Pattern

Number of sts divisible by 4, plus 3 sts.
1st and 2nd rows: (1st colour) 'plain knitting' (forward row k, backward row p).
3rd row: (2nd colour) edge st * k1, sl3 purlwise (thread in front of st), thr.o., put thread over the needle from back to front. From * rep. Row ends with k1, edge st.
4th row: (2nd colour) edge st, p1 * let the thread-over of previous row drop, p3, sl1 purlwise (thread to front). From * rep. Edge st.
5th and 6th rows: (1st colour) 'plain knitting'.
7th row: (2nd colour) edge st, k2 * k1 st with the horizontal thread tog., sl3 purlwise (thread in front), thr.o., in so doing put

thread from the back to the front. From * rep. Row ends with k1 st with the horizontal thread tog., k2, edge st.

8th row: (2nd colour) edge st, p2 * sl1 purlwise (thread to front), let the thread-over of previous row drop, p3. From * rep. Row ends with sl1 purlwise (thread to front), p2, edge st.

9th and 10th rows: (1st colour) 'plain knitting'.

11th row: (2nd colour) edge st, k1 * sl3 purlwise (thread to front), thr.o. (as before), k1 st with the horizontal thread tog. From * rep. Row ends with sl3 purlwise (thread to front), thr.o., k1, edge st.

4th–11th rows: rep. continuously.

218 Knitting Pattern in Three Colours

Number of sts divisible by 8, plus 2 edge sts.
1st–4th rows: (1st colour) 'plain knitting'.
5th row: (2nd colour) edge st * k7, sl1 purlwise (thread to back). From * rep. Edge st.
6th row: (2nd colour) edge st * sl1 purlwise (thread to front), p7. From * rep. Edge st.
7th and 8th rows: (2nd colour) as 5th and 6th.
9th row: (3rd colour) edge st, k3 * sl1 purlwise (thread to back), k7. From * rep.

Row ends with sl1 purlwise (thread to back), k4, edge st.
10th row: (3rd colour) edge st, p3 * sl1 purlwise (thread lies in front), p7. From * rep. P4, edge st.
11th and 12th rows: (3rd colour) as 9th and 10th.

5th–12th rows: rep. continuously (begin with 1st colour).

219 Knitting Pattern

Number of sts divisible by 5, plus 1 st.
1st row: (1st colour) k.
2nd row: (1st colour) p.
3rd row: (2nd colour) edge st * k4, sl1 purlwise (thread to back). From * rep. Row ends with k4, edge st.
4th row: (2nd colour) edge st * p4, sl1 purlwise (thread lies in front). From * rep. Row ends with p4, edge st.
1st–4th rows: rep. continuously.

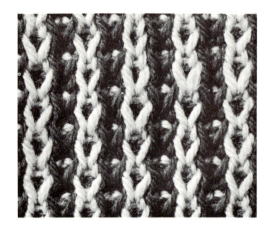

220   Knitting Pattern

Any number of sts.
1st row: (2nd colour) edge st, k1, p1, sl1 purlwise (thread behind st), p1. From * rep. Edge st.
2nd row: (2nd colour) work sts as they appear, again sl the slipped st purlwise, with thread in front of st.
3rd row: (1st colour) edge st * sl1 purlwise (thread behind st), p1, k1, p1. From * rep. Edge st.
4th row: (1st colour) as 2nd.
1st–4th rows: rep. continuously.

221   Knitting Pattern

Number of sts divisible by 6, plus 5 sts.
1st row: (1st colour) edge st * k1, sl1 purlwise (thread to the back), k1, sl3 purlwise (thread behind st). From * rep. Row ends with k1, sl1 purlwise, k1, edge st.
2nd row: (1st colour) edge st * p3, sl3 purlwise (thread in front). From * rep. Row ends with p3, edge st.
3rd row: (2nd colour) edge st * sl3 purlwise (thread to back), k1, k1 purlwise, k1. From * rep. Row ends with sl3 purlwise (thread to back), edge st.
4th row: (2nd colour) edge st * sl3 purlwise (thread in front), p3. From * rep. Row ends with sl3 purlwise (thread to front), edge st.
1st–4th rows: rep. continuously.

222   Knitting Pattern

Number of sts divisible by 5, plus 2 edge sts.
1st row: (1st colour) edge st * k1, k2 (with each st put thread 3 times around needle), k1, sl1 purlwise (thread to the back). From * rep. Edge st.
2nd row: (2nd colour) edge st * p1, sl4 purlwise (thread in front of work—the loops drop and make a long st). From * rep. Edge st.
3rd row: (2nd colour) edge st * k1, sl2 purlwise (thread to back), k2. From * rep. Edge st.
4th row: (2nd colour) edge st, p2 * sl2

purlwise (thread in front), p3. From * rep. Row ends with sl2 purlwise (thread in front), p1, edge st.

5th row: (2nd colour) as 3rd.

6th row: (2nd colour) edge st * p1, sl4 purlwise (thread in front). From * rep. Edge st.

7th row: (2nd colour) edge st * sl4 purlwise (thread to back), k1. From * rep. Edge st.

8th row: (1st colour) edge st * sl1 purlwise (thread in front), p1, draw the next 2 sts over the 1st st, and p, then p the 1st st, p1. From * rep. Edge st.

9th and 10th rows: (1st colour) 'plain knitting'.

1st–10th rows: rep. continuously.

223 Colour Change during Knitting

With faultless work, colour change takes place without any unevenness. The illustration shows vertical change of colour, and with this the following has to be watched: if the last st has been knitted light and the next st has to be dark, then put the light thread over the dark thread and continue working in dark. In this way the light thread embraces the dark, and a connection has been made. The illustration shows the back row: work with the dark colour is finished and light colour is to be started. The dark thread is being brought in front.

224 Diagonal Colour Change

The colour change here is diagonal upwards, and there is no need to intertwine the 2 colours. Should the colour be changed only in every row by 1 st, then it is necessary to intertwine the thread in the intermediate rows, as in paragraph 223.

225 Diagonal Stripes

Cast on 2 sts and inc. by 1 st at the beg. of every row. This is done by picking up the cross thread between the 1st 2 sts, to work as a new st. The illustration shows a work 'smooth-knitted' (k forward, p backward row). If, say, a pullover is worked in this way, one starts with the right or left lower corner of the garment. When, by increasing evenly, the correct lower width is reached, then continue to inc. by 1 st on the side seam to the beg. of the arm cut-out, and on the other side dec. in every row by 1 st. Further work is done to a paper pattern. If the work has to finish with an even edge (cushion covers, etc.) and the required height on the side seams has been reached, start decreasing by 1 st at the beg. of each row until all sts have been used.

Norwegian Patterns

226 Knitting Pattern

'Smooth-knit' according to the chart, in forward rows continually from * to **, in backward rows continuously from ** to *.
1st–8th rows: rep. continuously.
Explanation of drawing:
☐ = 1st colour.
✕ = 2nd colour.
1 pattern = 4 sts.

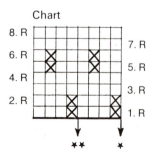

Chart

227 Knitting Pattern

Use the chart, 'smooth knitting' in forward rows continuously from * to ** and once from ** to ∅, in backward rows once from ∅ to ** and continuously from ** to *.

1st–12th rows: rep. continuously.

Explanation of illustration:

□ =1st colour.

✕ =2nd colour.

1 pattern =10 sts.

Chart

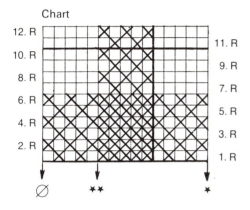

228 Knitting Pattern

Work from a chart in 'smooth knitting'; forward rows continuously from * to ** and once from * to ∅, in backward rows once from ∅ to ** and continuously from ** to *.

1st–8th rows: rep. continuously.

Explanation of illustration:

□ =1st colour.

✕ =2nd colour.

1 pattern =8 sts.

Chart

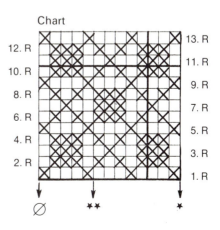

229 Knitting Pattern

Work according to the chart in 'smooth knitting': forward rows continuously from * to ** and backward rows continuously from ** to *.

1st–6th rows: rep. continuously.
Explanation of illustration:
□ = basic colour.
× = decorative colour.
1 pattern = 6 sts.

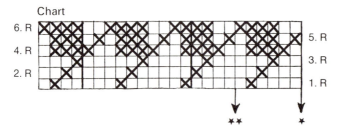

Chart

6. R
4. R
2. R

5. R
3. R
1. R

** *

230 Knitting Pattern

Work from chart in 'smooth knitting': forward rows continuously from * to **, backward rows from ** to *.

Explanation of illustration:
□ =1st colour.
✕ =2nd colour.
1 pattern = 12 sts.
(The photograph of this pattern appears on p. 204.)

Chart

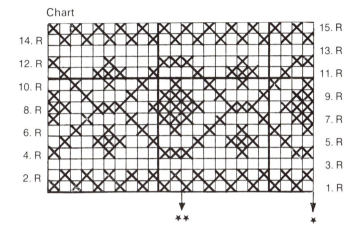

231 Knitting Pattern

231 Knitting Pattern *continued*

Work from chart in 'smooth knitting': in forward rows continuously from * to **, in backward rows from ** to *.

☐ = basic colour.
✕ = decorative colour.
1 pattern = 13 sts.
(Photograph of this pattern appears on preceding page.)

Chart

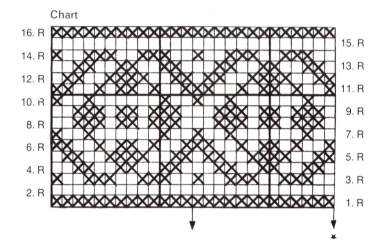

232 Knitting Pattern

Work from chart in 'smooth knitting': forward rows continuously from * to **, backward rows from ** to *.

☐ = basic colour.
✕ = 1st decorative colour.
● = 2nd decorative colour.
1 pattern = 14 sts. This pattern can be worked in 1 or 2 decorative colours according to choice.

Chart

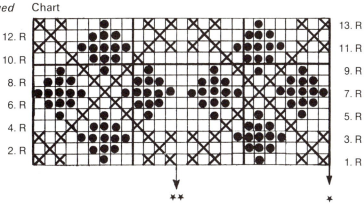

Chart

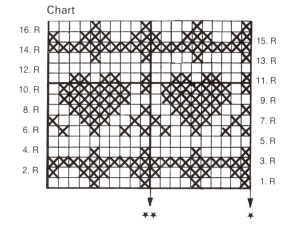

233   Knitting Pattern

Work from the chart in 'smooth knitting'.
☐ = basic colour.
✕ = decorative colour.
1 pattern = 10 sts.

234 Knitting Pattern

Work from the chart in 'smooth knitting', in forward rows continuously from * to **, in backward rows from ** to *.

□ = 1st colour.
× = 2nd colour.
1 pattern = 28 sts.

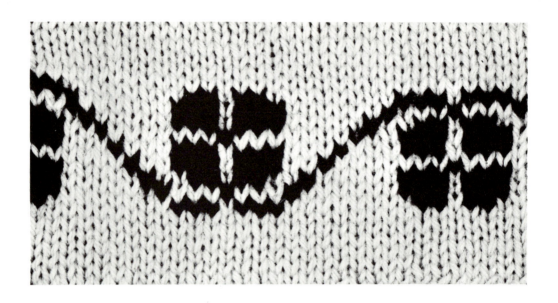

Chart

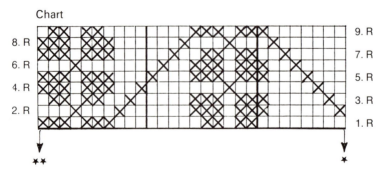

235 Knitting Pattern

Work from chart in 'smooth knitting'.

☐ = basic colour.
✕ = decorative colour.
1 pattern = 50 sts.

Chart

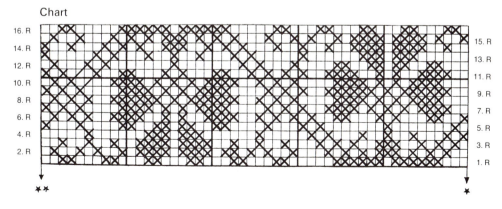

236 Knitting Pattern

Work from chart in 'smooth knitting', in forward rows continuously from ★ to ★★ and in backward rows from ★★ to ★.

☐ = 1st colour.
✕ = 2nd colour.
1 pattern = 14 sts.

Chart

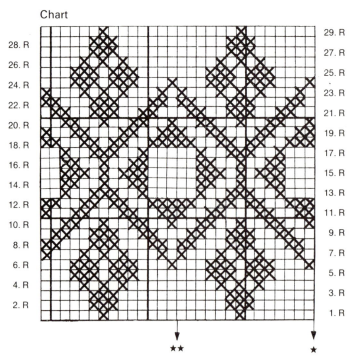

28. R
26. R
24. R
22. R
20. R
18. R
16. R
14. R
12. R
10. R
8. R
6. R
4. R
2. R

29. R
27. R
25. R
23. R
21. R
19. R
17. R
15. R
13. R
11. R
9. R
7. R
5. R
3. R
1. R

★★   ★

210

237 Knitting Pattern

Work according to chart in 'smooth knitting', in forward rows continuously from * to **, in backward rows from ** to *.

□ =1st colour.
✕ =2nd colour.
1 pattern =10 sts.

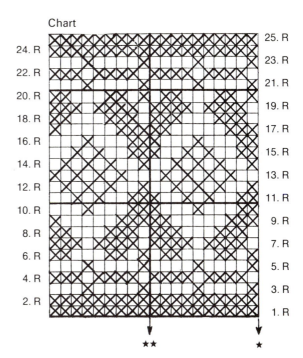

Chart

24. R
22. R
20. R
18. R
16. R
14. R
12. R
10. R
8. R
6. R
4. R
2. R

25. R
23. R
21. R
19. R
17. R
15. R
13. R
11. R
9. R
7. R
5. R
3. R
1. R

★★   ★

Chart

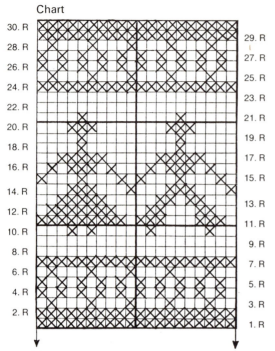

30. R
28. R
26. R
24. R
22. R
20. R
18. R
16. R
14. R
12. R
10. R
8. R
6. R
4. R
2. R

29. R
27. R
25. R
23. R
21. R
19. R
17. R
15. R
13. R
11. R
9. R
7. R
5. R
3. R
1. R

★★   ★

238   Knitting Pattern

Work according to chart, in 'smooth knitting',
in forward rows continuously from * to ** and
in backward rows from ** to *.
☐ = 1st colour.
✕ = 2nd colour.
1 pattern = 20 sts.

239 Knitting Pattern

Work according to chart, in 'smooth knitting', in forward rows continuously from * to **, and once from * to ⊘. In backward rows once from ⊘ to *, and continuously from ** to *.

☐ = 1st colour.
✕ = 2nd colour.
1 pattern = 32 sts.

Chart

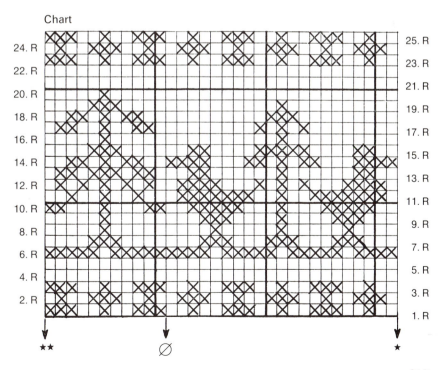

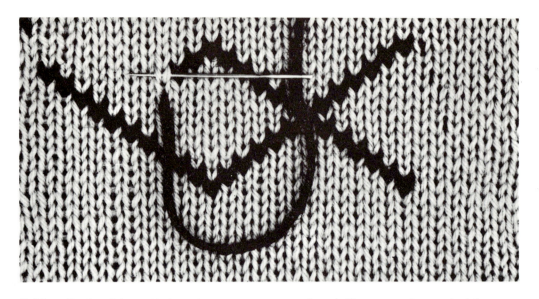

240 Embroidery Knit-stitch

On to a plain knitting embroider a pattern in different colours. The result is like a Norwegian pattern and it is easier to work. With extensive patterns especially embroidering is to be preferred. The st can be worked from every cross-st pattern. The embroidery thread should not be thinner than the knitting thread. Work as follows: insert from the back to front at the bottom of st, dr.thr. the st lying above (*see illustration*), insert again at the foot of st, draw thread to the back.

241   Knitting with a Knitting Machine

The knitting machine: a modern household apparatus, and what should be known about it.

The technique of this century has been increasingly devoted to the needs of domestic life. Technical appliances are today an integral part of a modern household, and no longer the privilege of certain social strata. Sewing and washing machines, electric irons and vacuum cleaners belong among normal household necessities.

Among such appliances, a newcomer which has already won for itself many friends is the knitting machine. It cannot yet be compared to the above-mentioned household appliances, since for most women knitting is not a purely domestic chore which must often be performed with more or less boredom, but is, on the contrary, for many women their chief hobby, a hobby which, year after year, produces work of enormous value, as well as enabling them to indulge their desire to create and to express their own personal tastes.

This prompts the question: does not the mechanization of knitting endanger that which one might describe as the artistic side of needlework?

Crochet, knitting and embroidery were, and are, for many people the essence of contemplation, and the clicking of the knitting needles conjures up a picture of domestic comfort and peace. But will not all this be brought into question by the use of machinery? Before answering this question let us consider the other aspect of needlework.

In an opinion poll many thousands of housewives were asked what gave them most pleasure in knitting. The answer was little concerned with peace, comfort, contentment, etc., but rather and unmistakeably with the enjoyment from seeing the finished product.

Isn't it a wonderful feeling when, say on May Day, one can wear a garment which one has made oneself, and in the creation of which all one's individual wishes and ideas have been realized?

But alas! many people lack the time, and perhaps the patience to knit by hand, and it is here that the knitting machine is a tremendous ally, whether one wishes to knit for the pleasure of it, or as a commercial proposition, for the machine saves time.

You, dear reader, have assuredly heard much about the knitting machine already: praise or blame, enthusiasm or reluctance, and the catch-phrases of advertisements. In the following sections we shall try to consider and to test the machine, in order to help you judge for yourself.

242   What Does a Knitting Machine Accomplish?

When one tries to estimate the value of any apparatus for one's own needs, the first question is, of course, what advantages accrue from the possession of it. In our introduction we have already asserted that one can never judge from a purely material standpoint, nor, in fact, should one. Nonetheless, we want to try to analyse the matter factually.

The first obvious advantage of the machine is the high knitting speed, though unfortunately one cannot answer the question: how much more quickly can one knit by machine than by hand?

The efficiency of the many different types varies a great deal, and personal skill plays a tremendous part, no less than the form and pattern, or the quality and character of the work.

243   What Cannot a Machine Do?

Bluntly speaking: a knitting machine cannot perform magic! Whoever acquires such a machine must be quite clear that it is not an automatic device which, when fed with wool, produces finished knitting. The knitting machine is a handicraft apparatus, and an aid to the head and hand of the knitter. In certain cases one can say that in hand knitting there are patterns which cannot, or only with very great difficulty, be produced on the machine. But at the same time, it can be said that the machine opens up pattern possibilities which go far beyond anything that the hand can achieve.

244   Handknitting: Machine Knitting; Differences and Similarities

Every young girl of today learns at school how to use a sewing machine, and we all have a clear idea as to how such a machine operates, and how it can be employed. But, generally speaking, this sort of knowledge concerning the knitting machine is completely lacking.

Nevertheless, as every schoolgirl learns to knit, it is best, when explaining the working of the machine, to link it to the basic teaching of hand knitting. One makes, then, the surprising discovery that basically the working methods of both machine and hand knitting are extensively the same. As in hand knitting, the stitch is formed by drawing the thread through the cast-on loop. The machine-knitted stitch looks exactly like the hand-knitted, and if we wish to give our knitting a definite form, we do this by increasing or decreasing the number of stitches. If we need to decrease, 2 stitches are knitted together: if we increase, an extra stitch is cast on. Machine-knitted work can be undone in precisely the same way as hand-knitted: we can work all types of patterns, and by using different colours we can adopt Norwegian styles. In short, the difference between hand and machine knitting lies in the apparatus, and not in the basic principles.

245   Is a Knitting Machine Profitable?

Next we'll deal with the question: when and in what circumstances does it pay to acquire a machine? We all know that knitted fashion is personal fashion, and home-knitted garments give the pleasure and satisfaction of personal achievement. Hand knitting is comparatively inexpensive, and it can present the true realization of personal taste. In short, knitting embraces ideal and material values and advantages. For those who take real pleasure in knitting, the creativity will outweigh all other considerations.

Nonetheless, the purely economic factors are obvious and weighty, and those who enjoy creating, those who prefer the personal note in their clothes, find that the handknitting machine is capable of producing many times the amount of work possible by hand.

Whether the machine is a business proposition one can easily work out for oneself. One has to take into consideration that through the speed of the appliance, completely new areas are discovered which go far beyond mere garment-making. If offers the possibility of making presents, domestic fabrics and to undertake profitable sidelines. If you weigh up financially all these opportunities, and consider also that the garment can be unravelled and the wool used again, you discover that the knitting machine, even when little used, pays for itself.

Of course the economic usefulness of a machine increases with the growth of the family, and with the preference for home-knitted clothing. A housewife with a family of 5 or more has hardly the time to cope with the need for knitted garments with hand knitting.

246 Is a Knitting Machine Difficult to Operate?

We have already mentioned at the outset that every young girl learns to knit, either at school or in the home, but whether or not the lessons are turned to good account depends on the inclinations of the individual concerned. The same applies to the machine. Knitting with the machine is, in principal, easier to learn than hand knitting, but, since, so to speak, we learn knitting from childhood onwards, it is in general easier than if one starts to learn to handle the machine as an adult.

Nonetheless, it can be said that anyone can learn to use the machine, and it depends, of course, on their natural aptitude whether the learning comes easy or not, and whether, after more or less effort, one learns to appreciate the advantages which the machine offers. But the fact is: the number of house-wives who work with the machine has already long passed the million mark.

This shows that it is as easy to learn to work with the knitting machine as with the sewing machine. Naturally, there are various essential differences between the several types, and one should therefore, before deciding on any particular make, investigate it carefully. Is it easy to manipulate, are its possibilities manifold, has the firm a good after-sales and information service and is a thorough and detailed instruction on the machine assured?

247 What Types of Wool May be Used?

Very frequently one meets with the belief that only specific materials and wools can be used on the machine, but this is quite untrue. On a good machine, as we have already seen, we can employ all the usual commercial yarns, natural wool and cotton, man-made fibres, metallic threads and even bast. Anyone who has knitted by hand will already know that different materials require different techniques, and with the machine, as with the hand, the best is a moderately strong and elastic woollen yarn. It is an elementary fact that the better the material the finer and the easier the actual work. A good brand of yarn works better and produces a much finer result than a cheap shoddy. The right firm is in a position to advise the owner of the machine, and those who buy their materials should remain faithful to the firm and to a branded product, then they will be better able to enjoy the fruits of their labours.

Of course one can knit with several sorts of yarn, and, as for example in the production of stockings, use a strong double thread for toes and heels. Interweaving with special materials, e.g. man-made fibres and metallic threads, is easily possible.

Beginners are recommended to start with with a good, fairly strong and stretchable thread.

248 How Does One Learn to Work with the Machine?

If a machine is bought from a good firm, one is given, with the machine, the opportunity of careful training, together with thorough working instructions. When one has completed the training one can be compared to a car-driver who has gained his driving licence; everyone knows that the mere possession of a licence does not make a skilled driver, but that his acquired knowledge must be developed through practice. This is just as true for the knitting machine, where practice also makes perfect, and it is obvious that the first pullover will not come off the machine so quickly and so faultlessly as the fifth and subsequent.

If a training course is taken, one is assailed by a host of new ideas which at first seem very complicated, but which in practice are quite simple. Anyone who takes such a course when buying a machine should in any case keep a few afternoons free to test in practice the lessons learnt. You will not achieve your target if you sit down straight away at your machine and try to produce a complicated piece of work. It is far more important to repeat the work done on the course, noting down any problems which arise. It is good practice to begin by knitting 4–8 oz of plain knitting, for by so doing one becomes fluent with the machine, one learns to know it and to acquire the touch necessary in handling it. After this repetition exercise, we take a simple garment, say, a pullover, or a child's jacket, and have close at hand a notebook or pad on which to jot down anything about which we do not feel absolutely sure. If there is an opportunity, we bring up these problems at the manufacturer's nearest advice bureau. It is a good idea to bring with one the finished knitting, so that one can discuss difficulties and ask advice about mistakes.

For those not technically minded the point may come when one feels unable to make any further progress, and when things simply won't work out one loses heart. But this is just a stage which we experience even as children when we learn to knit by hand, and which we have to go through again whenever we take up anything new. The simple truth is that patience certainly pays, and that there's hardly any case where, having passed 'the point of frustration', one ever forgets the sheer delight in completing one's very first finished work.

249 The Various Types of Knitting Machine and Their Technical Characteristics

We mention first the machine with the so-called 'open system'. Everyone will recall the primitive apparatus with which we, as children, made a knitted cord. By means of a hook and a nail stitches can be made, and with this simple system one can produce knitting somewhat more quickly than by hand. This may be the reason why this type of machine is scarcely still on the market, and so we can omit any further description of it.

Today the machines with the 'tongue-needle' dominate the market, and of these there are two types, viz, the so-called 'single-bed' and the 'double-bed'.

Before we clarify the essential differences between the two, we must explain how the tongue-needle works. This is a needle with the front (pointed) end bent into a hook. This hook can be closed or opened by a moveable 'tongue'. If we lay a stitch in this needle, and using the hook like a crochet-hook, pull thread through the loop of the first stitch, we make a new stitch. In this machine many such hooks are arranged side by side, and by means of an ingenious mechanism these needles are moved up and down, enabling row after row of knitting to be worked one after another.

This system is already over 100 years old. Before this an American, named Lamb, developed a knitting machine which works by means of tongue-needles laid side by side and motivated by a shuttle. The principle of our modern machines goes right back to this primitive form.

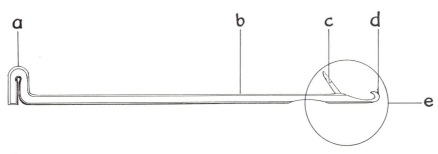

The Tongue-needle
(a) Foot, (b) Shaft, (c) Tongue, (d) Hook, (e) Head

The so-called 'Lamb Principle' is comparatively simple to explain. In the hook of the tongue-needle hangs a stitch. The needle itself is pulled right back in the needle-bed, and if the shuttle is moved from left to right, or vice-versa, the needle is pushed up from the bed. The stitch hanging in the hook glides back, opens the tongue and drops behind it. Simultaneously the thread guide brings the new thread into the hook. The shuttle now draws the needle back again and the old stitch closes the tongue. The new thread, trapped by the hook and tongue, is drawn loopwise through the stitch. This process occurs with each needle and in this way a piece of knitting is created which is generally known as 'plain'.

Besides this system, a new method of activating the needle has recently been developed. As in the Lamb system the tongue only opens when the needle comes out of the 'bed', and at this point it is necessary to rely on the mechanism for guiding the thread—the 'thread guide'. Knitting Norwegian patterns, or several parts next to one another, or forming vertical necklines, armholes, slits and buttonholes is made rather more difficult by this method.

Because of this, in the new system, the needle lies in its normal position with open tongue *outside* the needle-bed. The last stitch lies already behind the tongue. Now the needle can be laid in by hand without the thread guide, and, as the case may require, different colours or parts can be knitted next to one another with the same yarn.

When the shuttle is now moved, the needle is

drawn back, the last stitch closes the tongue and the new thread is drawn through the last stitch to form a new one.

Then the needle moves upwards once more, the new stitch opens the tongue and lays behind it, and you are back in the starting position again.

These two systems are used by different types of machine. If you have followed carefully our description of the needle action, and, with the aid of the illustrations, tried to imagine the separate processes, you will see that for a smooth and efficient follow-through of the whole operation it is necessary that the stitches on the machine can easily be pulled under. Only in this way can the opening and closing of the needle be achieved and the creation of stitches made possible. Drawing-off the work follows according to various systems. Many machines use, similar to industrial machines, the so-called 'weight draw-off'. By the use of combs which are either themselves heavy, or on which weights can be hung, the work can be pulled downwards. But as a piece of knitting, when pulled lengthways, does not stretch evenly, but diagonally, and the needles on the edges have more strain on them than those in the middle, and there is the danger that the edge stitches may jump off.

In order to counteract this, on machines with 'weight draw-offs' it is necessary to have weights on both edges of the knitting, so that an even draw-off is achieved. As the work progresses, these weights must be raised so that they never hang lower than 2—4 inches below the needle-bed.

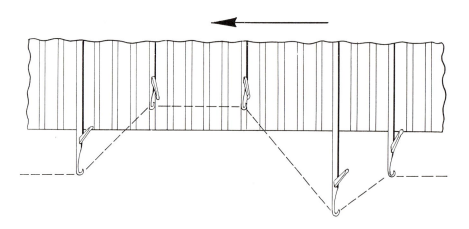

Forming the stitches

With the other system of draw-off, known as the 'friction draw-off', the knitted work is pulled down by a 'stripper' which is connected to the shuttle, and this is always operating where the shuttle happens to be. With this method the work is not pulled lengthways so strongly, and the finished work comes loosely off the machine. It is, however, necessary to apply special holders for the edge stitches, to ensure a regular draw-off.

In the third system the draw-off is achieved by a so-called 'platina'. These are flat parts fitted with hooks, lying on a spring-fitted needle-bed, and which, by means of a curved part (guided by the shuttle) draw the finished stitches down as they are made.

From these descriptions one sees that the function of tongue of the needle is most important. If this process is disturbed, by vibrations, etc., so that tongue which should be open, is closed, a stitch will drop because the new stitch cannot correctly be drawn through the old.

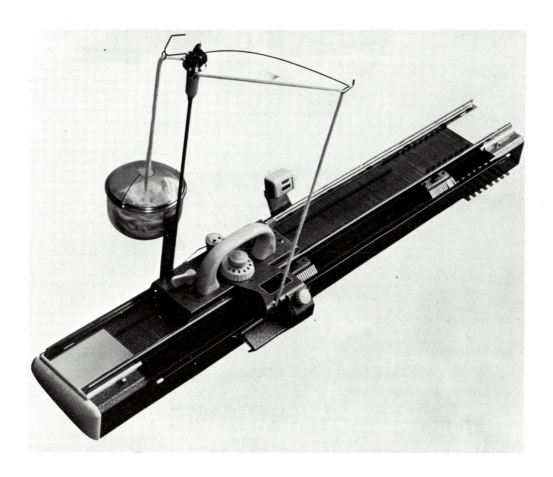

To prevent this mishap brushes are fitted to the machine, which have the duty of brushing open closed tongues. In new types of machine a special tongue-needle is used, in which the tongue is so springy that it opens itself, preventing stitches being dropped. These machines do not require brushes.

The number of available needles determines the number of stitches which can be knitted, and so, of course, the width of the knitting. In several machines on the market the number of needles varies between 160 and 200. The number of stitches and the width of the work depends, as can be seen, on the strength of the yarn. Twenty stitches in a thick wool give a greater width than 20 in thin wool. It pays, therefore, always to choose a machine with the greater number of needles, since one is less limited in its potential. One does not wish to be confined to one sort of work, but to be able to knit with wools of all thicknesses. The size of the knitted stitches on a machine are governed by 2 factors. We have already shown that the shuttle pulls down the needle and thereby the yarn is drawn through the last stitch to form a new one. If the needle then moves very far back, a large stitch is made; if it moves only a short distance, we get a small stitch. By appropriate adjustments to the shuttle the length of travel of the needle can be determined, and the resulting size of the stitches. But the distances between the

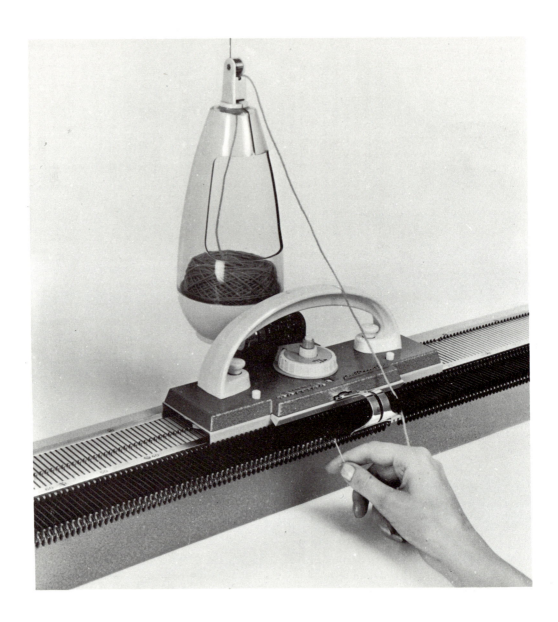

needles also have a big influence, and industrial machines have different needle spacings for different yarns.

At this point we must mention the so-called 'division'. The best average spacing is shown to be 5 needles to the inch, as being the most practical, though there are machines with a higher number which can work fine wool better. But on the other hand these are limited to large stitches with coarser yarns.

A little technical trick can help the knitter in those cases where the needle spacings and larger stitch settings are not sufficient to knit loosely a coarse yarn. One can put every 2nd needle out of action and work with the remaining half. In good machines it is even possible to work with every 3rd or 4th needle only, enabling one to knit very thick wool.

The type of knitting possible on a single-bed, tongue-needle machine is known generally as 'plain knitting', and this type is usually found in home-knitted garments. The work comes off the machine with the reverse side facing the knitter.

The basic knitting can be varied to countless types of patterns by the appropriate settings. How these patterns are worked is shown in section 250 *et seq*.

If one wishes to make an article in alternate 'knit one, purl one' it is necessary that the stitch-making operation already described be done in the opposite direction. On a simple single-bed machine one can achieve this in a smooth-knitted article by letting every 2nd,

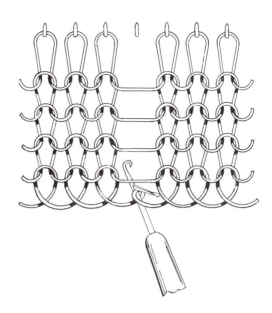

4th, 6th, 8th, etc., stitch drop, by drawing back the needles without laying in the thread, and then, with the help of a special manual tongue-needle crochet up in the opposite direction. This takes skill and practice and tends to slow-up the work.

For this reason several manufacturers have developed an attachment for single-bed machines, which works on the same principle as the basic apparatus, but in the opposite direction. This attachment, which is fixed to the machine, and which can easily be removed when not required, permits the production of articles in 'knit one, purl one'.

And now we come to the new type of handknitting machine, which are constructed with 2 needle-beds, and generally described as 'double-bed machines', closely resembling the industrial machines. The shuttles are linked together and the needle-beds themselves can be arranged against each other. In comparison with the basic machine, the attachment has, at most, only half the number of needles. Consequently, one-bed machines with attachments are somewhat cheaper than the double-bed, but have fewer pattern possibilities.

In contrast, in double-bed machines, both needle-beds have an equal number of staggered needles. The basic stitch pattern is technically known as 'plain plain', both sides of the work presenting the same appearance of plain stitches. When going over to bands or edgings in a simple 'plain knitting', the article must be cut off and hung on to 1 of the 2 needle-beds.

Which of the two types—single- or double-bed—is preferred depends on various reasons. Single are generally more reasonable in price, simpler to work and to look after, and by means of the accessory attachments their range can be increased to do plain and purl and other patterns.

Double-bed machines are, on the whole, more difficult to operate and technically less easy to understand. They have to be screwed to the table and do not enable such good supervision of the work, but with them a higher speed in plain and purl knitting, and changes of pattern can be achieved.

In deciding which sort of machine is best for one's own purpose, one should carefully look over the various types and perhaps test some knitting on them.

250 Pattern Knitting

The delight of every enthusiastic knitter is pattern-knitting, and what opportunities does the machine offer? In order to give the reader a general idea. we are showing the various groups of patterns which can be produced on the machine.

251 Holed Pattern

This pattern is worked on the machine on exactly the same system as by hand. Two neighbouring stitches are knitted together, creating a hole in the knitting. The arrangement of the holes is left to the taste of the knitter and can be varied accordingly. The machine works the pattern thus: with the help of a little hook 1 stitch is transferred from one needle to the next (where there is already a stitch), and by working in this way you should have no difficulty in following any description or chart. Unlike in handknitting, where after every hole one has to thread yarn over, this is not necessary with the machine as the next row is automatically fully knitted.

252 Pattern Formed by Changing Size of Stitches

In hand knitting we can obtain striped effects by using needles of varying sizes, and this pattern can be worked quickly and easily on the machine, by simply altering the tightness of the stitches in different rows. In this way, wide or narrow stripes can be created, and even coloured patterns, by using coloured yarns on varying stitch sizes.

253 Patterns Created by Omitting Needles

Should we have cast-on, for example, 100 stitches on our machine, and now leave every 3rd or 4th needle out of action, then,

contrary to the previously described stripe effect, which is horizontal, we now have a vertical stripe with a hemstitch effect. By combining the 2 previous patterns (252 and 253) we achieve a check or rectangular pattern.

254 Plait Pattern

It is possible to work the plait pattern on the machine without difficulty. Usually various fittings are delivered with the machine, including the so-called double or treble needles for working this pattern. These are 2, or 3 needles fitted to a handle and spaced apart corresponding to the spacing on the machine. They have an eye at the upper end. Two of such tools are hooked by their eyes

next to each other into the hooks of the tongue needles. By drawing-up and pushing back these needles with the help of the plait needle, the appropriate stitches are brought from the tongue on to the plait needle and can now be crossed, i.e. we cross our plait needle with the stitches, hook the eyes in again and slip the stitches on to the tongue needles. In this way one can knit 2 or more plaits, but a limit exists insofar as one cannot work plaits with a width of more than 6 stitches.

255 Norwegian Pattern

With a good machine one can easily knit Norwegian patterns. One must not forget that the apparatus depends on our counting the pattern accurately from the chart. If we knit a row of a Norwegian pattern we knit at first in 1 colour, and bring those needles into working position whose stitches are to be knitted in that colour. The rest of the needles are put into inoperative position, i.e. they do not knit that thread but let it lie in the needle. Now, after finishing this row we bring back the shuttle, after inactivating the needles, put the remaining needles for the colour into knitting position, leaving the other at rest. Repeat this process.

One can see from this description that in the Norwegian pattern the counting is important. Recently an additional attachment has appeared on the market, which makes the counting of the needles unnecessary. For every pattern one uses special punched cards which are inserted into the appliance and are moved mechanically from row to row. They control the in-and-out movement of the needles for the particular pattern. This attachment is sold under the name of 'JAC 40'.

256   The Catch Pattern

This pattern group is the most interesting and comprehensive to be knitted by machine. With the technique in this pattern, one can achieve, simply, an almost unlimited number of different effects, as all sorts of variations are possible. This group of patterns is therefore of great importance to the machine-knitter.

These patterns are created by putting certain needles into unoperated positions so that when the shuttle is moved they do not form a stitch. In the next row all needles are brought back into working position and knitted. The character of the pattern is determined by how many needles are put into unoperated position and how many rows we knit without changing their position. If, in a new row, the same needles are used the pattern is moved to the right or left.

This short description shows how many variations are possible, and in the following pages you will find some patterns illustrated and described. Modern machines have special parts built into the shuttle for the knitting of the catch pattern. Needles are put into unoperated position and back into working position with the aid of a pattern comb, with sliding hooks which are put into the required position for the pattern. But these appliances must always be moved by hand after each operation.

The catch patterns, even when created with this special attachment possess the great attraction of presenting no limits to the fancy and imagination of the knitter, who, according to taste and inclination, can constantly discover new designs, and give to her work a distinctively personal note. Catch patterns are the darlings of the machine-knitter, and are particularly adaptable to the single-bed machine.

257 Knit or Purl Pattern

This type is worked on the single-bed machine with auxiliary attachment, or on a double-bed machine. They embrace a large number of variation and combination possibilities, but depend on the construction of the individual machine. The following are the three main pattern groups:
(a) plain knit
(b) half patent (purl patent)
(c) patent, or full patent.
The 'knit one, purl one' form is mainly used when a special elasticity is required, for example, in edges, borders and necklines. An attractive effect is obtained if 1 row is worked in knit one, purl one, and alternate row in half-patent. Working in catch pattern gives an interesting picture of stitches, especi-ally recommended for strong, warm pullovers and cardigans, and for sportswear.
The same applies to the half-patent group. They can also be combined with the usual 'knit one, purl one' rows and the catch pattern. The working technique of the half-patent pattern is done by the appropriate steering of the guiding element in the shuttle of 1 of the 2 needle-beds. In one row the stitches are lifted; in the next 2 stitches are knitted together.
In the patent (or full-patent) pattern the same process as just described for the half patent is carried out, but on *both* needle-beds.
This form is not suited for very strong, thick yarns, as the resulting work would be too heavy and clumsy. It has the disadvantage of requiring considerably more wool than ordinary knitting methods, and is much more liable to undesirable sagging and stretching.

258 Transfer Pattern

The last group of patterns are reserved for the double-bed machines. These are the so-called 'transfer patterns', which are created by moving the 2nd needle-bed across the 1st, during the knitting. In the various types of machine, the transfer possibilities may vary by up to 6 moveable needles. If we work 'knit one, purl one' on a double-bed machine and move the 2nd needle-bed after each row by 1 needle to the right, to the furthest limit and then back again, we create a zig-zag pattern extending over 6 rows.
If the needle-bed is moved alternately right and left after each row, a similar zig-zag pattern is formed. One can see that many variations on this theme are possible, and they are widely employed in the industry.

259 What to Watch for when Knitting Patterns

From the foregoing descriptions one can see the wealth of interesting possibilities of a handknitting machine. Naturally there are patterns which are very easily and quickly knitted, while with others special attention is needed, and the knitting speed consequently reduced. Such are those which require a special attachment, or in which the necessity of counting the stitches, slows down the work, as for example, the plait, holed and Norwegian patterns. The widest choice, embracing all types of stitches, is offered by the catch patterns, which are, however, techni-cally quite easy to work. It is important, when deciding on a pattern, to choose one which suits the material and the garment to be made. For example it would be wrong to use an 'effect' yarn, such as boucle or knopple wool in a pattern. The yarns enliven the surface of a garment, and would only serve to obscure the pattern.

Expecially strong, thick wool should not be chosen for a tight pattern, otherwise the garment would be too stiff. For summer dresses or evening pullovers, etc., it is best to choose a light, airy lace-type pattern. For skirts, of course, a tight pattern is essential, which shows little elasticity.

260 Practical Work with the Machine

If one has decided upon the garment, the material and the pattern, then the most important part of the preparation is the compiling of the technical timetable. In other words, one must translate the measurements of the pattern into the required number of stitches and rows.

The basis for this is the 'stitch sample' and to this we must pay particular attention, as this is the foundation of our whole knitting plan. If an error slips into the sample it is not surprising if the garment does not fit. We therefore recommend that special care be taken with the following:

1. The sample should be large enough to give a reliable number of stitches. It is best to cast-on 40, and to knit 50–60 rows, and only then take the piece from the machine.

2. The circumstances when making the sample should be exactly the same as when knitting the actual garment. If, in the sample, we have worked with a wool-guider, then we must use this on the garment. If one uses a hand-wound ball of wool, then we must use this also in knitting the garment, and of course we take careful note of the tension on the stitches.

3. It is as well to leave the sample for a few hours, and before counting the number of stitches, lightly press with a damp cloth.

261 Counting and Calculating

When counting-out we work on the basis of so many rows and stitches to 10 cm (4 inches) of knitting. Having noted how many such rows and stitches there are to 10 cm, then the calculations begin, and having done this once, it will be very simple.

Let us assume that:
10 cm width = 34 sts
10 cm height = 42 rows
and from our pattern measurements we see that we need for a specific part of a garment to cast-on 31 cm. From this we have the calculation:

10 cm width = 34 sts
 1 cm   ,,   = 3·4 sts
31 cm   ,,   = 3·4 × 31 = 105·4 sts, which in effect is, of course 105 sts.
So we begin our knitting by casting-on 105 sts. From the pattern or measurements we see that we have to knit 48 cm upwards. According to our sample:
10 cm = 42 rows
then
$$1 \text{ cm} = \frac{42}{10} = 4·2 \text{ rows}$$
and
48 cm = 4·2 × 48 = 201·6 = 202 rows.
Thus to obtain 48 cm we have to knit 202 rows. The further calculations in the pattern—the increasing and decreasing, the knitting of armholes and neck, etc.,—are done on the same principle as in handknitting.

The counting of the stitch sample is simple if we have worked plain knitting. If, however, we have worked a pattern we have to pay special attention to the various knitting operations. With the catch pattern we must not only count the visible rows; it is best when counting to use that side of the knitting which shows the purl pattern. But as catch patterns are easily recognized, and we know from the description how many rows form a pattern, this particular type is quite simple to work out.

In working with a half-patent pattern we must not forget to count the small stitches lying behind the purl. It is typical of this pattern that large and small stitches alternate, and because of the elasticity of the knitting the small stitches are easily overlooked. But, as alternation of large and small is regular, a simpler way is to count only the large and double the number.

With the full-patent pattern we adopt similar tactics and recognize only the large stitches; the number of rows has to be doubled.

262 Hints and Suggestions on the Care of the Knitting Machine

Knitting machines are precision tools, and therefore need a certain amount of care in order to be always fit for use, but this in general is quite simple and need not deter the knitter. It is essential that, when the knitting is finished, the machine is cleaned of all wool-fluff and dust with a soft brush.

When storing the machine remember that damp, extreme changes of temperature and leaving it standing unevenly are harmful. If the machine is accidently wetted it is essential to dry and clean it immediately.

Be sparing in the use of lubricating oil and take care that only good quality, acid-free oil is used. With a small brush apply a thin film of oil, especially to the needle-foot and to the rails which carry the shuttle.

Each make of machine will have its special instructions which should be strictly adhered to.

A handknitting machine should always be put on to a flat, level surface, for if it stands for a lengthy period on an uneven table this can lead to a warping of the basic parts, adversely affecting the free movement of the shuttle. Should a stoppage occur, do *not* use force, and if, after careful examination the reason cannot be discovered it is best to contact the advisory service of the factory.

Good machines normally require little maintenance, but one which is used a great deal should be overhauled annually or every 2 years at the factory, where there is expert attention. With good makes this is done at a reasonable charge.

263 Special Applications of Knitting Techniques

A machine opens up new possibilities and ways of knitting, and we would like to describe a selection of some of these in detail. If we work with a strong yarn and discover that our pattern is still too hard and stiff, and the stitches too tight, even after selecting the largest possible stitch, we knit then only with every 2nd needle, i.e. we put every alternate needle temporarily out of action. With good machines we can even work with every 3rd or 4th needle only. But we must check to see that the number of stitches thus available is

230

sufficient to obtain the desired width. With many knitted articles—skirts, shorts, etc.—a hollow edge is needed to take the elastic, and in the case of cardigans, jackets and so forth the garment is usually finished off with a double, or turned edge.

To form such a hollow edge we need about 20 rows, which are usually sufficient. For the 10th row we set the tightness of the stitches to its limit, after which we continue normally to the 20th row. The individual stitches of the lowest row are now hooked on to the needles and knitted together with the next row.

If we wish to have a clean edge then we let the last stitch drop and crochet it in the opposite direction with the help of a hook.

Skirts are often knitted diagonally and this method has the advantage that the skirt does not droop unevenly or 'timp'. In this way we can also knit a bell-shaped skirt, using the technique of shortening rows, i.e. we knit from one side more rows than from the other, by putting some of the working needles out of action in regular sequence.

The diagonal knitting technique also makes simple the knitting of pleated skirts. A pleated skirt is nothing more than a straight piece and the pleat effect is produced by the following method:

knit 12 rows normally, 1 row with maximum tightness

knit 23 rows normally, 1 row with double yarn. Of course we must knit this skirt exactly to measure, and because of this, work a sample pattern according to the a/m method, with 3 pleats, then measure the width and calculate the number of pleats to the width at the hips. A plissé-type skirt is knitted similarly. This effect is created by diagonal knitting in the following technique:

knit 4 rows normally, 2 rows with double yarn. The calculation of the width of the skirt is done as described for the pleated skirt.

264   Knitting Heels and Curves

If we wish to knit toes or heels, for instance, on a single-bed machine, this is done by the technique of the shortened rows. If, in knitting the foot of a sock or stocking we have, say, 36 stitches on the machine, we put, in every purl-and-knit row, 1 needle into inactive position, until each side of the knitting is reduced by a third. Then, with every row we bring back 1 needle into knitting position, and when the full number of needles is again in action, we have formed a sort of pouch which can serve various purposes, e.g., a heel, or, if we have chosen a larger number of stitches, a baby's bonnet, mittens, etc. The type of curve depends on the number of needles left in knitting position after the last decrease or before the next increase. For example, if a third of the needles are left in

the middle then we get the curve in the form of a heel. The fewer the needles the more pointed the effect we obtain. In this way, too, one can knit a neat collar edge.

265 Applying Diagonal Strengthening Pieces

If we wish to join a button-support we hook the stitches of a lengthwise-knitted piece diagonally into the machine, so that we hook alternately 5 full stitches and a knot on to the needles. To obtain an even edge, and, when sewing them together, a nice, neat seam, expecially in sloping work, one decreases 2 or 3 stitches *within* the work rather than at the edges. This method gives a clean and decorative seam in Raglan pullovers and cardigans.

266 Edges in Half-patent

In this pattern it can happen that the right edge is too loose. To avoid this, on the right side of the work, *two* needles into knitting position instead of 1 needle.

267 Knitted Cords

For belt trimmings, edges, etc., one often needs a cord, and these can be worked on the single-bed machine. Cast-on 5 stitches and switch-off the needle-lifter on the right side of the shuttle. The shuttle is brought back *without* the thread, and the thread is put under the needles, to the right. In this way we get the desired length of cord, but it is important to set the machine to a very close stitch.

268 Binding for V-necks, etc.

With V-necks faultless joining of seams is often difficult to achieve. It helps considerably if the binding is knitted-in. After the cast-on one knits 1 row on to all the stitches and then continues with shortened rows in such a way as to bring the necessary needles into unoperative position to form the V-neck. Should the strip be, say, 13 rows high, one brings, on 1 side, 6 times 2 needles into unoperated position.
The stitches are now cast-off, except the twelve above-mentioned needles, and put the loop of the last cast-off on to the 13th needle. Put the 13 stitches with their loops which have been formed in the shortened rows, on to a spare needle, and work the opposite binding by casting-on from right to left. The stitches of this 2nd binding are not taken on to a spare needle, but are turned on the machine, and now the stitches of the *first* half of the binding are taken from the spare needles and hooked back on to the machine so that both cast-off threads lie on the same side. Two stitches, and 2 stitches with loops are on 1 needle, and now we put all needles into inactive position and cast-off.

269　Buttonholes

For horizontal buttonholes one puts, on to as many needles as the buttonhole is wide, an auxiliary thread instead of the normal thread. After the garment is finished these threads are drawn out, leaving a buttonhole with open stitches which now have to be sewn.

To these technical hints now an important postscript!

The various types of handknitting machine differ from one another in their constructional details, and consequently tricks and dodges which can be done on one machine cannot always be done on another. It is, unfortunately, not possible to explain the differences of the various machines, and this is why we again recommend every owner of a machine to undergo a course of instruction, and to make a point of studying the machine and the instructions most carefully. This applies, no less, to the study of the patterns. While all basic types have been covered in the description of the patterns, and the technical

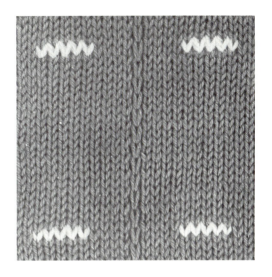

operations fully described, they still vary on the different types of machine. In the following examples we cannot, therefore, take any particular make or type into consideration, and only the technique of the pattern will be described.

Patterns

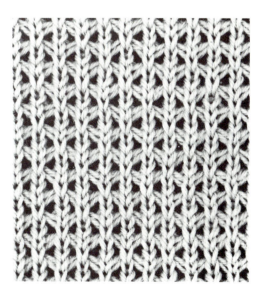

270　Knitting Pattern

1st: cast-on every 2nd needle.
2nd: of the above put every 2nd needle into inoperative position.
3rd: k 2 rows.
4th: bring needles from unoperated into knitting position.
5th: k 1 row.
6th: rep. operations 2–5, but move the pattern.

271   Knitting Pattern

1st: bring every 2nd, 4th, 6th, 8th, etc., needle into inoperative position.
2nd: k 2 rows.
3rd: bring needles into knitting position and put every 1st, 3rd, 5th, etc., needles into inoperative position.
4th: k 2 rows.
5th: bring needles back into knitting position.
6th: rep. operations 2–5.

272   Knitting Pattern

1st: Bring every 5th, 10th, 15th, etc., needle into inoperative position.
2nd: k 4 rows.
3rd: bring needles back into knitting position.
4th: move pattern by 1 needle to the right, i.e. put the 6th, 11th, 16th, etc., needle into inoperative position.
5th: k 4 rows.
6th: rep. operations 1–5, but always move pattern by 1 needle to the right.

273   Knitting Pattern

1st: Put 7th, 9th, 16th, 18th, 25th, 27th, etc., needles out of action.
2nd: Put the 8th, 17th, 26th, etc., needles into inoperative position.
3rd: k 2 rows.
4th: bring needles into knitting position.
5th: k 1 row.
6th: rep. process 2–5.

274   Knitting Pattern

1st: bring 4th, 8th, 12th, etc., needles into inoperative position.
2nd: k 4 rows with the 1st thread.
3rd: bring needles into knitting position.
4th: k 2 rows with 2nd thread.
5th: put 2nd, 6th, 10th, etc., needles into inoperative position.
6th: k 4 rows with 1st thread.
7th: bring needles back into working position.
8th: k 2 rows with 2nd colour.
9th: rep. operations 1–8.

275   Knitting Pattern

1st: put 2nd, 4th, 6th, 8th, etc., needles into inoperative position.
2nd: k 2 rows with 1st thread.
3rd: bring needles back into knitting position.
4th: k 2 rows with 2nd thread.
5th: put 1st, 3rd, 5th, 7th, etc., needles into inoperative position.
6th: k2 rows with 1st thread.
7th: bring needles into working position.
8th: k 2 rows with 2nd thread.
9th: rep. operations 1–8.

276   Knitting Pattern

1st: put 3rd, 5th, 8th, 10th, 13th, 15th, 18th, 20th, 23rd, 25th, etc., needles *out of action.*
2nd: put 4th, 14th, 24th, etc., needles into inoperative position.
3rd: k 6 rows.
4th: bring the inoperative needles (4th, 14th, etc.) into knitting position.
5th: bring every 9th, 19th, 29th, etc., needles into inoperative position.
6th: k 6 rows.
7th: bring inoperative needles (9th, 19th, etc.) into knitting position.
8th: rep. operations 1–7.

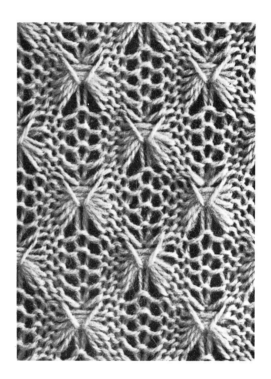

277   Knitting Pattern

1st: bring every 2nd, 4th, 6th, 8th, etc., needle into inoperative position.
2nd: k 3 rows with 1st thread.
3rd: bring needles back into knitting position.
4th: draw out the outer needle lever, k 1 row with 2nd thread, draw back shuttle and push lever in again.
5th: rep. operations 1–4 but move the pattern.

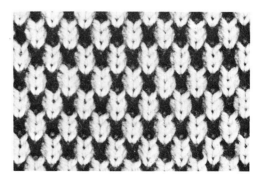

278   Knitting Pattern

3 needles in knitting position, 2 out of action.
1st: of the needles in knitting position put every 3rd one into inoperative position.
2nd: k 4 rows.
3rd: bring needles back into knitting position.
4th: put 1st needle of every group into inoperative position.
5th: k 4 rows.
6th: rep. operations 1–5.

279   Knitting Pattern

1st: put every 5th needle out of action.
2nd: of every group put 4th needle into inoperative position.
3rd: k 1 row.
4th: bring needles into knitting position, and every 1st needle of each group into inoperative position.
5th: k 1 row.
6th: bring needles in knitting position.
7th: rep. operations 2–6.

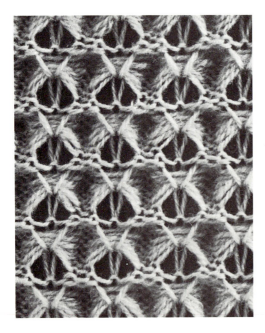

280   Knitting Pattern

1st: cast-on the 1st, 2nd, 4th, 6th, 7th, etc., needles: the 3rd, 5th, etc., remain always out of action, but are always counted in the instructions.
2nd: put 4th needle into inoperative position.
3rd: k 8 rows.
4th: bring needles into knitting position.
5th: k 2 rows.
6th: rep. operations 2–5.

281 Knitting Pattern

1st: put every 2nd needle into inoperative position.
2nd: k 3 rows.
3rd: bring needles into knitting position.
4th: k1, p1 for 3 rows.
5th: put every 1st, 3rd, 5th, 7th, etc., needle into inoperative position.
6th: k 3 rows.
7th: rep. operations 1—6.

282 Knitting Pattern

1st: put every 2nd needle into inoperative position.
2nd: k 4 rows with 1st colour.
3rd: bring needles into knitting position.
4th: k 2 rows with 2nd colour.
5th: put every 1st, 3rd, 5th, etc., needles into inoperative position.
6th: k 4 rows with 1st colour.
7th: bring needles back into working position.
8th: k 2 rows with 2nd colour.
9th: rep. operations 1—8.

283 Knitting Pattern

1st: put 6th, 12th, 18th, etc., needles into inoperative position.
2nd: k 3 rows.
3rd: bring needles into knitting position.
4th: k 3 rows.
5th: put 3rd, 9th, 15th, etc., needles into inoperative position.
6th: k 3 rows.
7th: bring needles back into knitting position.
8th: k 3 rows.
9th: rep. operations 1—8.

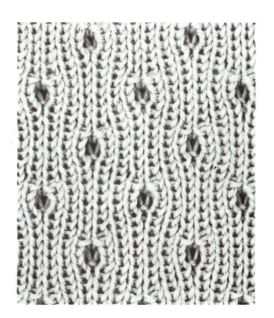

Practical Hints

Knitting Individual Parts

Hints on Knitting Stockings

1 When knitting a stocking by hand the seam is worked as follows: the last st of the 4th needle is purled in every row. From the calf to the heel, the stocking decreases on average by one quarter, therefore one must decrease 2 sts in every round, 1 st on each side of the purled seam-st.

1 The Seam and Decreasing for the Calf

This decreasing is done at first on the 4th, then on the 1st needle. Knit the 4th needle till 4 sts are left; knit the next 2 sts tog., and then k1, p1 (seamstitch). On the 1st needle, at first k2, then 2 tog. Between the individual decreasing rounds k6–10 rounds plain. The illustration (left) shows the decreasing for the calf without a seam.
Fourth needle: knit to the last 3 sts, knit the following 2 tog., then k1.
First needle: k1, knit following 2 sts tog., knit to the end of the needle.

2   The Heel

For the heel half the number of sts are used, and begins at the middle of the back. The 1st needle is knitted; turn, the 1st and 4th needles knit, then turn, and so on. The ordinary heel shows on both sides, besides the edge st, a double seam. In the forward row p the 2 sts before the edge st of the 1st needle, and the 1st 2 sts *after* the edge st of the 4th needle. The backward row is always purled. A third of the cast-on sts are used for edge and sea sts. For a smooth heel knit forward and purl backward rows. The illustration shows the heel with side seams. The 1st and last sts are ordinary edge sts (*see* p. 84).

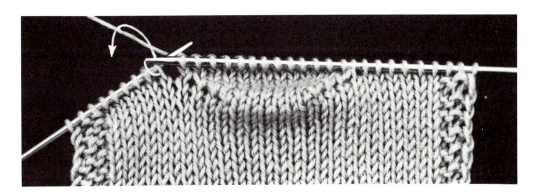

3   The Four-part Heel-cap

In a 4-part heelcap the number of sts of 1 needle is divided by 4. One begins in the middle of the front, i.e., if there are 16 sts on the needle, a quarter of that is 4, so k4 sts, turn, sl1 purlwise, p7, turn, sl1, k3.

In the 2nd row 5 sts are knitted on every needle before the work is turned. In the 3rd row k6 sts (i.e., always 1 st beyond the gap which has been created by the turning of the work), then turn, sl1, and work back. Continue like this until in front of, and behind, the gap, you have an equal number of sts, e.g. 8 sts in front of gap, 8 behind it.

From now on always knit together 1 st before and 1 st after the gap. In the forward row they are twisted and in the backward row, purled.

How to decrease: should the sts be knitted twisted, one has to insert into the *back* of the 2 sts and draw working thread through both sts. If a st is slipped purlwise, one purls 2 together. After decreasing, the work is turned and the 1st st slipped as described above. This is continued until the sts behind the gap have all been used by decreasing.

4 Three-part Heel-cap

This is started in the middle of the heel. The number of sts are divided by 3, e.g. with 18 sts k6, the 7th and 8th twisted tog., then turn the work. By this we form a gap.
Slip the 1st st purlwise and purl back to the middle, p6 more sts from the *other* needle. Purl together the 7th and 8th, then turn the work. Slip the 1st st and knit until 1 st before the gap. From now on, the sts before and behind the gap are, in the forward row, knitted together twisted, and in the backward row, are purled together, until the sts of the 1st and 3rd *third* have been used.

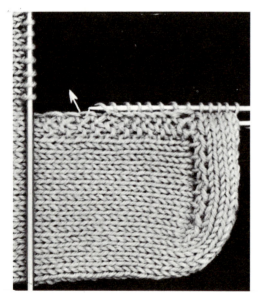

5 Joining the Heel and the Instep

For this the edge sts along the heel are picked up. Divide the sts of the cap on to 2 needles. Every needle picks up the sts along the heel, i.e. always the back link (*see* illustration). The same will be knitted twisted in the 1st round. So that no holes develop in the corners where the edge sts meet the sts of the instep, one should pick up a cross link.
One can also knit the corner sts as follows: by gripping both links from the front to the back, pick up thread and draw through. This method is recommended if no double seam is knitted.

6 Instep Decreasing

When the heel and instep sts have been arranged again on the needles, k2 rounds plain. Now begin the decreasing as follows: on the 1st and 4th needles:
1st needle; knit up to the last 3 sts, k2 tog., k1. On the 4th needle knit the 1st st, knit the 2nd and 3rd sts together twisted, knit to the end. Knit in this way until the number of sts on the needles is the same as the original number before commencing heel. Above the decreasing round always k2 plain rounds.

7 Plain Toe

In the final decreasing, 2 decreases are worked on each needle, once in the middle and once at the end. Example: there are 18 sts on 1 needle.

1st decreasing round: k7, dec., k7, dec., and so on. K 7 rounds.
2nd decreasing round: k6, dec., and so on, k 6 rounds.
3rd decreasing round: k5, dec., and so on, k 5 rounds.
4th decreasing round: k4, dec., and so on, k 4 rounds.

5th decreasing round: k3, dec., and so on, k 3 rounds.
6th decreasing round: k2, dec., and so on, k 2 rounds.
7th decreasing round: k1, dec., and so on, k 2 rounds.
From now on, decrease in every round until the round counts 8 sts, then break the thread and with the help of a long darning needle, draw it through the sts. The thread has to be drawn once again through the 1st 2 sts. Sew in thread at back of the work. This form is called 'circular decreasing'.

8 A Different Method of Decreasing for Plain Toe

This method, decrease on every needle only once, by knitting the 3rd- and 2nd-last sts together. In the first 3rd of the decreasing rounds, k2 plain rounds after the decrease. In the second 3rd k1 round plain after every decreasing round. For the final 3rd, decrease every round until 8 sts are left to draw up for toe. To calculate the decreasing rounds, begin by counting 8 sts, e.g. if the round has 68 sts, 60 have to be 'lost' by decreasing. In every decreasing round one loses 4 sts, so this makes 15 rounds for the 60. Divide this: k 5 times 2 plain rounds above decreasing round, 5 times 1 plain round above decreasing round, and 5 rounds without plain round.

9 Working the Flat Toe

The decreasing is done at the end of the 1st needle, the beginning of the 2nd, the end of the 3rd, and the beginning of the 4th needle. Knit the 1st needle till there are 3–4 sts left (depending on the width of the strip), decrease, knit either 1 or 2 sts.
2nd needle: k 1 or 2 sts twisted.
3rd needle: as the 1st.
4th needle: as the 2nd.
After the 1st decreasing round, k3 plain rounds, after the 2nd and 3rd decreasing rounds k2 plain rounds, and after each of the 4th, 5th and 6th decreasing rounds k1 plain round. From now on, decrease in every row until 1 or 2 sts are left on each side of the strip. Put the sts of the 1st and 4th needles on to 1 needle, and the sts of the 2nd and 3rd needles on to another, and join the opposite sts together by means of a knitted seam.

10 Ankle Socks; size 9

Materials: 1 set of double-pointed needles (2 mm).
Cast on 68–72 sts. Work 13–14 cm in rib pattern to the heel, k1 twisted, p1. Before the heel k4–5 rounds plain, in the 1st round decrease 1 st on each needle. The height of the heel double seams. Measure the length from heel to toe with a sock of the required size (*see* pp. 242 and 243 for details of heel, instep and toes).

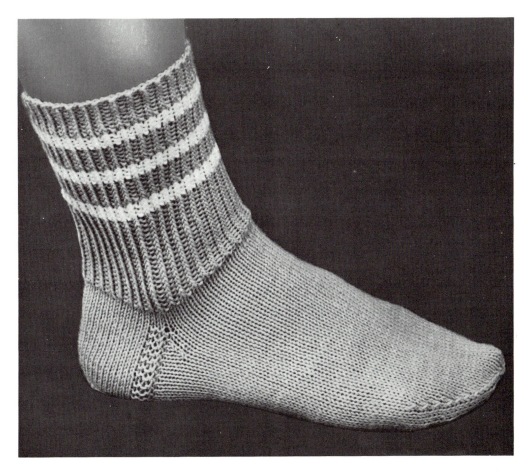

11   Plain Knitted Sock

Materials: 130 g of sock wool, 1 set of double-pointed needles (2 mm).
Cast-on to 4 needles 20 sts each, and in a round k2, p2, or k1 twisted, p1, for 8 cm, i.e. for about 40 rounds. Now knit 18 cm (90 rounds) plain. From here for details of heels, instep and toes, *see* pp. 242 and 243.
Measure the length of the foot with a sock of the required size.

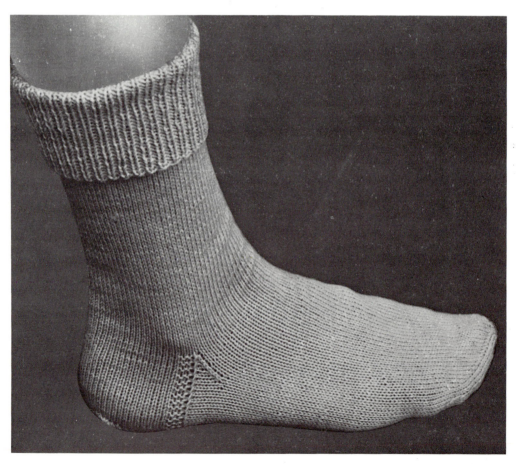

Children's Mittens

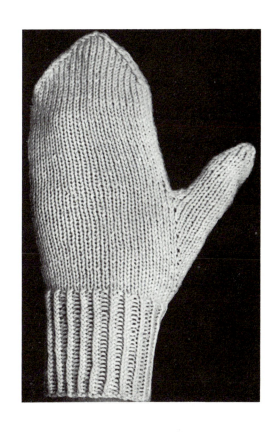

12 Mittens for Children (8-10 years)

Materials: 80 g of medium wool, 1 set of needles (2·5 mm). Cast-on 42 sts. For the cuff band about 6 cm (25 rounds) in k1 twisted, p1. Knit 7 rounds plain before starting the thumb.

At the beginning of 1st needle, increase by 1 st (pick up the horizontal link and knit twisted), k1 and again make 1. K2 rounds without increase. Then increase to the right and left of the sts previously made (make 1 at the beginning of the needle, k3 and then again make 1). K2 rounds. Increase again to the right and left of the previously made sts. Continue in this way until the wedge has about one 3rd of the number of the cast-on. (In this case 15 sts.)

247

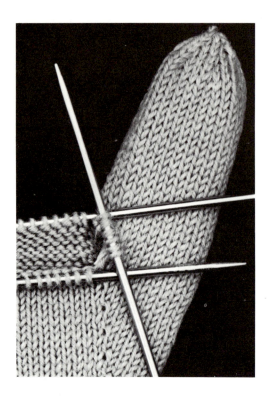

The thumb: divide the sts used for the wedge on to 3 needles. To these cast-on a further 5 sts with a spare needle, then knit the thumb in the round. Reduce the 5 cast-on sts in every 2nd row, in wedge form. Of these 5, the 1st is knitted twisted together with the st in front of it, the 5th knitted twisted with the st behind it. In the 2nd following round repeat this again (16 sts). Now k13 rounds (the length of the thumb is usually proportional to the length of the wedge).

One finishes off thus: k2 sts between the decreasing, then 2 rounds, then k1 st between the decreasing and k1 round. Draw the last 4–6 sts together.

After finishing the thumb pick up the 5 cast-on sts and put to the remainder of the sts. As for the thumb, these are decreased in wedge form. For the palm one needs 58 rounds from the wrist-band to the start of the decreasing. The 4th illustration shows the decreasing. On the 1st needle knit the 2nd and 3rd sts together. On the 2nd needle knit the 3rd and 2nd-last. On the 3rd needle the 2nd and 3rd sts, and on the 4th needle the 3rd and 2nd-last. Decrease in every 2nd round.

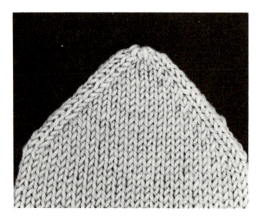

Hints on Knitting Gloves

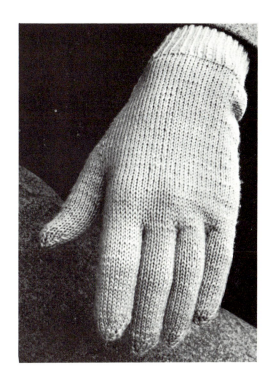

13 Gloves

Materials: 100 g of Nomotta Regina 4-ply. 2 sets of needles ('PERL INOX') 2 mm and 2·5 mm.

Cast-on 60–68 sts (2 mm needles). Work 30 rounds in rib pattern (k2, p2, or k1 twisted and p1). Knit a further 10 rounds, or use any pattern according to taste (needles 2·5 mm). **Knitting the wedge for the thumb.** After completing the straight part as above, begin the wedge for the thumb. This is worked as for the child's mitten (*see* section 12). But the increasing is continued till the wedge totals one 3rd of the sts originally cast-on (e.g. 64 sts = 21 sts, 72 sts = 24 sts, etc.). The thumb is worked as for a child's mitten (*see* section 12, 3rd illustration).

After finishing the thumb pick up the 5 sts cast-on for the wedge, and put them with the rest of the sts. As in the case of the thumb, they are decreased in wedge form, then k18 rounds before knitting the fingers. So that the thumb lies a little inwards to the palm of the hand, put 5 sts from the 4th on to the 1st needle.

When dividing the number of sts for the 4 fingers, allot 4 more for the index finger. Take these 4 sts from the number originally cast-on, and divide the remainder by 4.

For example, if 64 were cast-on:

64 minus 4 = 60, divided by 4 = 15

so the 3 smaller fingers each have 15 and the index has 19 sts. The little finger is knitted first. For this take 8 sts from the palm and 7 from back of hand, and with a spare thread

cast on 3 sts, so that there are now 18. With these knit until the desired length is reached then for the point decrease as described for thumb. Draw the spare thread out of the newly cast-on sts, and put these to the remaining 49 and k2 complete rounds.

Ring (3rd) finger. 3 newly cast-on sts, with 7 from palm and with the spare thread cast on 2 new sts, 8 sts from the back (20 sts in all).

Middle (2nd) finger. Draw spare thread out of the 2 newly cast-on sts, and in so doing pick up horizontal thread as a st, 7 sts from palm, with spare needle cast-on 3, and 8 sts from the back of hand (21 sts in all).

Index (1st) finger. To the 3 newly cast-on sts for the middle finger put the remaining 19 (total 22).

The 2nd glove is worked in the opposite direction. Before dividing the sts put 5 from the 1st onto 4th needle.

Details for Knitted Garments

Different Hems

14 Knitting a Hem with a Toothed (Picot) Finish:

The necessary number of sts are cast-on out of 1 st (*see* section 1: Introduction to Basic Stitch; Single Cross Cast-on), then according to the width of the seam, knit a few rows in 'plain' knitting (=forward rows knit, backward rows purl).

Then a 'pierced' row (forward row): * thr.o. (put working thread from front to back over right needle), k2 sts tog. From * rep. Again knit a few sts 'plain', 1 row more than in front of pierced row (in the 1st, i.e. backward row purl all sts and thread-overs).

Knitting up the hem
With a spare needle pick up the cast-on sts from back to front. Put this spare needle with the cast-on sts behind the needle and knit together the 1st st of the front needle with the 1st st of the back needle. Take care not to get the vertical rows out of alignment.

15 Securing a Knitted-on Hem at Conclusion of Work

An edge or hem (e.g. of a skirt) can be secured thus: after the full depth of the hem has been knitted, it is put on its reverse side and the hem sewn on with a darning needle. * Put the darning needle from back to front through the 1st st, and grip a horizontal link in the appropriate row chosen for the hem. From * repeat continuously. Always grip the horizontal link. The illustration is in 2 colours to show the process clearly.

16 An Edge on 'Smooth-knitted' Garments

It is well known that edged in 'smooth-knitted' garments are prone to curl, and not even by steaming can this be avoided. It is therefore advisable, after the cast-on, to work several rows 'curled' (knit backward and forward rows). Continue this form up the edges with about 3 or 4 sts.

Edges and Corners

A perfect garment demands accurate edges and corners, and we show here various possible methods.

17 Smooth Edges

Turn up the seam and make sure that the edge is very true and accurate, and corresponds exactly with the vertical rows of sts. Sew the hem to the desired width with invisible sts, or pick up the cast-on sts and knit to the garment.

18 Edge with Purled Rib

The row which is to become the edge of the hem, purl on the right (i.e. the outer) side. The hem is then sewn or knitted as in section 17 above.

19 Front Edge—'Smooth-knitted'

Smooth-knitted front edges are *double-knitted*, as otherwise the edge curls and is not firm. To achieve an especially neat, strong edge, work the st which runs along the edge as follows:

Right side of work: k1 st.
Reverse side: sl1 st, with thread in front of work.

In ready-made garments the hem is turned-up and the edge is sewn with invisible sts. Take special care that the edge runs exactly along the st, as described above.

No less important is the execution of corners, whether right-angled or rounded. The best knitted jacket loses its *chic* if the lower corners are crooked or unevenly worked. We now describe several working methods.

20 Right-angled Corner: First Method

Let us assume, for example, that the hem at the side and bottom is to be 4 cm. Then, if one wants a double seam at side and bottom (under no circumstances must the knitting be of treble thickness), for the lower edge cast on 8 cm less in width, and knit up to 4 cm. Now cast-on on front edge in a different-coloured thread (this is removed later), st to the width of 8 cm and continue knitting the front part of the garment.

When the work is finished and steam-pressed, the coloured thread is withdrawn so that 3 sts remain in a width of 8 cm. The front edge is turned-in 4 cm, and sew together the sts which lie opposite each other (*see* p. 278), then at the bottom turn in 4 cm and sew on invisibly. The slit which remains on the front edge is neatly sewn together from the outside with invisible zig-zag sts (*see* paragraph 40).

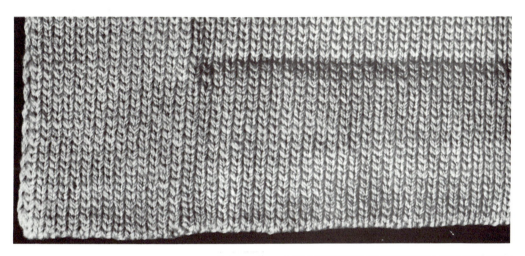

21 Right-angled Corner: Second Method

If the width of turn-in at side and bottom is 4 cm, then one begins again with sts 8 cm less. Increase by 1 st on every needle on the front edge. After 4-cm height, work up the 2nd st from the lower edge, as a st, which forms the front edge, and during the next 4 cm, again increase at front edge by 1 st at the beginning of every needle. Then continue knitting the front part of the garment.

When finishing and steam-pressing the front parts, the lower and front edges are turned up and inwards 4 cm, and sewn as described above (paragraph 20), and the sloping slits closed from outside with invisible zig-zag sts (*see* paragraph 40).

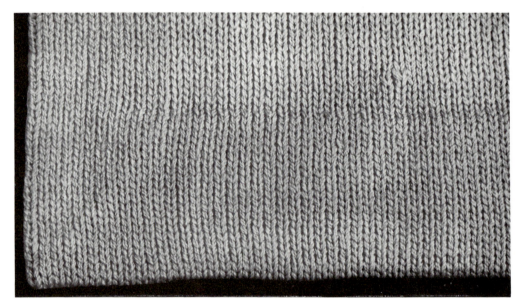

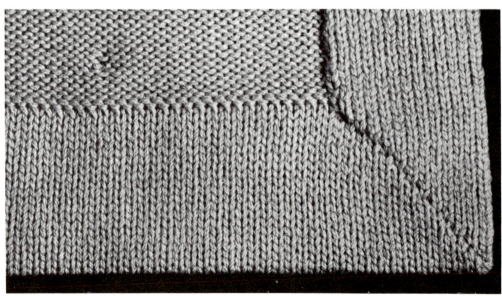

22　Rounded Corners

The turn-in is knitted along the full width of the front of the garment, then one calculates, according to the pattern, the number of sts and rows involved in the rounding of the corner, and knits this in shortened rows. Then cast-on sts to the width of the turn-in and continue knitting the garment.

Our example is 30 sts wide and 42 rows in height (= 10 cm). The turn-in is 2·5 cm high, thus 7 sts wide and 11 rows high. The rounding is knitted with 30 sts in 30 rows. The width of the front panel is 25 cm = 75 sts.

Cast-on 75 sts and k11 full rows, then follow on with the knitting of the shortened rows (*see* p. 90, section 29). Beginning on the side edges, first k45 sts, turn, knit back, and in the next row 5 sts more, then once 4 sts, once 3 sts, 6 times 2 sts and 6 times 1 st more.

When all sts have been knitted cast-on for the front edge and the turn-in 7 new sts, and finish the front panel according to the pattern. The calculation of sts and rows for the rounding can make the knitting sample much easier. Simply put the sample under your pattern and count the sts and rows.

As preparation for the steam-pressing, it is most essential that the front rounding is pinned up exactly according to the pattern

(the lowest cast-on row of the turn-in *must not* be stretched). After the steaming turn in the hem and sew with invisible sts as already described. The slit which remains is finally sewn together from the outside with a zig-zag st.

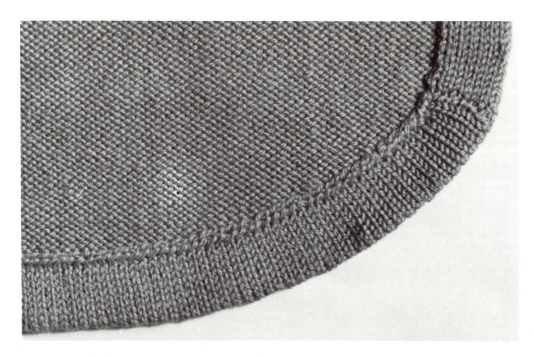

Necklines and Collars

23   Neck

In the knitted model the neckline often forms a special feature, and therefore extra care has to be taken here. In the following sections we offer various suggestions:

1. Close-fitting neckband
The neck sts of the straight back are not cast-off, but remain for the band. In the front edge of the neckline insert marking threads at a distance of 1 cm apart. Now work out with a st sample the number of sts needed for the complete neckband, and divide these by the number of cms. The resulting figure gives the number of sts which have to be knitted out of each cm of the edge. The sts for the band are not knitted out of the actual edge sts, but from the sts immediately below. If these lie too far apart, then make a st out of the horizontal links between them.

One knits round, or in the technique of k1, p1 alternately. If the neckline is very tight a zip fastener is to be worked-in at the back. After about 5 cm cast-off loosely, and turn in half of the band and sew on lightly with a loose st. If the wool is very thick it is enough to knit only 2 cm, but cast-off the sts very carefully.

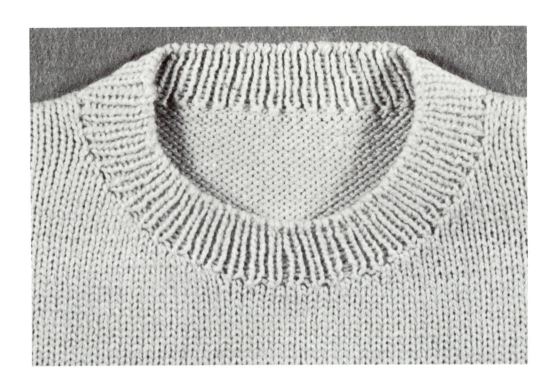

2. Square neckline

The sts for the neckline, in the middle of the pullover, are put on to a spare thread (not cast-off). When deciding on the depth of the neckline one must remember that the band will be 2 cm wide. Knit the rest of the sts up to the shoulder line. When the shoulder seams have been joined together, pick up the edge sts all around on 4 needles (calculating the distribution and knitting of sts as described above) and knit the band around in the technique of k1, p1.

Forming a corner:

1st row: slip the 2nd st before the corner st, knit the following st and draw the slipped st over. Knit the corner st. Knit the next 2 together.

2nd row: slip the 2nd st before the corner st, knit the next and draw slipped st over, purl the corner st and knit the following 2 sts.

Repeat these 2 rows continuously. At the end, cast-off loosely.

If a corner has to be worked into an edge strip, one begins with a cast-on appropriate to the outer size of the edge.

1st row: k.

2nd row: k up to 1 st before the corner, then knit the corner st together with the sts before and behind it (slip the st in front of corner, knit together the corner st and the st behind it and draw slipped st over).

Repeat these 2 rows until the strip has the desired width. Cast-off. (*See* p. 82.)

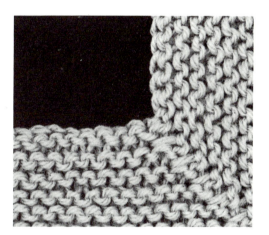

3. V-Neck (Rib pattern)

The sts of the back neckline are not cast-off, but remain for the band. The calculation, distribution and knitting of sts out of the front of the neck are as in the 1st neckline. To get a nice, trim edge, the 1st round is purled. For the following rounds k2, p2. The corner in the centre is formed thus: (2 knitted sts run up the middle).

1st row: knit together the 1st corner st with the previous st, slip the 2nd corner st, knit following st and draw the slipped thread over.

2nd row: purl st in front of corner st, put thread in front of needle, slip corner st, put both sts on to left needle, draw corner st (without knitting it) over, and put the st from the left back on to the right needle. Purl together the 2nd corner st with the following st.

If the neckband is worked in k1, p1, then the point in the front is knitted as in the square neckline.

259

4. V-Neck; plain knitted

Work the pullover to the beginning of neckline, then knit separately a triangle for the beginning of the turn-in. Begin with 1 st, and on the right side of the work, out of the horizontal link, to the right and left st of the middle st, k1 twisted.

When the triangle has reached a width of 4 cm, then the sts are divided and knitted with the separate fronts as a turn-in.

At a distance of 4 cm (2 cm as turn-in, 2 cm as border) from the new edge st, begin the decreasing and continue this at regular intervals, depending on the depth and width of neckline.

24 Collars

1. Roll collar

Work exactly as with a close-fitting neckline (*see* section 23) but knit a straight tube about 10 cm long and cast-off loosely. Suitable st for a roll collar is k2, p2.

2. Plain-knitted collar with straight corners but curly edge

According to a pattern knit the 'smooth-knitted' part, beginning with the inner edge. Out of the edge sts of the side edges knit sts and now along the 3 outer edges k6 rows 'curled'.

On the reverse side, out of the corner sts work 2 sts each time. Beginning at the outer edge of the collar, cast-on sts for the outer edges (lower and side) and mark the 2 corner sts. Now follow 6 rows 'curled'. On the reverse side of the work knit the corner sts once together with the st in front, once with the st behind it. The sts of the side edge remain.

On the sts of the lower edge, knit the 'smooth-knitted' part, and at the end of every needle knit together a st of the curled with a st of the smooth, and cast them off.

When all the sts of the curled edge have been used, pick up the edge sts of the curled knitting and cast-off all sts.

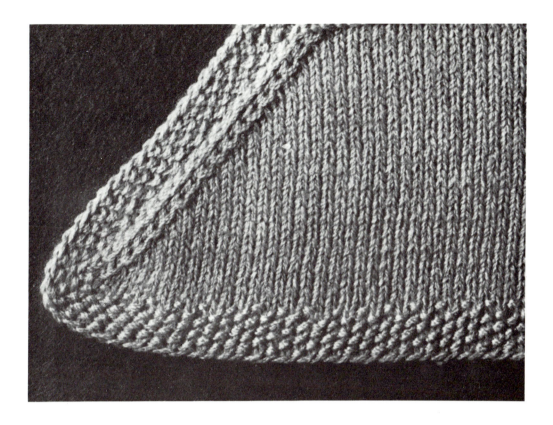

3. Collar with pointed corners

This collar is worked in exactly the same way as that with straight corners, but on both sides of the smooth-knitted parts sts are increased according to pattern.

4. Tapered revers in plain (smooth) knitting

In tapered revers the st which forms the folded edge is carried straight on. The increasing which widens the revers begins on the outer edge for the turn-in, and for the buttonhole, etc., it starts on the side. Mark on the pattern the point at which the revers begins, then calculate the additional width desired: e.g. additional width to be 25 sts and 75 rows to the shoulder. The number of sts from the middle of the front to the shoulder sloping is 25.

So in every 3rd row (75 divided by 15) increase by 1 st, once to the side of the buttonhole (or strengthening strip for button) and twice on the edge of the turn-in (1 st for the tapering and 1 for the straight turn-in). The increasings at the side of buttonhole or button strip are not above one another, but moved by 1 st to the side. On the side edge of the turn-in increase 1 st after the edge st and 1 st after a further two sts. After 25 increases the rever is completed.

Fold the turn-in and join the sts opposite each other, beginning with the middle st.

25 Pockets

Special care must be taken when working pockets. They can be set in, or afterwards sewn on.

1. Straight pocket

Straight set-in pockets are worked by knitting the sts for the width of the pocket with a thread of a different colour. Put these sts back on to left needle and knit them once again with the wool of the garment.

After completion of the work, draw out the coloured thread, and pick up the now-open upper and lower sts on to 2 needles. Knit the smooth lining of the pocket on to sts of the upper needle and, on to the sts of the lower needle knit the pocket edge.

If the pocket requires a double lining, one has to knit twice its length.

The working of the border of the pocket depends on the style of the garment: it can be worked simply in k1, p1, 'curly' knit or in a different colour. If the pocket is to be unobtrusive, then knit according to the basic pattern about 2 cm and finish the upper edge with a tight crocheted st. The edges of the pocket have to be very carefully and invisibly sewn on.

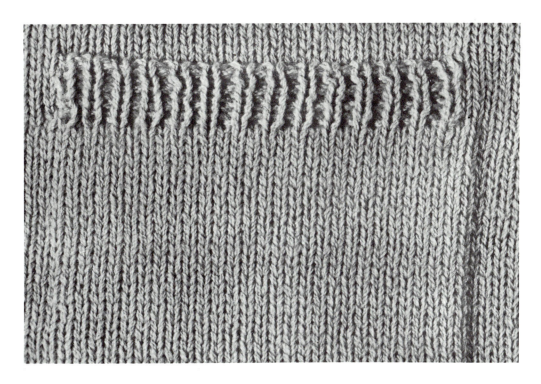

2. Sloping pocket with lining

Work the garment to where the pocket slit begins. The sts between pocket and side-seam remain unknitted. With the sts which remain knit the sloping thus:

(a) On the front side, in forward row knit the last 2 sts together (therefore no edge st). In backward row slip the 1st st, purl the 2nd and draw the slipped st over. With the *left* pocket purl in the backward row the last 2 sts

265

together on the reverse side. On the right side slip the 1st st, knit the 2nd and draw the slipped st over.

In this way the sloping is worked until the width of the pocket is reached, and at the same time the sts between the front edge and the pocket are worked.

(b) Pocket lining, cast-on as many sts as the pocket is wide, and knit the height of the pocket up to the beginning of the slope. Pick up the sts between pocket and side-seam which had been left on the needle, and continue knitting until the number of rows are the same as in previously knitted part and the highest point of the sloping is reached.

Now all sts are worked together again and the lining is invisibly sewn-on on the reverse side.

The lining can also be knitted on. For this, instead of casting-on anew, pick up the sts of the lower pocket edge, on reverse side, to the width of the sloping. Pick up horizontal links from back to front on to the needle.

(c) Flap: pick up the inner links of sts on upper pocket edge (insert from back to front) and knit them twisted. Out of every 6th st make 2. The flap is knitted 'curled' (i.e. knit forward and backward rows). At the lowest point of the sloping increase at the end of every forward row by 1 st (pick up the horizontal link between 2nd and 3rd-last sts and knit twisted). At upper end of slope decrease at the end of backward rows (knit 2nd and 3rd-last sts together). When the flap has the necessary width, cast-off and turn to the outside, and sew invisibly the edges both sides.

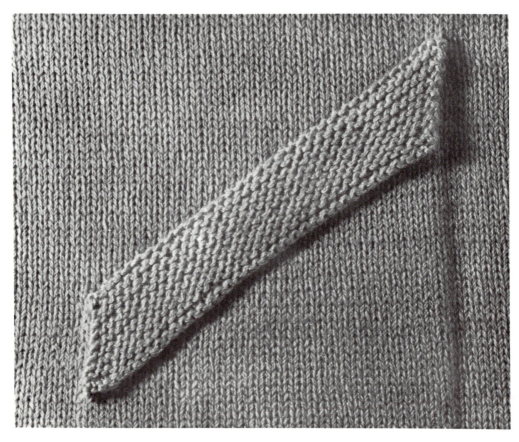

3. A free-hanging pocket with knitted-on band

Knit to the beginning of the pocket-slit, putting on as many sts on to spare needle as the pocket is to be wide. With these sts knit about 10 rows 'smooth' or plain. In 1st row increase on each side by 1 seam-st, then continue to knit in the basic pattern until twice the depth of the pocket is reached. Now decrease 1 st on each side and put the sts of the pocket back on to the main needle and continue the garment. Close the side seams of the pocket: 8 rows of the 'plain-knitted' edge remain visible.

26   Pleats and Box Pleats

Number of sts divisible by 30, plus 2 edge sts.
1st row: edge st * k4, sl1, k4, p1, k10, p1, k4, sl1, k4. From * rep.
2nd row: k sts as they appear. P the slipped sts.
1st and 2nd rows: rep. continuously.
Instead of a pleat depth of 4 sts, as described above, more sts can be used. Then, between the 2 slipped sts there must be double the number of sts for the pleat, and between the 2 purl sts, the double number, plus 2.
The closing of the pleats.
Edge st * put 1st 4 sts and slipped st on to a spare needle, the following 4 sts and purl st on to a 2nd spare needle, and turn these. Now lay all 3 needles parallel next to each other and knit the 3 foremost sts of these needles

together (1 st from each needle). Then put following 5 sts on to the 1st spare needle, the purl st and the 4 knitted sts on to 2nd spare needle, and turn. Lay the 3 needles again parallel, knit always the 1st sts of each needle together. From * repeat.

27   Double-decreasing with Taking-up of Middle Stitch

The number of sts has to be uneven. The double decreasing is always done on the front of the work. Mark the middle st and knit up to 1 st before it. Slip this st and put the middle st on to the spare needle. Knit together the sts in front and behind the gap. Now put the middle st and the joined st on to the left needle and draw the middle st over the joined st. Knit the remaining sts, and purl backward row. If the number of sts is to remain constant throughout the work, then at the beginning of every forward and backward row pick up the horizontal link between the 1st and 2nd sts and knit twisted.

28   Pleated Stripe on Plain-knit Base

The stripes can be as wide as desired. Between the individual stripes a relief st is brought up, which is slipped in forward and purled in backward row. Assuming the stripe is to be 14 sts wide at the bottom.
Number of sts divisible by 15, plus 2 edge sts.
1st row: edge st * sl1 purlwise (thread behind work), k14. From * rep. Edge st.
2nd and all further backward rows: p.
3rd, 5th, 7th and 9th rows: as 1st.
11th (decreasing) row: edge st * sl1 purlwise, k2 tog., k10, sl1 purlwise, k1 and draw slipped st over. From * rep. Edge st.

13th, 15th, 17th, 19th and 21st rows:
edge st * sl1 purlwise, k12. From * rep.

23rd (decreasing) row: edge st * sl1 purlwise, k2 tog., k8, sl1 purlwise, k1 and draw slipped st over. From * rep. Edge st.

Repeat 1st–12th rows continuously, but after each decreasing row the stripe is 2 sts narrower. Calculate how many smooth rows are to be knitted between the two decreasing rows thus:

The difference between the upper and lower width of the garment gives the full number of sts which have to be decreased. This number is divided by the number of stripes, and from this you will get the number of sts to be decreased in each stripe. Now work out with a knitted sample how many rows are necessary for the full length of the completed garment. This number of rows is divided by the number of 'decreasings' in 1 stripe, and then doubled (as in 1 decreasing 2 sts of a stripe are lost) and this gives the distance between the 2 decreasing rows. If it is desired that the stripe should become wider instead of narrower, then reverse the process and increase instead of decrease.

29 Pleated Stripe on Purled Base

Work exactly as before (as in section 28), but the st between the relief sts is purled in forward and knitted in backward row. In the decreasing rows the 2 sts in front of, and behind the relief st are purled.

Knitting and Crocheting According to a Pattern

Practical Hints and Details for the Production and Finishing of a Garment

30   Making a Pattern

For a well-fitted garment an accurate pattern of the exact size of the garment is absolutely essential. In the following we explain how to enlarge a smaller pattern to the required size.

The numbers given *outside* the pattern show the measurement in cms: the numbers *inside* show the numbers of sts.

Fold a sheet of paper in half and lay it on the table with the creased edge to the left side. Then about 3 cm from lower edge draw a horizontal line which will be the lower limit of the pattern.

On to the paper write the measurements of the reduced pattern. Always start from the zero points, measure from the lower left edge along the crease.

25·5 cm—beginning of zip-fastener

32 cm—beginning of neckline for front

37 cm—highest point of shoulder and start of neckline for the back, from right lower edge to the left

1·5 cm—vertical dotted line shows width of waist

5 cm—beginning of waistband

18 cm—upper end of waistband

3·5 cm—horizontal dotted line shows beginning of width of waist following the waistband

20 cm—beginning of armhole

35·5 cm—horizontal dotted line shows lowest point of shoulder seam

37 cm—highest point of shoulder from right upper corner to left

3·5 cm—vertical dotted line, for lowest point of shoulder

13 cm—highest point of shoulder and beginning for neck-line for front and back.

Enlarging by Drawing Apart

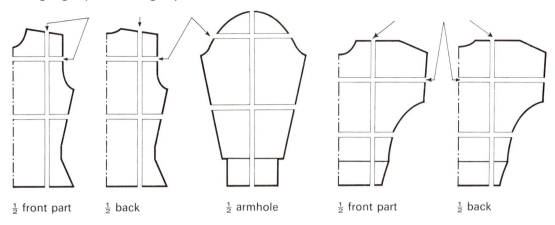

½ front part   ½ back   ½ armhole   ½ front part   ½ back

Reducing or Diminishing by Overlapping

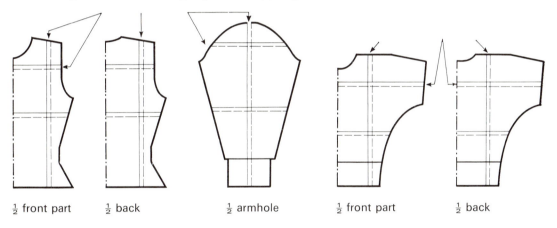

½ front part   ½ back   ½ armhole   ½ front part   ½ back

The marked points are joined as described in the pattern, and treat the other patterns in the same way. After transferring the pattern, mark it with the correct measurements.

In enlarging the pattern or making it smaller, the back and front parts are cut twice vertically, i.e. through each part at about the middle of the shoulder seams, and twice horizontally—once below the armhole and once within the armhole. A sleeve is cut once down the middle and twice horizontally, through the middle and through the upper arm.

For enlarging or reducing the pattern it is essential that the upper horizontal cut runs through the sleeve so that the lower edge (wrist and elbow) are also enlarged (or reduced).

In this way patterns can be enlarged or decreased, as the measurements require. The already cut parts of the paper pattern are put on to a new paper and every vertical and horizontal cut is drawn apart, or overlapped as the measurements require.

271

31 Measuring

Please be precise! To take the measurements is the first essential for every knitted garment, for without it there is no guarantee of a correct pattern and good fit.
Take all measurements correctly and write them down.

(a) *Width of neck.* Put tape measure around neck and measure from collarbone to collarbone.

(b) *Shoulder width.* The correct measurements are from neck to shoulder, even if the fashion demands a long shoulder.

(b1) *Chest and back width.* From the left to the right points of shoulder.

(c) *Bust.* Put the tape measure round the widest point of chest and back. The tape should not be tight.

(d) *The tape measure is put straight around the waist.* With children and stout people it is often difficult to determine the waistline, in which case mark it with the help of a ribbon.

(e) *Shoulder to waist.* From the highest point of the shoulder, at the neckline, bring the tape-measure over furthest point of bust and down to waist, and there read the measurement.

(f) *Sleeve length.* Measure from point of shoulder over lightly bent elbow to the wrist (inclusive).

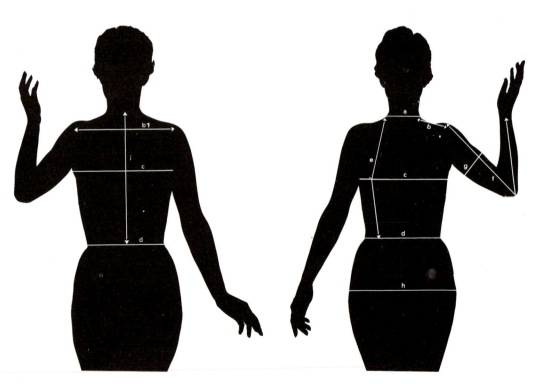

(g) *Width of upper arm.* This is measured round the muscle of the upper arm, but so loosely as to leave plenty of freedom for movement.

(h) *Hip.* Measure the hips at the broadest, about 16–18 cm below the waist. For skirts allow an extra 4–6 cm and for straight skirts about 8 cm to allow freedom of movement.

(i) *Back (neck to waist).* Let the tape-measure drop from the neckband down to the waist and there read the measurement.

All high-necked garments, e.g. pullovers, are knitted according to the length of the front. But with open-fronted garments such as blouses, jackets, cardigans, front and back are knitted according to their respective lengths. Differences of length up to 2 cm can be corrected at the side edges: with bigger differences darts must be knitted in the front panel (about 2 cm below the armhole).

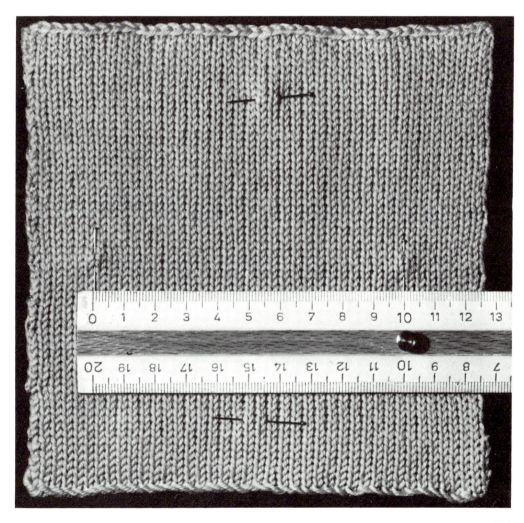

32 Stitch Sample

This is essential when working with a pattern and knitting instructions. To ensure the correct fitting of a garment it is necessary to make a stitch sample, whether you crochet, knit by hand or with a machine. With this sample you can calculate how many sts to cast-on for the individual parts, how many to increase or decrease, etc.

The sample remains with the pattern during the whole work so that at any time, should you have had to interrupt it, you can put yourself again in the picture. Besides, it is very nice

to have at hand a small box containing such samples: it increases the pleasure in the work and stimulates one afresh.

Knit or crochet, in the basic pattern of the work on which you are engaged, a square of about 12 cm. Carefully lay it flat and tack down with rustproof pins, and steam-press. Count the rows and sts of a 10-cm square in the centre and compare these with the tension in your knitting instructions. If these correspond you can confidently commence work. If there are differences, then take the trouble to calculate for yourself from your sample how many sts and rows are to be worked. This is quite simple.

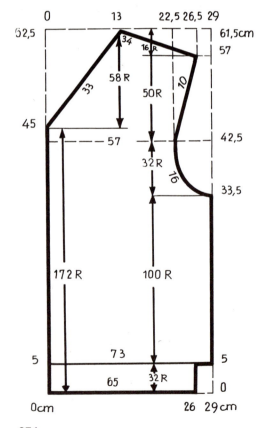

33 Calculation of Stitches and Rows According to a Pattern

As the basis for the calculations we need a pattern in the correct size. And on to this is written all sts, increasing and decreasing of rows.

Example: If the stitch pattern shows:
10 cm wide = 25 sts
10 cm high = 35 rows
then one calculates as follows:
Cast-on: our model is 26 cm wide.
If for 10 cm 25 sts are cast-on, then
for 1 cm 2·5 are cast-on
for 26 cm 26 × 2·5 = 65 sts.

Border.
if Border is 5 cm high, then
5 × 35 : 10 = 18
To beginning of Armhole.
Knitting to beginning of armhole!
increase in 33rd row by 3 cm, evenly divided.
thus: 3 × 25 : 10 = 8 sts, so that the whole row

274

consists of 73 sts. Continue knitting for 28·5 cm, i.e.

$$28·5 \times 35 : 10 = 100 \text{ rows.}$$

Armhole.
For the armhole the sts must be decreased by 6·5 cm, so

$$6·5 \times 25 : 10 = 16 \text{ sts}$$

which means we must decrease once 5 sts, once 3 sts, twice 2 sts and 4 times 1 st (i.e. 16 sts in all).
At about 9 cm after beginning the armhole increase the width by 4 cm in a height of 14·5 cm:

$$4 \times 25 : 10 = 10 \text{ sts}$$
$$14·5 \times 35 : 10 = 50 \text{ rows}$$

which means increasing by 1 st in every 5th row.

Shoulder sloping.
In a height of 4·5, 13·5 cm of sts have to be decreased, thus:

$$13·5 \times 25 : 10 = 34 \text{ sts}$$
$$4·5 \times 35 : 10 = 16 \text{ rows}$$

i.e. in every 2nd row cast-off 6 times 4, and twice 5 sts.

Neck.
At the same time as the armhole is being formed, the neck begins at 49 cm height, i.e.

$$49 \times 35 : 10 = 158 \text{ rows}$$

at a height of 16·5 cm, 13 cm must be decreased, thus

$$13 \times 25 : 10 = 33 \text{ sts}$$

in $16·5 \times 35 : 10 = 58$ rows
that is to say, every 2nd, 4th, 6th, 7th, 9th, 11th and 12th rows are continuously decreased by 1 st.

Tidying Loose Ends and Joining New Threads

34 Tidying Loose Ends and Joining New Threads

When joining a new thread, under no circumstances knot it to the old one, for even when lying in the wool a knot is visible and it distorts the evenness of the sts, and even when drawn through to the reverse side a knot betrays its presence.

It is best to join a new thread on the side edge which is later to be used as a seam. Even if you have to knit back a whole row, don't shirk the effort. The thread which has been cut off the finished work can be used later to sew the seams.

For ways of securing a loose end, *see* illustration at the foot of preceding page.

35 Working-in Elastic Threads to Give Strength and Resilience

The elastic thread is drawn through with a darning needle, on the reverse side. It is drawn through the right link of every knitted st in every 2nd row.

Finishing the garment correctly

36 Preparation for Steaming and Pinning out the Parts

It is essential to pin-out the individual parts with special care. It is extremely important for the straightness of the seams and for the shape of the complete garment.

The pinning-out is best done on a thick, but not too-soft underlay, a felt or an old woollen blanket folded into several thicknesses, over which a white cloth has been stretched. Now lay the paper pattern from which the garment has been knitted, on the white cloth, and on top of it, reverse side uppermost, the knitted part. If this has been knitted correctly it will match with very little stretching. Never overstretch a piece of knitting, as this will distort the sts and certainly will not make a too-tight knitted garment fit, for during use the overstretched sts will resume their original size.

With rust-proof pins, at intervals of 1 cm, pin the knitting by its edges to the edge of the paper pattern. Press softly with the left hand on the material and push it slightly back, and with the right hand insert the pins at a slight angle so that they will not be bent by the iron. The closer the pins are, the neater the

edges. Under no circumstances must the edges be wavy or crinkled. Pin buttonholes with 1 or 2 pins into the correct shape.

Edges and borders which are not to be steam-pressed are not pinned as described, but just lightly secured.

37 Steaming

Often insufficient importance is given to the steaming, and then it is not surprising if the garment fails to present the desired appearance Every type of knitting has to be treated differently. Use only clean, absorbent cloths and watch the exact temperature of the iron. Look under the iron occasionally; rust spots must be removed at once with vinegar water because they can penetrate the cloth and into the knitting. Should that happen the only remedy is to dab it with hydrogen peroxide and let it bleach in the air but not in full sunlight.

Over the knitting lay the damp cloth and go over it lightly with the moderately hot iron, never allowing the iron to remain stationary, so that only the steam works upon the wool. Heavy pressure would press the knitting flat, while steaming enlivens the wool, brings out the 'fullness' and enhances the knitted pattern.
Heavier wool can stand slight pressure.
Patent, plait and similar patterns are merely covered with a damp cloth which is left on the knitting until dry. Never steam elastic edges, as this causes the elasticity to disappear.
Leave the damp cloth on the knitting until it is completely cold and dry.

Seams

Seams mean the completion of a knitted work, and are decisive in the fit of a garment.

After the parts have been steam-pressed and cooled, they are sewn together with accurate sts, edge to edge if the edges have been well worked. If this is not the case, then they are sewn ½ cm at the most, from the edge. The seams must be absolutely straight, for if crooked they distort the work and spoil its appearance completely.

For sewing thread use the same wool as for the knitting, but if it is too thick, divide it. Do not sew too tightly, as this is apt to split the seams.

Here are different types of seams:

38   Quilting Seam

The thread is not drawn too tightly through the sts, so that the seam retains the same elasticity as the knitting. This type of seam is recommended for almost all cases, and particularly for side-, sleeve- and shoulder-seams, for fitting-in sleeves, and for skirts.

39   Knitted Seam

Here again, it is important not to draw the thread too tight. Keep it as the same tension as the knitting, then the st and the knitting will match and the seam be completely invisible.

(a) Joining plain knitting.

If 2 rows of sts are to be joined the least visible method is by the knitted seam. Both rows of sts are put on to knitting needles (to show the sts more clearly, in the illustration they have *not* been put on to the needles). The upper needle has one st less than the lower, because on each side of the upper remains half a st. Into the 1st st on lower needle insert from back to front and slip the st. Into the upper half-st insert from front to back, at the same time taking the next st from back to front and on to the needle, drawing through and slipping the st off the needle. Into the lower st from which the needle as previously emerged, insert from front to back. Take the next st from back to front on to the needle, draw through, and slip the st.

Into the upper st from which the needle previously emerged, insert. Put the next st on the needle from back to front, draw through, etc., etc.

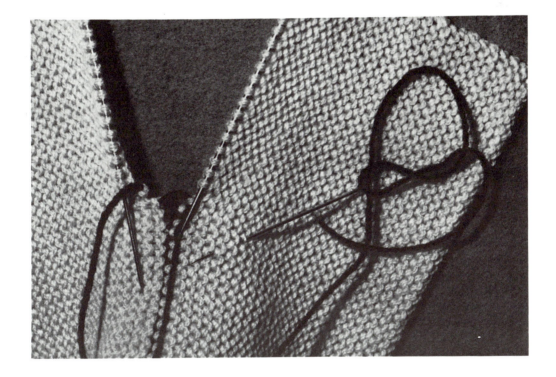

(b) Joining p1, k1, with k.st.
Put the knitted and purled sts each on to a separate needle (i.e., 4 needles in all) and lay them parallel. First connect the knitted sts of the right side as in (a), then turn the work to the reverse side and join the sts which appear knitted, in the same way. This seam is especially useful for neck-trimmings.

279

40　Seam with Zig-zag Stitch

This seam is used when sewing together wrist- and waistbands, etc., which have been knitted in rib pattern (either k1, p1, or k2, p2). This st is invisible, so that the bands can be worn inside or outside.

When knitting, care has to be taken that the pattern matches at the edges (i.e. in a k1, p1 edge, begin with a k.st and finish with a p.st). Put the two edges next to one another and insert with the knitting needle into the 1st two horizontal links of the edge, and draw through. Now draw thread through the 1st two horizontal links of the opposite edge, and so on. The insertion is always into the exit of the previous st.

In this way plain-knitted edges can be joined without being visible from the outside.

41 Buttonholes

The clean finishing of buttonholes is very important for the smart appearance of a garment. Worked-in buttonholes, whether vertical or horizontal, are finished with the same wool as the knitting, and in close buttonhole st. If the wool is too thick it should be divided.

If one wishes to make buttonholes in a finished work, cut a thread in the middle of the intended hole, and draw the loose threads to the right and left of the sts, depending on the width of the buttonhole, so that one now has open sts. The ends of the thread are secured. Draw a woollen thread through the open sts and sew them evenly in buttonhole st, as described above.

In a plain-knitted edge which has to be half turned-in (*see* p. 252) it is advisable to make the buttonholes when the work is completed. At even distances from the edge, open sts according to width of buttonhole, once for the outside, once for the turn-in.

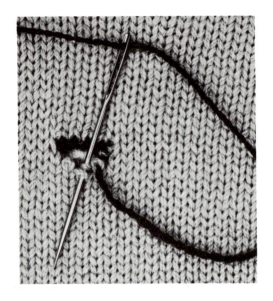

In the turn-in, the open sts of both parts must correspond exactly. Sew these corresponding sts together.
In this case it is not necessary to finish with a buttonhole st, as by sewing the sts together we get a clean edge.

42   Inserting Zip-fasteners

Crochet with tight sts around the opening into which the zip-fastener is to be inserted, splitting the wool if it is too thick. Slightly tighten the edge during the crocheting. The zip-fastener must never be too long, or it will tend to become wavy during use.
After fitting the zip and tacking it, sew it in with matching silk thread, in small quilting st. Sew the outer edge of the tape with small, invisible sts. Take great care when sewing the upper edge of the zip-fastener to the knitting. Turn in the upper end of the tape with a slight slope, and cut off the small protruding piece.

Finish by sewing it with small, neat sts. If the upper edge of the garment has a turn-in, then push the tape into the hollow edge.

The same procedure is adopted with zip-fasteners which can be separated. The correct length is very important, and the flexibility of the knitting has to be taken into account. How untidy is a jacket in which the side seams than the zip-fastener in the front edge permits, and the converse is also true—when the zip-fastener is too long and the front edge is wavy.

A pleasing effect is achieved when a strip of about 2 cm plain knitting is worked and then sewn with invisible sts over the zip-fastener tape, on the reverse side.

Making Fringes, Cords, Tassels and Pom-pons

43 Spinning a Cord

Decide on the length of the cord and multiply it by 3. For a cord of medium thickness take 4—6 times that length, but do not cut it. In the finished cord this will make 8—12 strands. Put the loops of one end over a door-knob and into the loops at the other end put a pencil or knitting needle. Stand back far enough for the strands to be taut, grip with left hand close behind the pencil and with the right hand twist in one direction till the strands are twisted tightly. When the tension is slackened slightly, small knots should form. Now take the pencil out, loosen the loops slightly and put them also on the door-knob, keeping the strands taut. Into the new loop which has been formed put the pencil and twist in the opposite direction, then take the loops off the door-knob, sew them together and trim any loose ends.

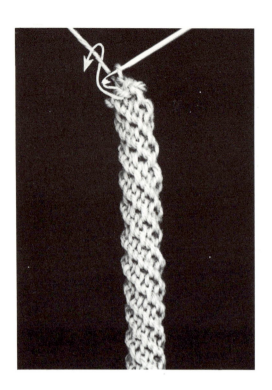

44   Crocheting a Cord

Start with 4 chain sts and close them into a
ring. Into each chain st work 1 crochet st. In the
following 2 or 3 rows into each single
crochet st work again a single crochet st.
To the end of the cord work from the inside,
i.e. in all the following rows insert from the
inside through the horizontal link which lies
between the 2 single sts on the outside of
previous row. This forms spiral ribs the whole
length of the cord (*see* illustration). If the
cord is to be thicker, cast-on more sts.

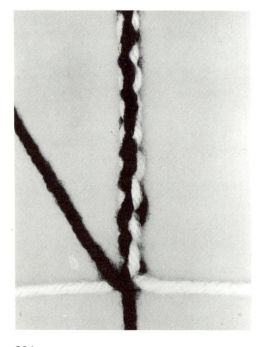

45   Plaiting a Cord in Two
Colours

Take 2 woollen threads in harmonizing
colours, and lay them crossways above each
other and with the lighter thread on top. Pin
them together at the crossing point. The 2
dark threads are to be vertical, the light
horizontal. Alternately lay the dark threads
over the light at the crossing point, and vice-
versa. Thus * Bring the upper dark thread down
over the x point, and the lower dark thread
upwards. Bring the left light thread over x
point to the right, and the right thread to the
left. From * repeat. If the finished cord is
required to be 80 cm one needs about 100 cm
of each colour (20 cm is lost in the plaiting).

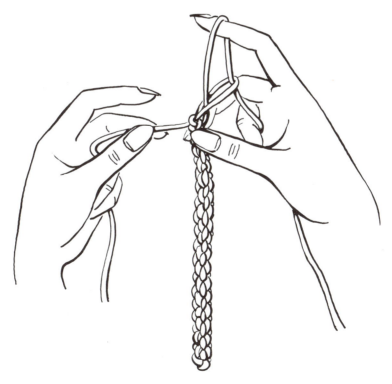

46   Knotted Cord

With a single or double thread.

The knotting is done with both ends of the wool. The wool is wound, without breaking it, into 2 balls. First lay a loop in the middle of the thread, as if to crochet a commencing st. Put the right index finger into the loop and hold the crossing between thumb and middle finger of the same hand. It is now clearly seen that one thread runs to the right and the other to the left. * With the left index finger take the left thread through the loop (*see* illustration) which is over the right index finger, and draw the thread up into a new loop.

Now put the cross-point (i.e. the knot) between thumb and middle finger of left hand, draw right index finger out of the loop and draw the right thread tight with right hand. Through the left loop draw the right thread with right index finger into a new loop (*see* illustration, p. 285).

Take the knot into right hand between thumb and middle finger, draw left index finger out of the loop and tighten the working thread. From * repeat. Never let the working thread drop out of the hand, but guide it over the ring and little finger.

47   Fringes

Fringes are indispensable for the shawls and stoles so popular today. The longer and fuller the fringe, the more elegant the garment. Especially fashionable effects are achieved if the fringe is in a restrained, contrasting colour, or multi-coloured.

Cut a strip of cardboard 1 cm longer than the fringe is to be, and around it wind the wool (but not stretched). Depending on the thickness of the wool, allow 2–6 windings for each tassel. Cut the wool along the lower edge of the cardboard strip, and with the help of a crochet needle, each tassel is knotted on the edge of the knitting. Insert with the crochet needle from back to front, into the edge and grip the middle of the tassel-bundle, and draw this into a loop to the back of the work (*see* illustration). Through this loop draw the open ends of the bundle and tighten evenly the knot which has been formed. When all the tassels are through and knotted, trim them to an even length.

If more rows of knots are required, the tassels must be made longer. After completing the 1st row, as described above, take half the threads of the 1st, with half of the 2nd tassel, at about 2 cm from the edge of the knitting, and knot them (*see* illustration). The 2nd half of the 2nd tassel is knotted with the 1st half of the 3rd, and so on. If desired the whole procedure can be repeated yet again, making a 3rd row of knots.

48 Tassels

Cut a cardboard strip the length of the tassel and around it wind the wool evenly: the thicker the tassel the more windings. With the end of the wool tie the bundle at the upper end firmly together, and finish off by crocheting a few chain-sts. Cut the wool at the lower end and take out the cardboard. Now wind a new thread around the tassel at the upper end, at about $\frac{1}{2}$ to 3 cm from the top (depending on size of tassel and thickness of wool).

49 Pom-pons

According to the desired size cut 2 matching circular rings, and wind several strands of wool together evenly through the rings until the central opening is tightly filled. Then cut the wool between the 2 rings. With doubled wool bind the cut threads tightly between the 2 rings, leaving this binding thread as long as possible as it will be used to sew on the pom-pon or to make a little cord.

When it is securely bound, cut the cardboard rings away. Trim the pom-pons evenly around, then hold over steam.

The illustration shows two finished pom-pons.

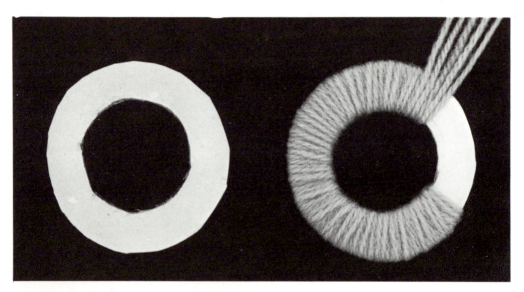

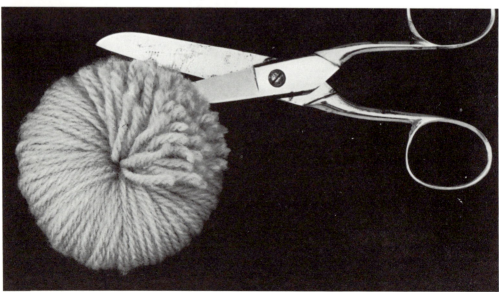

Pom-pons with different coloured rings are obtained if coloured wools are wound in even rows around the cardboard ring.

Polka-dot pom-pons are easy to make by interrupting the basic colour at intervals with coloured wool, which is wound around about 20 times. Even-out the winding in the basic colour, then work a new dot the same way in a different place.

50   Renovating and Modernising Old Garments

Wool is almost everlasting if it is not attacked by 'enemies'. With children these are usually sharp stones, rusty nails, tearing corners and so on, which cause holes. And in the case of adults it often happens that the elbows work through and edges fray. If you don't feel inclined to unravel the garment, many defects may be made good. In the following sections we shall discuss modernising an unfashionable garment as well as repairs to worn or damaged clothes.

The hole in a pullover
If it is still small we can repair it with knitted sts.

Darning with the knitted stitch
This type of darning is suitable for coarse knitting and small holes, and it can be done in such a way that the darn will be invisible.
First cut the hole square and expose the sts of the upper and lower edges. At each end undo 1 or 2 sts more. It is best to put these 2 rows of loose sts on 2 safety-pins. Each of the side edges are turned back vertically on to a row of sts.

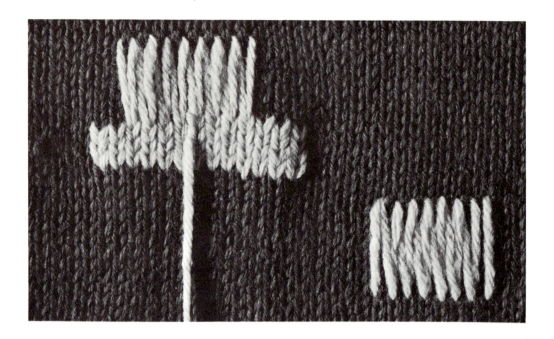

Now span the hole by drawing the thread from st to st vertically across it, starting by inserting into the 1st open st at lower right corner. Use the same wool as in the garment.

Making the new loops begins at the lower right corner, 2 sts *before* the vertical spanning-threads and finishes 2 sts behind them.

Insert under the first 2 vertical threads, and insert again back into the st from which the thread has emerged. The sts should be drawn to the same tension as the knitting in the garment. Take care not to catch the vertical threads, as they are to be drawn out at the finish, to give the darning the same elasticity as the knitting. It is best to use a blunt darning-needle.

In the turning at the end of the row the last st is formed as the others, but instead of inserting horizontally into the next st, insert from back to front vertically above the last st. This is the beginning of the 2nd row. Turn the whole work so that one can again work from right to left. During the inserting into the st of the previous row, st *between* the 2 vertical threads, while for the new st, go *under* these threads. In the last row insert into the st of the upper edge.

As the edges are now well secured, threads and the sts on the side edges can be cut off and the vertical threads drawn out.

The beauty of this st depends very much on the correct position and tension of the threads. It is advisable to tack the part to be patched on to a piece of cardboard of suitable size, for if done over the hand the fabric may contract.

Renewing a wristband

For this one unravels the complete band, and since one normally starts the knitting at the band, this is difficult to do, as one is going against the direction of the st.

To simplify this, with a needle pick up a stitch in the last row of the band, draw up and break the thread. It is now easy to part the band from the sleeve. Pick up the sts of the sleeve and knit on the new band.

Modernising an old garment

It is possible to alter the whole 'cut' of a garment. Undo all seams and pin the parts out over a paper pattern. Steam them and mark with chalk the alterations which are desired, e.g. if the rounding of the upper arm is too large, it can be set in a cm or 2 deeper

290

into the armhole. If sleeves have been made narrower, steam the seams flat so that the now-wider laps do not bulge.

The length of an old pullover can be changed if a row is unravelled where desired (*see* 'Renewing a wristband'). The new part can now be knitted on, in the opposite direction, or perhaps even crosswise, but it should never be knitted in the same pattern or the same colour, as these cannot match the old work and will only spoil the look of the garment. For even if the wool is washed there is always a visible dividing-line between the old and the new.

If you wish to change the upper part, then undo as much of that as you desire, but it is recommended that you insert a different-coloured stripe to bridge the division. A narrow coloured stripe never offends the eye, especially if it is in a lighter tone of the same colour.

In a 'plain-knitted' pullover, a shoulder panel done in 'curled' st would look well: a coarser pattern would be too heavy for the purpose.

If a neckline no longer appeals, take off the old collar and so much of the front that the new collar can be accurately fitted. To conceal the division between old and new, we recommend a pastel colour, a change of pattern, or embroidery with pearls or beads. You can also use different sts, or crochet around the dividing-line, but *never* carry on from old to new without making this sharp interruption. Your old garment would not look renewed but on the contrary, badly repaired.

You may have a pullover which is slightly 'felted' and which cannot be unravelled, and which you'd like to remake for your young daughter, or perhaps you'd prefer a cardigan! One should really never do it, but in this case take the scissors and cut the front opening vertically down. Now, with the hand or sewing machine sew a few rows up and down so that the edge cannot fray. Work a double strip in plain knitting and put the sewn edge of the old pullover down the middle of this strip. Fold the strip and sew on both sides. Repeat this with the other cut edge so that the front opening of the cardigan is secured on both sides and will not unravel.

51   Re-heeling

1. Count the lower width and the height of the heel.

2. Remove and pick up the lower heel sts. Cut open the 2nd right edge st, unravel to the left edge and back again to the middle, and pick up the sts on 2 needles.

3. Cut open both sides between edge st and 1st st from the botton to the cap. Draw out the threads and pick up the exposed sts with the 2 needles on which are already the heel sts.

4. Knitting the height of heel.

This is done in the method of the 3-part cap (or flap). The last st of the heel is knitted together with the next side-edge st (in front row twisted, in backward row purled).

After turning, slip this st. Repeat this until all side sts have been knitted.

5. Knitting the cap.

Take care that the sts of the cap match those

of the foot. For this adopt the method of the 4-part cap. Begin with the knitting of a quarter of the number of sts. After every row add 1 more st until in the middle there are the right number of sts to sew on to the foot.

6. Sewing on the cap with a knitted seam. Both rows of sts are put on to needles. The upper needle (that with the sts of the foot) has 1 st more than the lower, as on each side of the upper remains half a st.

Insert from back to front of the 1st cap st and slip the upper st. Take on to the needle the half-st from front to back, and at the same time the next st from back to front; draw through; slip st.

Into the lower st from which the needle has emerged, insert from front to back, and take the next st from back to front on to the needle, draw through and slip the st.

Insert into the upper st from which needle has emerged, take next st from back to front on to the needle, draw through, etc.

52   Re-heeling a Round Heel

In machine-made stockings heels are knitted round, and in such cases it may be desired to replace with the same type.

The heel is completely removed. Pick up sts on to 4 needles, taking care that on both sides of heel no gap appears. Knit 4 rows plain. In the 5th row begin the seam-decreasing. These decreasing rows are the same as in a stocking toe (*see* p. 244) except that *between*

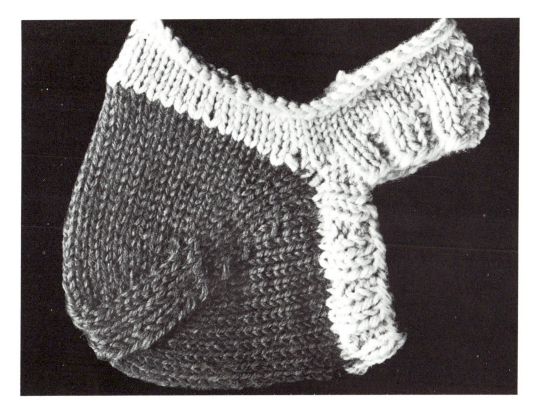

the decreasing rounds knit once 3 rounds, twice 2 rounds and once 1 round, plain knitting.

When you have decreased in every round you will have 12 sts left: connect these with a knitted seam.

The care of woollen garments

It pays to take care of your woollens, and the life and wear of your clothes can be greatly extended by careful maintenance. The care begins with their storage: fold and lay them in a drawer. Never must they hang as their own weight pulls them out of shape and leaves bulges that can never be eradicated. White and light-coloured articles should be kept in a protective bag to prevent dusty edges.

Tips for Washing Woollens

It is important to use a large basin and make sure that the washing powder or soap-flakes are *completely* dissolved in cold or luke-warm water. Have another bowl for rinsing.

Colour Test

With coloureds we recommend a colour test, especially before the first washing.
Dip a small point of the article into the suds and press it out between a white cloth. If it leaves a stain wash the article quickly in cold water, and add a little vinegar to the rinsing water.

Delicate Articles

Woollen articles washed hot: lay them loosely into the soapy water and squeeze them carefully again and again, and move them around, but *never* rub them.
Spots are easier to find in the washing if you have marked them with white cotton. Carefully rub a thick soap solution on to the spot and immediately squeeze them again in the water.

Squeezing

When the garment is washed, take it immediately out of the soapy water, and by squeezing
it (as in the illustration) most of the soapy
water is extracted. *Never wring!*

Rinsing

Thorough rinsing is most important. Never
leave the wet garment 'lumped' together. Put
it in the 2nd bowl and rinse in luke-warm
or cold water till the water remains clear.
With delicate colours add a little vinegar to
the rinsing water.
If you wish your woollens to be particularly
soft and fluffy, add a little fabric softener to
the last rinsing water.

Preliminary Drying

Here again, just squeeze out the water—*never
wring*—then spread the article out on a white
turkish towel. Small towels inside the garment,
in sleeves and pockets, prevent the coloured
parts being in direct contact with each other.

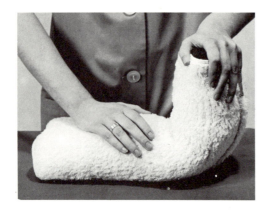

Roll the article tightly in a towel, and press the roll, (as in illustration) with folds or sharp creases. A lot more water will be thus extracted. With thick woollens it is advisable to use a 2nd towel.

Drying

After the rolling, the garment is always dried-off flat. Spread the article on to a clean, smooth sheet or towel, in its correct shape. Wool should be dried out of direct sunlight and away from fire.

Care for woollens in this way and they will always give you satisfaction!

The Correct Needles

The better the tools, the finer the work! The correct needle is essential for every form of knitting and crocheting. Wrong needles damage the wool and are a source of much irritation, but good equipment adds an additional pleasure to the work. Ladies with an inclination to rheumatism in the hands are advised to use needles with an insulating coating (e.g. Perl-Inox). The size of the needle is, of course, matched to the strength of the wool and to the pattern.

In closely-knitted patterns formed of cross-sts (plait and weaving patterns, etc.) thicker needles are recommended, while for patterns which in the course of wear, and through washing tend to flatten, use thinner needles.

For cardigans, pullovers and similar garments, quick-knitting needles (Perl-Inox-Tric, and Inox-Tric) are advised.

Very thick and bulky yarns are best knitted with needles of 8 mm and above: use plastic (Imra-Galalith).

Tubular articles are worked with circular needles (Imra-Plastic). Socks and gloves require a *set* of needles, depending on the work.

The same principles naturally apply to crocheting: only the best hooks will give good results. Test that the hook and the ridge are faultless (e.g. Perl-Inox and Inox). Especially popular is the Perl-Inox crochet hook with the plastic grip.

The true sizes of the needles are shown on p. 298.

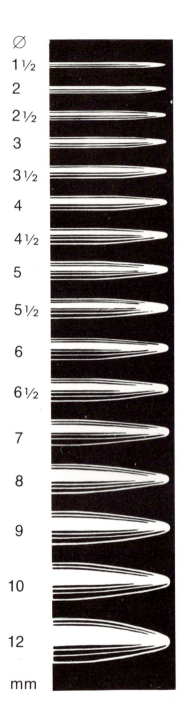

∅
1½
2
2½
3
3½
4
4½
5
5½
6
6½
7
8
9
10
12
mm

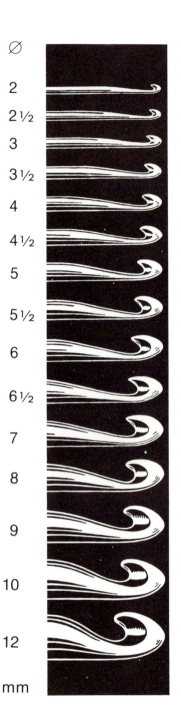

∅
2
2½
3
3½
4
4½
5
5½
6
6½
7
8
9
10
12
mm

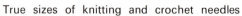

True sizes of knitting and crochet needles

List of Abbreviations

k =knit; p =purl; sl =slip; Ch. =chain; st(s) = stitch(es); k.st =knit-stitch; p.st =purl-stitch; sl.st =slip-stitch; Ch.st =chain stitch; Cl.st = cluster stitch; SC =single crochet; DC = double crochet; TC =treble crochet; thr.o. = thread over; dr.thr. =draw through; dr.l.thr. = draw loop through; inc. =increase; dec. = decrease; tog. =together; rep. =repeat; beg. = beginning.

Explanation of Terms:

Double-decrease =slip 1 st, knit 2 together and draw the slipped st over.
alternately =repeat a small group of sts continuously (e.g. k2, p2, alternately).
From * repeat =repeat a larger group of sts continuously, these groups being enclosed by some sign.

thread over = In crochet it occurs in every st. In knitting the thread-over is needed in holed, pierced, or patent patterns. The thread is laid over the needle as in purling.
to move the pattern =when repeating the pattern in the next row, so that it appears to the right or left of the pattern below.

Explanation of symbols for the charts

Patterns which are accompanied by charts can be worked according to these as well as, or instead of, the written instructions. The empty squares and spaces in the individual pattern rows are determined by the construction of the pattern, and are to be ignored in the knitting.

The edge-sts have been omitted in the charts, but must be added in the knitting.

r = knit.

I = purl.

U = thread over.

╱ = knit 2 together.

╲ = slip 1, knit 1 and draw slipped st over.

Λ = slip 1, knit 2 together and draw slipped st over.

⌒ = slip 1 purlwise, purl 2 together and draw slipped st over.

Λ = slip 1 purlwise, knit 2 twisted together, draw slipped st over.

■ = slip 2 together, k1, and draw slipped st over.

╲ = slip 1, knit 2 and draw slipped st over.

◇ = knit 1 twisted.

◆ = purl 1 twisted.

● = knit 1 twisted, out of horizontal link between sts.

a = slip 1 purlwise, thread to the back.

d = slip 1 purlwise (thread to back) and at same time pick up horizontal link at the back of st of last-row-but-one and draw through the slipped st.

✳ = slip 1 purlwise and with that pick up the thread behind the st in the last-row-but-one, and draw the st; then put the st back on to the left needle and knit it.

◇ = knit 2 twisted together.

╱ = purl 2 together.

╲ = purl 2 twisted together.

⏝ = slip 2 purlwise (thread to back).

⏜ = slip 2 purlwise (thread to front).

⋀ = knit 3 together.

3 = purl 3 together.

V = out of 1 st, knit 3 (k1, k1 twisted, k1, or k1, p1, k1).

◣ = knit edge st with following st together.

◤ = slip the last st with edge st and in following row purl 2 together.

⑵ = out of thread-over of previous row make 2 sts (p1, k1).

f = drop st.

— = drop thread-overs of previous row.

⎵ = slip thread-over of previous row purlwise.

⎵⎵ = slip double thread-over of previous row purlwise as 1 thread over.

V5 = out of 1 st make 5 (e.g. k1, k1 twisted, k1, k1 twisted, k1, or k1, p1 alternately).

⟋5⟍ = knit 5 together put first 3 sts on to right needle and draw 1st 2 sts over 3rd st, then put them back on to left needle and draw 4th and 5th over the 3rd st, and knit these.

▲ = knit edge st with first 2 sts together.

△ = slip last 2 sts with edge st and in following row knit together.

= put 2 sts on to spare needle, leave behind work, knit 1st slipped st of previous row, then put the 2 sts of spare needle together.

= put the 2 sts of previous row on spare needle and leave in front of work; knit 2 together then knit sts on spare needle.

◇3 = insert into next 2 sts as if to knit them together, put them on to right needle and back again on to left so that the 2nd st is now in front. Now knit these 2 sts twisted together with the next st.

▤ = join 5 threads of previous row together with purl 1, knit 1.

✕ = put next st on to spare needle in front of work, miss the following st and knit the next. Now knit the missed st

300

and let slip both sts of left needle. Knit spare needle st.

∞ = put 2 sts on spare needle in front of work, knit 2, and knit the spare needle sts.

N = out of next st make 6 sts (e.g. k1, k1 twisted, k1, k1 twisted, k1, k1 twisted) and draw these sts, one after another, over last loop.

⋈ = put next 2 sts on to spare needle and leave in front of work, knit next 2 sts together, knit 1, knit spare needle sts.

B = put following 3 sts on to spare needle and leave behind work, knit 2, then knit the 1st 2 spare needle sts together, knit 3rd spare needle st.